Paradigms for a Metaphorology

signale
modern german letters, cultures, and thought

Series editor: Peter Uwe Hohendahl, Cornell University

Signale: Modern German Letters, Cultures, and Thought publishes new English-language books in literary studies, criticism, cultural studies, and intellectual history pertaining to the German-speaking world, as well as translations of important German-language works. *Signale* construes "modern" in the broadest terms: the series covers topics ranging from the early modern period to the present. *Signale* books are published under a joint imprint of Cornell University Press and Cornell University Library in electronic and print formats. Please see http://signale.cornell.edu/.

Paradigms for a Metaphorology

Hans Blumenberg

Translated from the German with an afterword by Robert Savage

A Signale Book

Cornell University Press and Cornell University Library
Ithaca, New York

The translation of this work was funded by Geisteswissenschaften International–Translation Funding for Humanities and Social Sciences from Germany, a joint initiative of the Fritz Thyssen Foundation, the German Federal Foreign Office, the collecting society VG WORT and the German Publishers & Booksellers Association.

Originally published under the title *Paradigmen zu einer Metaphorologie,* by Hans Blumenberg. © Hans Blumenberg 1960. All rights reserved by Suhrkamp Verlag Frankfurt am Main.

First published 2010 by Cornell University Press and Cornell University Library

Printed in the United States of America

Library of Congress Cataloging-in-Publication Data

Blumenberg, Hans.
  [Paradigmen zu einer Metaphorologie. English]
  Paradigms for a metaphorology / Hans Blumenberg ; translated from the German with an afterword by Robert Savage.
     p. cm. — (Signale : modern German letters, cultures, and thought)
  Includes bibliographical references and index.
  ISBN 978-0-8014-4925-3 (cloth : alk. paper)
  1. Metaphor.   I. Savage, Robert (Robert Ian)   II. Title.   III. Series: Signale (Ithaca, N.Y.)

  PN228.M4B61613 2010
  808—dc22   2010013565

Cloth printing   10 9 8 7 6 5 4 3 2 1

The Unicode Greek font SymbolGreekU™ used to print this work is available from Linguist's Software, Inc., PO Box 580, Edmonds, WA 98020-0580 USA tel (425) 775-1130 www.linguistsoftware.com.

CONTENTS

A Note on the Translation

I have tried to follow the presentation of Blumenberg's text as closely as possible, generally only deviating from this principle where he quotes in Greek, Latin, Italian, or French. On these occasions I have provided English translations in the main text and consigned the original wording to the footnotes, except in the case of very short quotations, where the phrase in the original language follows in parentheses upon the English translation. My insertions in the text and notes are enclosed in square brackets. Unless otherwise noted, all translations are my own.

I wish to thank Bryan Cooke for insisting that I translate this book, Peter Uwe Hohendahl for accepting it for publication, David Roberts and Paul Fleming for offering valuable feedback, and Helen Slaney for sharing her expertise in Greek and Latin. During the revision process I benefited greatly from consulting Didier Gammelin's French translation, *Paradigmes pour une métaphorologie* (Paris: Vrin, 2006). An Ernst Keller Travelling Fellowship from the Australian Academy of the Humanities, combined with a Marbach Stipend, allowed me to spend a month at the Deutsches Literaturarchiv researching and writing the afterword; my thanks to Marcel Lepper for the friendly interest he showed in my work, and to Dorit Krusche for guiding me through Blumenberg's posthumous papers. Finally, I am grateful to Bettina Blumenberg, Henning Ritter, and Peter Rothacker for graciously granting me permission to quote from Blumenberg's unpublished postdoctoral dissertation, "Die ontologische Distanz," and from his correspondence with Joachim Ritter and Erich Rothacker in my afterword.

INTRODUCTION

Let us try for a moment to imagine that modern philosophy had proceeded according to the methodological program set out for it by Descartes, and had arrived at that definitive conclusion that Descartes himself believed to be eminently attainable. This 'end state' of philosophy, which historical experience permits us to entertain only as a hypothesis, would be defined according to the criteria set out in the four rules of the Cartesian "Discours de la méthode," in particular by the clarity and distinctness that the first rule requires of all matters apprehended in judgments. To this ideal of full objectification[1] would correspond the perfection of a terminology designed to capture the presence and precision of the matter at hand in well-defined concepts. In its terminal state, philosophical language would be purely and strictly 'conceptual': everything *can* be defined, therefore everything *must* be

---

1. Descartes defines the characteristics of clarity and distinctness as follows: *Claram voco illam (sc. ideam) quae menti attendenti praesens et aperta est . . . (Oeuvres,* ed. Adam-Tannery, VIII, 13) [I call a perception clear when it is present and accessible to an attentive mind . . .]; *Distinctam autem illam, quae, cum clara sit, ab omnibus aliis ita seiuncta est et praecisa, ut nihil plane aliud, quam quod clarum ist, in se contineat* (VIII, 22) [I call a perception distinct if, as well as being clear, it is so sharply separated from all other perceptions that it contains within itself only what is clear; René Descartes, *The Philosophical Writings of Descartes,* trans. John Cottingham (Cambridge: Cambridge University Press, 1985), 1: 207–8]. The debt to the Stoic doctrine of knowledge and its ideal of cataleptic presentation is unmistakable, although it has yet to be sufficiently clarified.

defined; there is no longer anything logically 'provisional', just as there is no longer any *morale provisoire*. From this vantage point, all forms and elements of *figurative* speech, in the broadest sense of the term, prove to have been makeshifts destined to be superseded by logic. Their function was exhausted in their transitional significance; in them, the human mind rushed ahead of its responsible, step-by-step fulfillment; they were an expression of the same *précipitation* regarding which Descartes, likewise in the first rule, states that it ought carefully to be avoided.[2]

Having arrived at its final conceptual state, however, philosophy would also have to relinquish any justifiable interest in researching the *history* of its concepts. Seen from the ideal of its definitive terminology, the value of a history of concepts can only be a critical and destructive one, a role it ceases to perform upon reaching its goal: that of demolishing the diverse and opaque burden of tradition, summarized by Descartes under the second of his fundamental critical concepts, *prévention* (corresponding to Francis Bacon's 'idols'). History is here nothing other than precipitancy (*précipitation*) and anticipation (*prévention*), a failing of that actual presence whose methodical recuperation renders historicity null and void. That the logic of the first rule eviscerates history was first recognized by Giambattista Vico, who set against it the idea of a "logic of fantasy." Vico proceeded from the assumption that the clarity and distinctness called for by Descartes were reserved solely for the creator in his relationship of insight to his work: *verum ipsum factum*. What remains for us mortals? Not the 'clarity' of the given, but solely that of whatever we have made for ourselves: the world of our images and artifacts, our conjectures and projections—in short, the universe of our 'imagination', in the new, productive sense of the term unknown to antiquity.

In the context of the task of a "logic of fantasy" there falls also, indeed in an exemplary fashion, a discussion of 'transferred' speech or metaphor,[3] a subject previously confined to the chapters on figures in handbooks of *rhetoric*. The traditional classification of metaphor among the ornaments of public speech is hardly fortuitous: for antiquity, the logos was fundamentally adequate to the totality of what exists. Cosmos and logos were correlates. Metaphor is here deemed incapable of enriching the capacity of expressive means; it contributes only to the *effect* of a statement, the 'punchiness' with which it gets through to its political and forensic addressees. The perfect congruence of cosmos and logos rules out the possibility that figurative language could achieve anything for which common speech (κύριον ὄνομα) could not furnish an equivalent. In principle, the orator and poet can say nothing that could not just as well be presented in a theoretical, conceptual way; only how they say it is specific to them, not what is said. The possibility and potency of persuasive

---

2. [René Descartes, *Discourse on Method and the Meditations,* trans. F. E. Sutcliffe (Harmondsworth: Penguin, 1968), 41.]

3. [The Greek verb from which the word *metaphor* is derived literally means "to translate," "to transfer."]

speech had been one of the elemental experiences of life in the polis—so elemental, in fact, that Plato could present the decisive phase of his mythic cosmogony in the "Timaeus" as the rhetorical act by which Necessity (*Ananke*) was swayed. It is difficult for us today to overestimate the importance of rhetoric, an importance that explains just how crucial it was that philosophy interpret persuasive force as a 'quality' of truth itself, and oratory, with all its 'tools of the trade', as nothing but the fitting implementation and amplification of that quality. The battles fought over the functional classification of rhetoric, the contestation of the Sophistic claim of autonomy for the technique of persuasion: these were fundamental processes in the ancient history of philosophy that we have barely even begun to investigate. The Platonic subordination of rhetoric, sealed by the church fathers, definitively transformed the objects traditionally assigned to rhetoric into the merely technical armaments of 'persuasive means', even if these were now to be found stockpiled in the armory of truth itself. Whether the rhetorical artifice of *translatio* could do anything more than arouse 'pleasure' in the truth to be communicated remained undiscussed. Of course, the fact that this question was not asked and could not be asked does not mean that metaphors had not in fact always already yielded such a surplus of expressive achievement. Otherwise the task of a metaphorology would be doomed from the outset; for we will see, curiously enough, that the *reflective* 'discovery' of the authentic potency of metaphorics devalues the metaphors produced in the light of that discovery as objects of a historical metaphorology. Our analysis must be concerned with detecting the logical 'perplexity' for which metaphor steps in, and an aporia of this kind is most conspicuously evident precisely where it is not 'admitted' by theory in the first place.

These historical remarks on the 'concealment' of metaphor lead us to the fundamental question of the conditions under which metaphors can claim legitimacy in philosophical language. Metaphors can first of all be *leftover elements*, rudiments on the path *from mythos to logos;* as such, they indicate the Cartesian provisionality of the historical situation in which philosophy finds itself at any given time, measured against the regulative ideality of the pure logos. Metaphorology would here be a critical reflection charged with unmasking and counteracting the inauthenticity of figurative speech. But metaphors can also—hypothetically, for the time being—be *foundational elements* of philosophical language, 'translations' that resist being converted back into authenticity and logicality. If it could be shown that such translations, which would have to be called 'absolute metaphors', exist, then one of the essential tasks of conceptual history (in the thus expanded sense) would be to ascertain and analyze their conceptually irredeemable expressive function. Furthermore, the evidence of absolute metaphors would make the rudimentary metaphors mentioned above appear in a different light, since the Cartesian teleology of logicization in the context of which they were identified as 'leftover elements' in the first place would already have foundered on the existence of absolute translations. Here the presumed equivalence of figurative and 'inauthentic' speech proves questionable; Vico had already declared metaphorical language to be no less 'proper' than the language commonly held to be such,[4] only lapsing into the Cartesian schema in reserving the language of fantasy for an earlier historical epoch. Evidence of absolute metaphors would force us to reconsider the relationship between logos and the imagination. The realm of the imagination could no longer be regarded solely as the substrate for transformations into conceptuality—on the assumption that each element could be processed and converted in turn, so to speak, until the supply of images was used up—but as a catalytic sphere from which the universe of concepts continually renews itself, without thereby converting and exhausting this founding reserve.

Readers familiar with Kant will at this point recall §59 of the "Critique of the Power of Judgment," where the procedure of "the transportation of the reflection" is thematized under the heading "symbol," even if the expression 'metaphor' does not appear in this context. Kant proceeds from his basic insight that the reality of concepts can be secured only through intuitions. With empirical concepts, this occurs through examples; with pure concepts of understanding, through schemata; with concepts of reason ('ideas'), to which no sensible intuition can ever adequately correspond, it occurs through the provision of a representation that has only the "form of the reflection" in common with the intended referent. Kant has his reasons for not wanting to concede the expression 'symbol' to "recent logicians"; we no longer have them, or rather we are only too pleased to be rid of this overfreighted term. Kant gives the name "characterization" to thetic expressions that function as mere "means of reproduction," whereas his "symbols" correspond fairly exactly to metaphors, as the term will continue to be used here. This is clearly shown in Kant's paradigms, among which we reencounter Quintilian's *pratum ridet.*[5] Our 'absolute metaphor' appears here as "the transportation of the reflection on one object of intuition to another, quite different concept, to which perhaps no intuition can ever directly correspond." Metaphor is clearly characterized as a model invested with a pragmatic function, from which a "rule of the reflection" can be gleaned that may then "be applied" in the use of the idea of reason; it is thus "a principle not of the theoretical determination of what an object is in itself, but the practical determination of what the idea of it ought to be for us and for the purposive use of it." In this sense, "all our cognition of God is merely symbolic" (in the Kantian terminology), an argument intended to skirt the twin perils of anthropomorphism and deism. Or to take another of Kant's examples: the metaphor of the machine, when applied to the state, signifies that "between a despotic state and a hand mill there is, of course, no similarity, but there is one between the rule for reflecting on both and their

---

4. *Opere,* ed. Ferrari[2], V, 186. [Giambattista Vico, *New Science,* trans. David Marsh (London: Penguin, 1999), 162.]

5. ["The meadow laughs" (*pratum ridet*) is a stock example of metaphor commonly (but erroneously) ascribed to Quintilian, the first-century author of "The Orator's Education."]

causality." Immediately following this example there appears the sentence that provided the initial stimulus for the present study: "This business has as yet been little discussed, much as it deserves a deeper investigation . . ."[6]

To be sure, the task of a metaphorological *paradigmatics* can only be to lay the groundwork for that 'deeper investigation'. It endeavors to stake out the terrain within which absolute metaphors may be supposed to lie, and to test criteria by which they may be ascertained. That these metaphors are called 'absolute' means only that they prove resistant to terminological claims and cannot be dissolved into conceptuality, not that one metaphor could not be replaced or represented by another, or corrected through a more precise one. Even absolute metaphors therefore have a *history*. They have a history in a more radical sense than concepts, for the historical transformation of a metaphor brings to light the metakinetics of the historical horizons of meaning and ways of seeing within which concepts undergo their modifications. Through this implicative connection, the relationship of metaphorology to the history of concepts (in the narrower, terminological sense) is defined as an ancillary one: metaphorology seeks to burrow down to the substructure of thought, the underground, the nutrient solution of systematic crystallizations; but it also aims to show with what 'courage' the mind preempts itself in its images, and how its history is projected in the courage of its conjectures.

---

6. *Übertragung der Reflexion über einen Gegenstand der Anschauung auf einen ganz andern Begriff, dem vielleicht nie eine Anschauung direkt korrespondieren kann . . . Regel der Reflexion . . . ein Prinzip nicht der theoretischen Bestimmung des Gegenstandes . . . , was er an sich, sondern der praktischen, was die Idee von ihm für uns und den zweckmäßigen Gebrauch derselben werden soll . . . alle Erkenntnis von Gott bloß symbolisch . . . zwischen einem despotischen Staate und einer Handmühle . . . zwar keine Ähnlichkeit (ist), wohl aber zwischen der Regel, über beide und ihre Kausalität zu reflektieren . . . Dies Geschäft ist bis jetzt noch wenig auseinander gesetzt worden, so sehr es auch eine tiefere Untersuchung verdient . . .* [Immanuel Kant, *Critique of the Power of Judgment,* trans. Paul Guyer and Eric Matthews (Cambridge: Cambridge University Press, 2000), 225–27.]

I

Metaphorics of the 'Mighty' Truth

Anyone who set out to write a history of the concept of truth, in a strictly terminological sense aimed at definitional stringency, would have little to show for his efforts. The most popular definition, purportedly lifted by Scholasticism from Isaac ben Salomon Israeli's book of definitions—*veritas est adaequatio rei et intellectus* [truth is the match of thing and intellect][1]—provides leeway for modification only in the shortest of its elements, in the neutrality of the 'et'. While the definition

---

1. Thomas Aquinas cites the definition thus, adding *Isaac dicit in libro De definitionibus* [Isaac says in his book of definitions]; *Summa theol.* 1 q. 16 a. 2 ad 2 and in *De veritate* q. 1a. 1. This wording is not to be found in the corresponding §24 of Isaac's book of definitions, however. Cf. A. Altmann, and S. M. Stern, *Isaac Israeli: A Neoplatonic Philosopher of the Early Tenth Century; His Works Translated with Comments and an Outline of His Philosophy* (Oxford, 1958), 58: *Definition of 'true'* (haqq): *That which the thing is.* D. H. Pouillon (in *Revue Néoscholastique de Philosophie* (1939): 57ff.) has investigated how the misattribution of the definition arose. He shows that the formula originates in Avicenna and was initially cited without acknowledgement by William of Auxerre, Philip the Chancellor, Alexander of Hales, and others. Philip the Chancellor also quotes Isaac's definition, although he takes it from Augustine's "Soliloquies" (II 5, 8: *quidquid est, verum est* [whatever is, is true]); in doing so, he mistakenly attributes the book of definitions to Augustine as well: *Item Augustinus in Libro soliloquiorum 'verum est', inquit, 'id quod est'. Item Augustinus in libro De definitionum collection idem dicit.* [Likewise, Augustine says in his *Soliloquies:* "What is, is true." Augustine says the same thing in his book of definitions.] Albertus Magnus subsequently mentioned Isaac in citing his authentic definition: *secundum Isaac et secundum Augustinum verum est id quod est* [According to Isaac and according to Augustine, truth is that which is], but now it seemed only natural to connect the previously anonymous formulation with the wrong name.

should be understood, in keeping with its Aristotelian origins, as leaning toward the *adaequatio intellectus ad rem* [match of the intellect to the thing], the Middle Ages was to discover in it the supplementary possibility of determining absolute truth in the divine spirit as the *adaequatio rei ad intellectum* [match of the thing to the intellect]. This latitude in the concept of truth has basically sufficed for all philosophical systems. But is the demand voiced in the age-old question "What is truth?" thereby satisfied? The terminological material tells us precious little about the full import of this question. If, however, we pursue the history of the metaphor most closely linked to the problem of truth, the metaphor of *light,* the question explicates itself in a concealed plenitude never yet hazarded by any system.[2] The metaphorics of light cannot be translated back into concepts; analysis seeks to disclose the questions to which answers are sought and risked, questions of a presystematic nature whose intentional fullness 'provoked' the metaphors, as it were. We should not shrink from the supposed naïveté of spelling out these fundamental questions, regardless of whether they were ever actually posed in so many words. To what extent does mankind partake of the whole truth? What situation do those who seek the truth find themselves in? Can they feel confident that what exists will freely reveal itself to them, or is knowledge to be acquired only through an act of violence, by outwitting the object, extorting information from it under duress, interrogating it on the rack? Is our share in truth meaningfully regulated by the economy of our needs, for example, or by our aptitude for superabundant happiness in accordance with the idea of a *visio beatifica?* These are all questions that barely a philosophical school has attempted to answer with systematic means; we nonetheless maintain that everywhere in the language of philosophy, *indications* can be found that answers to these questions have always already been given in a subterranean stratum of thought, answers that, although they may not be contained in the systems in propositional form, have never ceased to pervade, tincture, and structure them. The categorial equipment needed to grasp and describe such indications is still far from complete and methodologically operational. When we classify philosophical 'dispositions' as optimistic or pessimistic, for example, we basically stick to the sullenness or cheerfulness of a given physiognomy, without reaching back to the *orientations* in relation to which such apparently emotional 'settings' are first constituted. These settings are 'read off' quite elementary *model representations* that push through to the expressive sphere in the form of metaphors.

To illustrate these settings, a group of truth metaphors in which truth is ascribed a particular kind of 'comportment', an energetic quality, will be presented here in a series of paradigms. Although it does not constitute a legitimate object of theology, a fundamental conviction of this kind can also assume a theological guise. Milton

---

2. See my essay "Licht als Metapher der Wahrheit," in *Studium Generale* X (1957): 432–47. [Hans Blumenberg, "Light as a Metaphor of Truth," trans. Joel Anderson, in *Modernity and the Hegemony of Vision,* ed. David Levin (Berkeley: University of California Press, 1993), 30–62.]

writes: "God himself is truth . . . We cannot suppose the Deity envious of truth, or unwilling that it should be freely communicated to mankind."[3] On the same topic, we read in Goethe's "Maxims and Reflections": "If God had wanted human beings to live and act in truth, he would have had to set things up differently."[4] Here there is at least a hint of what is meant by 'truth' in the naïve questions formulated above: a certain transparency of the structure of the world, an ultimately straightforward publicity of the creative will, a lack of inhibition in the self-disclosure of what exists, the 'intensity' of the *veritas ontologica*. Of course, whether such publicity of Being is seen to attest to God's goodness will depend, in turn, on how the relationship between human happiness and the possession of truth is conceived. If it is deemed more salutary for people to imbibe knowledge only in measured doses, then God's goodness will reveal itself precisely in the economy with which he distributes truth to them: ". . . that portion of truth which he (the Father of Light) has laid within the reach of their natural faculties."[5] The premises clothed here in the language of theology can also appear as attributes of the hypostasized truth itself, which can withhold and conceal itself or assert itself in triumph, be characterized as almighty or impotent, impose itself against our will or forcibly be brought under our control.

Aristotle, for whom the history of his philosophical predecessors points teleologically toward his own insights and culminates in them, sees in this preparatory orientation the tacit striving of the 'matter itself': "But as men proceeded in this way, the very circumstances of the case led them on and compelled them to seek further."[6] The motive for inquiry is not sought in the subject; it is as if truth itself were pressing its claims, manifesting itself from the very beginning in turns of phrase that seem to anticipate insight without yet possessing it, "as though truth itself drove them to it in spite of themselves."[7] The epistemic situation presupposed by the Stoics, by contrast, is one in which the early scenario of vague intimations and hints has long since given way to a surfeit of competing sectarian opinions and dogmatic offers; the full force of the evidence is required to compel the Stoic subject, mistrustfully tarrying in its customary position of ἐποχή, to give its assent to what is brought before it (συγκατάθεσις). This compulsion is described by the concept

---

3. *Second Defence*, cited in B. Willey, *The Seventeenth-Century Background: Studies in the Thought of the Age in Relation to Poetry and Religion* (London, 1953), 243.

4. *Wäre es Gott darum zu tun gewesen, daß die Menschen in der Wahrheit leben und handeln sollten, so hätte er seine Einrichtung anders machen müssen. Werke,* ed. E. Beutler, IX, 611.

5. Locke, *Essay concerning Human Understanding,* IV 19, 4. Cf. ibid., Introduction 6 (ed. Frazer, I, 31): *Our business here is not to know all things, but those which concern our conduct.*

6. αὐτὸ τὸ πρᾶγμα ὡδοποίησεν αὐτοῖς καὶ συνηνάγκαζε ζητεῖν. *Metaph.* 984a18; b8–11. [Aristotle, *Metaphysics, Books I-IX,* trans. Hugh Tredennick (Cambridge, MA: Harvard University Press, 1922), 23.]

7. ὥσπερ ὑπ᾽ αὐτῆς τῆς ἀληθείας ἀναγκασθέντες. *Phys.* 188b29 sq. Cf. *De part. an.* 642a18–20. [Aristotle, *The Physics, Books I-IV,* trans. Philip W. Wickstead and Francis M. Cornford (Cambridge, MA: Harvard University Press, 1957), 57.]

of the 'apprehensive presentation' (καταληπτικὴ φαντασία); yet it is by no means obvious who is being compelled here by whom. The original Zenonian idea seems to have been that a 'cataleptic' presentation is one that seizes and masters the object as it exists 'itself', bringing it to presence in the fullness of its concrete characteristics. The second meaning of the cataleptic presentation appears to have dawned at a later date: the mind seized and overwhelmed by the evidence of the presentation is now the object of κατάληψις. The classical metaphor of light, brought into play through the derivation of φαντασία from φῶς in Stoic etymology,[8] is indifferent to the 'direction of action' of cataleptic compulsion and points rather to the theory (θεωρία) of the classical period, with its attitude of restful enjoyment and trusting contemplation: "Just as light shows both itself and the things that stand in the light, so too the presentation shows both itself and that which it calls forth." Such 'showing' no longer satisfies the demands made by the Stoics on the strength of the evidence; a metaphorics of *imprinting* takes the place of the light metaphor. The apprehensive presentation can then only be interpreted as a molding of the epistemic organ, as an "imprinting upon the soul" (τύπωσι ἐν ψυχῇ), like the impress of a seal.[9] The almost violently compulsive effect of the utmost presentational 'thickness' is conveyed still more vividly in the report of Sextus Empiricus, for whom the 'apprehensive presentation' seizes us by the hair and drags us off to give our assent.[10] A metaphorics of this kind is instructive not only for the ideas underlying the Stoic doctrine of knowledge, but equally for the attitude of theoretical resignation that characterized Hellenism as a whole, an attitude that felt itself obliged to place enormous demands on a truth before being prepared to accept it.

The Aristotelian metaphor of the truth paving its own way became a popular patristic expression for the Christian doctrine supposedly prepared and foreshadowed by the ancients. Classical poets and philosophers could be cited in support of monotheism, not because they had already been in possession of the truth as knowledge, but because the truth is so mighty that no one can entirely deny its penetration and radiance.[11] It is highly characteristic that here, too, a *resistance* to truth on the part of the subject is presupposed, a further heightening of Hellenistic indifference and abstention. Thus Plotinus, in demonstrating the inconsequentiality of

---

8. *Stoicorum Veterum Fragmenta*, ed. Arnim (= *SVF*) 11, fr. 54. Cf. Sextus Empiricus, *Adv. math.* VII, 442.

9. *SVF* 11, fr. 55. The irrefutable evidence of the 'apprehensive presentation' is brought out very forcefully in the report of Sextus Empiricus as well, *Adv. math.* VII, 248: It is "imaged and stamped in the subject in accordance with that existing object." [Sextus Empiricus, *Against the Logicians,* trans. R. G. Bury (Cambridge, MA: Harvard University Press, 1957), 137.]

10. VII, 257. [Sextus Empiricus, *Against the Logicians,* trans. Bury, 137.]

11. Lactantius, *Divinae institutiones* I 5, 2: . . . *non quod illi habuerint cognitam veritatem, sed quod veritatis ipsius tanta vis est, ut nemo possit esse tam caecus, qui non videat ingerentem se oculis divinam claritatem.* [. . . not that they had ascertained the truth, but that the force of the truth itself is so great, that no one can be so blind as not to see the divine brightness presenting itself to his eyes; *Ante-Nicene Fathers,* ed. Alexander Roberts and James Donaldson, trans. William Fletcher (Peabody, MA: Hendrikson Publishers, 2004), VII, 13.]

the Stoics with regard to their own materialism, lets them unwittingly testify that the essence of the soul must be something higher than the body.[12] We again encounter the characteristic *se ingerere* [forcing or presenting itself] from the passage in Lactantius cited above in the typical account, related by Anselm of Canterbury in the preface to his "Proslogion," of how he discovered the proof of God's existence thereafter associated with his name. Anselm refers to his "Monologion," where he tells how "through silent reasoning with himself" he wrestled with the "meaning of faith." After his painstaking and time-consuming search for a "single argument that for its proof required no other save itself" had proved fruitless, he had all but resigned himself to failure: "Finally, in desperation, I was about to give up." He had abandoned his efforts, and even turned to pursue fresh interests, when he was startled by the flash of insight: "However, when I had decided to put aside this idea altogether, lest by uselessly occupying my mind it might prevent other ideas with which I could make some progress, then, in spite of my unwillingness and my resistance to it, it began to force itself upon me more pressingly."[13] We find the Aristotelian formulation once again in Thomas Aquinas's commentary to "De anima" (I 4, 43), where he says of Empedocles and Plato that they arrived at their doctrine of the soul "as though compelled by the force of truth itself; they dreamed, as it were, of the truth."[14] The double meaning of 'truth' is here anything but a play on words. Thomas can make truth the efficient cause (not the formal cause!) of knowledge when he writes in "De veritate" I, 1: "Cognition is the result of a truth."[15] That looks like an imageless, purely terminological statement, a typical example of 'pure Scholasticism', no less, but it proves on closer inspection to be oriented toward a metaphorical background, toward what we propose to call an "implicative model." This means that metaphors, in the function discussed here, do not need to appear as such in the lexical sphere of expression; but a collection of statements suddenly coalesces into a meaningful unity if the leading metaphorical representation from which these statements were 'read off' can be hypothetically ascertained.

---

12. *Enneades* IV 7, 4: μαρτυροῦσι δὲ καὶ αὐτοὶ ὑπὸ τῆς ἀληθείας ἀγόμενοι, ὡς δεῖ . . . [Our opponents themselves are driven by stress of fact to admit the necessity . . . ; Plotinus, *The Enneads,* trans. Stephen MacKenna (London: Faber & Faber, 1980), 344.]

13. *tacite secum ratiocinando . . . ratio fidei . . . argumentum quod nullo alio ad se probandum quam se solo indigeret . . . Sed cum illam cogitationem, ne mentem meam frustra occupando ab aliis in quibis proficere possem impediret, penitus a me vellem excludere: tunc magis ac magis nolenti et defendenti se coepit cum importunitate quadam ingerere. Opera,* ed. F. S. Schmitt, I, 93. [Anselm of Canterbury, *St. Anselm's Proslogion,* trans. M. S. Charlesworth (Oxford: The Clarendon Press, 1965), 103.] The report continues: *Cum igitur quadam die vehementer eius importunitati resistendo fatigarer, in ipso cogitationum conflictu sic se obtulit, quod desperaveram, ut studiose cogitationem amplecterer, quam sollicitus repellebam* [So it was that one day when I was quite worn out with resisting its importunacy, there came to me, in the very conflict of my thoughts, what I had despaired of finding, so that I eagerly grasped the notion which in my distraction I had been rejecting].

14. *quasi ab ipsa veritate coacti, somniabant quodammodo veritatem.* [Aristotle, *Aristotle's* De Anima *in the Version of William of Moerbeke and the Commentary of St. Thomas Aquinas,* trans. Kenelm Foster and Silvester Humphries (London: Routledge & Kegan Paul, 1951), 71.]

15. *Cognitio est quidam veritatis effectus.*

The metaphor of the self-activating power of truth survives well into the modern age. In his introduction to book V of his "Harmony of the World," Kepler expresses his astonishment that Ptolemy had already achieved in his "Harmony" what Kepler had stumbled across independently and by taking a different route: "The very nature of things was setting out to reveal itself to men, through interpreters separated by a distance of centuries. This identity of conception, on the conformation of the world, in the minds of two men who had given themselves wholly to the study of nature, was the finger of God, to borrow the Hebrew phrase, since neither had guided the other to tread this path."[16] Disregarding the fact that 'nature' has here taken the place of hypostasized 'truth', we can see that the subjective ingredient, the painstaking study of nature, complements and even conditions the obliging self-revelation of nature. It is significant that in Vico,[17] the metaphor of the force of truth (*vis veri*) is built into a theory of error. The human mind is struck to the core by the mightiness of truth, "for the mind is always put under compulsion by truth," but the will counters this force and neutralizes it by means of a language drained of meaning, unfulfilled, and mired in mere 'opinion': "But words very often, by the will of him who is lying, escape the force of truth and desert the mind."[18] The 'fate' of truth is increasingly consigned to the immanent play of subjective faculties, even if the "Dictionnaire de l'Académie" of 1694 still speaks in good 'medieval' fashion of "the force of truth, which is to say the power that the truth has over the mind of men."[19] While "the invincible force of truth" may still play a role in the vocabulary of the Enlightenment, there it is rather a topos of modesty serving to conceal the self-consciousness of a spirit that illuminates with its own light.[20]

It is interesting to note how the link between 'truth' and 'force' is transformed and even perverted in the writings of a skeptic like David Hume. Whereas the traditional version of the metaphor represents 'force' as a legitimate attribute of truth, emphasizing the self-assertion of a primordial metaphysical right, for Hume force has become the sole 'substance' of truth. 'Truth' is simply the name we give to the fact that particular representations prevail over others in human consciousness,

---

16. [Johannes Kepler, *The Harmony of the World*, trans. E. J. Aiton, A. M. Duncan, and J. V. Field (Philadelphia: American Philosophical Society, 1997), 391.]

17. *Opere*, ed. Ferrari², II, 96; III, 110.

18. *mens enim semper a vero urgetur mens enim semper a vero urgetur . . . verba autem saepissime veri vim voluntate mentientis eludunt ac mentem deserunt.* [English in Benedetto Croce, *The Philosophy of Giambattista Vico*, trans. R. G. Collingwood (London: Howard Latimer, 1913), 68.]

19. *La force de la vérité, pour dire le pouvoir que la vérité a sur l'esprit des hommes.*

20. I cite as evidence the preface to the work on Joachim of Fiore by François Armand Gervaise (*Histoire de l'Abbé Joachim, surnommé le prophète* [Paris, 1745], I, 4): *. . . je tâcherai de mettre jour dans tout son génie, son charactère, ses inclinations, ses vues, ses pensées, ses écrits, sa conduite: par-là j'espère que l'Abbé Joachim ne sera plus un problème et que les sentiments du public, jusqu'à présent si partagé a son sujet, se réuniront dans un seul. Telle est la force invincible de la vérité: elle se fait jour à travers les ténèbres les plus épaisses.* [I will strive in everything to shed light on his genius, his character, his inclinations, his views, his thoughts, his writings, his conduct: by this means I hope that Abbot Joachim will no longer pose a problem and that public opinion, until now so divided on this subject, will reach a consensus. Such is the invincible force of truth: it dawns through the deepest gloom.]

and so attain to the status of 'belief', due to the sheer amount of energy they have on their side; the criterion for distinguishing true ideas from false is thus the "superior force" of true ideas, or better: that class of ideas that are thereby declared to be 'true'.[21] "When I am convinc'd of any principle, 'tis only an idea, which strikes more strongly upon me." Here, truth no longer *has* a power; rather, we theoretically legitimate as true whatever has power over *us*. Admittedly, this is not so positivistic a claim as it may sound, since a covert teleological implication stands behind it as a proviso: in the power over us that we interpret as 'truth', 'nature' reveals itself to be an agency that has our own best interests at heart, one whose 'practical' care we 'theoretically' reconceptualize under the heading of truth. The metaphor has here ceased to be a metaphor; it has been 'taken at its word', naturalized, and become indistinguishable from a physical proposition.

---

21. *Treatise of Human Nature* (1738), I 3, 7–8.

II

METAPHORICS OF TRUTH
AND PRAGMATICS OF KNOWLEDGE

In the treatise on Alexander Pope he wrote in collaboration with Mendelssohn, Lessing speaks of the philosophical use of what in rhetoric are called 'figures', a category that includes metaphor: "And wherein consists the essence of the same?—In their never sticking strictly to the truth; they say now too much, now too little— only a metaphysician of Böhme's ilk can be forgiven them."[1]

What Lessing raises here is the question of the truth of metaphor itself. It is self-evident that metaphors like that of the power or impotence of truth *do not admit of verification,* and that the alternative already decided in them one way or the other is *theoretically* undecidable. Metaphors are unable to satisfy the requirement that truth, by definition, be the result of a methodologically secure procedure

---

1. *Und worin bestehet das Wesen derselben?—Darin, daß sie nie bei der strengen Wahrheit blieben; daß sie bald zu viel, und bald zu wenig sagen— —Nur einem Metaphysiker, von der Gattung eines Böhmens, kann man sie verzeihen.* Pope ein Metaphysiker!—*Werke,* ed. P. Rilla, VII, 233. The paragraph I have just cited was undoubtedly written by Lessing. Compare this statement, published in 1755, with what Bouhours had already written about metaphors in his 1687 text "La manière de bien penser dans les ouvrages de l'esprit": *Le figure n'est pas faux et la métaphore a sa vérité aussi bien que la fiction* [Figurative language is not false, and metaphor has its truth just as much as fiction]. On Bouhours's aesthetics, see E. Cassirer, *Die Philosophie der Aufklärung* (Tübingen, 1932), 400 ff.

of verification. They therefore not only fail to say 'nothing but the truth', they do not say anything truthful at all. Absolute metaphors 'answer' the supposedly naïve, in principle unanswerable questions whose relevance lies quite simply in the fact that they cannot be brushed aside, since we do not *pose* them ourselves but find them already *posed* in the ground of our existence. We must bear in mind here that a metaphorology cannot result in any method for *using* metaphors, or for addressing the questions that announce themselves in them. On the contrary: as students of metaphorology, we have already deprived ourselves of the possibility of finding 'answers' in metaphors to those unanswerable questions. Metaphor, as the theme of a metaphorology in the sense that will concern us here, is an essentially *historical* object whose testimonial value presupposes that the witnesses did not possess, and could not have possessed, a metaphorology of their own. Our situation is therefore characterized by the positivistic program of a resolute critique of language in its 'guiding function' for our thinking, whereby an expression like 'true' becomes immediately superfluous (Ayer), *or* (or rather *and*) our situation is characterized by the 'transference' of the operation formerly deposited in metaphors to *art*[2]—the latter taken to persist in unhistorical and unmediated productivity—whereby the urgency of those questions proves to be ungainsayable. The task and method of metaphorology may therefore take us beyond the historical sphere of objects to a selective interpretation of expressive elements in art.

Having voiced these reservations, we ask once again about the relevance of absolute metaphors, their *historical* truth. This truth is *pragmatic* in a very broad sense. By providing a point of orientation, the content of absolute metaphors determines a particular attitude or conduct [*Verhalten*]; they give structure to a world, representing the nonexperienceable, nonapprehensible totality of the real. To the historically trained eye, they therefore indicate the fundamental certainties, conjectures, and judgments in relation to which the attitudes and expectations, actions and inactions, longings and disappointments, interests and indifferences, of an epoch are regulated. "What genuine guidance does it give?"[3] This form of the "truth question," formulated by pragmatism, is pertinent here in a sense that has nothing to do with biology. A question like "What is the world?", with its demand as imprecise as it is hypertrophic, cannot serve as a point of departure for theoretical discourse; but it

---

2. Incidentally—but not irrelevantly—these considerations shed light on the contemporary importance of art as the *real metaphysical activity of this life* (Nietzsche), pertaining to an age that, in its omnivorous will to historical understanding and self-understanding, has almost everywhere destroyed its freedom of genuine expression, and that has created in its art something like a sanctuary, maintained by popular consensus, for a historically conscious ahistoricism. The Absolute, which modern man seems most likely to encounter in his aesthetic experiences (at least if the flourishing metaphysics of art is to be believed), presents itself here as something untouched by the distortions wreaked by historically reflective consciousness. Hence the widespread predilection, seldom differentiating precisely between naïveté and refinement, for "Fauvist" tendencies of all kinds. Just how highly a future metaphorology will rate the documentary value of productive imagination for our age will depend on how we answer the fundamental question as to whether such *ekstasis* from the historically reflected situation has been successful, indeed whether it can succeed at all.

3. [English in original.]

does bring to light an implicit need for knowledge that, in the 'how' of an attitude, knows itself to be reliant on the 'what' of an all-encompassing and sustaining whole, and that seeks to give itself a modicum of stability by taking its bearings from that whole. Time and again, this implicit questioning has 'lived itself out' in metaphors, and it has induced from metaphors different styles of relating to the world. The truth of metaphor is a *vérité à faire*. Although it has been idle, ever since Kant's antinomies, to make theoretical assertions about the totality of the world, the quest for images to 'stand in' for this objectively unattainable whole is by no means a trifling matter. In his "Auswahl aus des Teufels Papieren" |Selection from the Devil's Papers|, Jean Paul writes: "I will never regret instructing everyone here, so far as is possible with good analogies, what this world really is. It can be the *cul de sac* in the great city of God or a mere *provincial town* in comparison with other planets. It is the *baby walker or baby runner* of mankind, designed to teach us to get around on our own two feet. It is . . . the *wings* and dressing room of another world, in which we will first play our parts not without approbation. It is a *dark chamber* (camera obscura) into which a ray of light transmits and depicts reversed and contracted images of a finer chamber without; . . . it is the *numerator* to a yet invisible denominator; truly, I say, it is almost nothing at all."[4] That is a tidbit of scurrilous wisdom, informed by a venerable metaphorical tradition, which appears to stand precisely on the border of ironic reflectiveness, where it forfeits its ahistorical innocence. It may be juxtaposed with a quotation from a recent work of philosophy: "What the world really is—not what we ordinarily imagine it to be, but the authentic, the true, the whole and hale world, which by no means stands there for all to see but is entirely concealed from view, perhaps not even here today, perhaps never there at all but always to come—that is the fundamental question motivating Heidegger's thought. In his later writings he answers this question by defining the world as 'the enowning mirror play of the unifold of earth and sky, divine and mortal.' And purely poetic words speak the answers to the question of what these four might be . . ."[5] What the world really is—this least decidable of all questions is at the same time the never undecidable, and therefore always already decided, question. That it is 'cosmos' was one of the constitutive decisions of our intellectual history, a metaphor heard again and again in its original meaning despite its early nominalization,[6] and spun out in

---

4. *Es wird mich niemals reuen, wenn ich, so gut es mit guten Gleichnissen möglich ist, hier Jeden lehre, was diese Welt eigentlich ist. Sie kann gar wol das* Sackgäßchen *in der großen Stadt Gottes sein oder eine bloße* Provinzialstadt *in Vergleichung mit andern Planeten. Sie ist der* Gängel- oder Laufwagen *der Menschheit, um sie aufschreiten zu lehren. Sie ist . . . die* Kulisse *und Anziehstube für eine andere Welt, in der wir erst unsere Rollen nicht ohne Beifall machen. Sie ist eine* dunkle Kammer *(camera obscura), in die ein Strahl umgewendete und zusammengezogene Bilder einer schönern trägt und malt; . . . sie ist der* Zähler *zu einem noch unsichtbaren Nenner; wahrhaftig, ich sage, sie ist fast gar nichts.* "Auswahl aus des Teufels Papieren," XII.

5. W. Bröcker, *Dialektik—Positivismus—Mythologie* (Frankfurt, 1958), 35. |I borrow the ugly neologism "enowning" (*ereignend*) from Parvis Emad and Kenneth Maly's translation of Heidegger's *Contributions to Philosophy* (Bloomington: Indiana University Press, 1999).|

6. If the much-discussed fragment 124 of Heraclitus (Diels B) really does equate the beautiful cosmos with "a heap of sweepings, piled up at random," then this surely presupposes that the populace had forgotten the meaning of 'cosmos'. Even in Epicurus, we can easily see that the mechanistic chance

the metaphors of the cosmic polis and the world organism, the *theatrum mundi* and the clockwork universe. Only relatively seldom is it possible to adduce *documentary* evidence for what was *pragmatically* signified in each case—ultimately, we cannot measure our demands on the documentation by the yardstick of our current capacity to 'interpret' ourselves historically at the level of our most deep-seated motives. I must admit that here, discovering authenticating material is largely a matter of chance, however much one may develop a feeling for where to rummage for such material. Thus the Stoic cosmic polis resurfaces, refunctioned in an interesting way, in Tertullian, who defends the outlawed church by characterizing the state as a matter of complete indifference to Christians. They are consequently immune to the temptation to meddle in politics and foment unrest: "Nothing is more foreign to us than the state. One state we know, of which all are citizens—the universe."[7] If the cosmic polis originally consoled the Stoics by reconciling them to the breakdown of the Hellenic state system, it is now conceived as the superordinate neutralization of an overbearing and hostile state perfection. According to a well-known apocryphal saying attributed to Jesus: "The world is a bridge. Pass over it, but do not build your dwelling there."[8] Here the pragmatic amplification has been included. The following statement is ascribed to Rabbi Elieser, the son of Jose the Galilean: "The world is like a shop that stands open for business, and like a table that is always set, but a book lies open on it, and a hand is registering everything in that book. The merchant borrows, but the creditor lives and reigns."[9] In Alexandrine *allegoresis,* the colorful robe worn by the high priest is interpreted as the cosmos, while the high priest himself represents the godhead; this leads to the *rejection* of an understanding of the cosmos as the garb of God, the disavowal of an aestheticizing view of the world.[10] Allegory may well be heterogeneous to metaphor—it is not "the thought born immediately in the image," to use Fontane's expression[11]—but it can retroactively spring into

---

arrangement of atoms cannot fully assert itself against the fundamental Greek decision for the cosmos. Indeed, the thesis of purely hyletic primordial processes only has its intended therapeutic effect (or is credited with having such an effect) because, in the end, it is self-evidently always the same eidetically unique cosmos that 'comes out' in an unforeseeable plurality of copies. Preliminary decisions for particular images thus by no means rely for their explanation on specific systems; their force suffices to tincture systems of a very different stamp.

7. *at enim nobis . . . nec ulla magis res aliena quam publica. unam omnium rem publicam agnoscimus, mundum. Apologeticum* 38, 3. [Tertullian, *Apology,* trans. T. R. Glover (Cambridge, MA: Harvard University Press, 2003), 173.]

8. A version can be found on the Buland Darwasa in Fatehpur Sikri containing words explicitly attributed to Jesus: *The world is a bridge; cross it, but do not build a house upon it; it lasts only for an hour.* M. Lasky, "Reise nach Indien," *Der Monat Heft* 118 (1958): 65.

9. M. J. bin Gorion, *Der Born Judas,* 2nd ed. (Leipzig, 1959), II, 296.

10. *Sapientia Salomonis* 18, 24.

11. I quote the entire passage owing to its relevance for our topic: *Es muß der Gedanke gleich im Bilde geboren werden, dann kann das Bild schöner und frappanter sein als das einfache Wort; wird das Bild aber erst als Extrakleid genäht und dann angezogen, so sitzt es nicht und ist eine Last und kein Schmuck.* [The thought must be born immediately in the image, then the image can be more beautiful and striking than the simple word; but if the image is first sewn as an additional article of clothing and then put on, it does not sit well and is a burden, not an ornament.] (Theater review from 19 February 1881: Laube, *Die Karlsschüler.*)

the function of metaphor through an inversion of the projective relationship.[12] For Thomas Browne the world is "not an Inne, but an Hospitall."[13] For Vauvenargues it is a social event governed by obscure factors and conventions: "Whoever has seen the masks at a ball . . . can get an idea of the nature of the world."[14] For Melville, metaphorizing his novel "White-Jacket, or, The World in a Man of War" in its final chapter, the world is a man-of-war that has quit its port forever and is sailing with sealed orders toward a final haven unknown to all on board. The old destiny metaphor of the "ship at high seas" is here combined with a new consciousness of universal entropy to take the form of the *voyage metaphor,* which has its timeless source in Homer's "Odyssey" but now assumes the counterform of denied homecoming, irreversibility, noncircularity. That reads almost like the outline of a rather enticing research project that still remains to be written.[15] What I am submitting here is only semifinished product, and the perfection and comprehensiveness with which one can deal with 'Being' is quite unattainable in this field.[16]

After this attempt to illustrate and methodically unpack the pragmatic meaning of absolute metaphor, let us return to the metaphorics of the mightiness of truth to test the procedure of pragmatic interpretation there as well. The amount of effort required to access the truth will stand in inverse relation to the power attributed to it. There can be no doubt that the vitality of the metaphor of the mighty truth has a certain quietism as its correlate. The tepidity with which a Lactantius advocates 'his' truth is explicable in the light of his truth metaphorics: "The power of truth is so great that it defends itself even in small things by its own clearness."[17] Tertullian, by contrast, comes across as an attorney desperately pleading for a lost cause, but only because he is adamant that matters first be placed on a sound procedural basis

---

12. Examples in E. Stein, *Die allegorische Exegese des Philo aus Alexandria,* Beih. Z. Ztschr. f. atl. Wiss. 51 (Gießen, 1929). On the historical evaluation of allegory, see H. G. Gadamer, "Symbol und Allegorie," *Archivio di Philosofia* 1958, 27: *The concept of allegory is closely bound up with dogmatism: with the rationalization of the mythical (as in the Greek Enlightenment), or with the Christian interpretation of Scripture in terms of doctrinal unity (as in patristics), and finally with the reconciliation of the Christian tradition and classical culture, which is the basis of the art and literature of modern Europe and whose last universal form was the baroque. With the breakup of this tradition allegory too was finished. For the moment art freed itself from all dogmatic bonds and could be defined as the unconscious production of genius, allegory inevitably became aesthetically suspect.* [H. G. Gadamer, *Truth and Method,* trans. W. Glen-Doepel, rev. Joel Weinsheimer and Donald G. Marshall (New York: Crossroad, 1989), 79.]

13. *Religio Medici* (1642) II, sect. 11 [Thomas Browne, *The Major Works* (Harmondsworth: Penguin, 1977), 153]. The motif recurs in T. S. Eliot, *Four Quartets,* "East Coker" IV: *The whole earth is our hospital / Endowed by the ruined millionaire . . .*

14. *Die französischen Moralisten,* ed. F. Schalk (Leipzig, 1938), I, 122. [*Quiconque a vu des masques, dans un bal . . . peut se faire une idée du monde*; Vauvenargues, *Oeuvres complètes* (Paris: Hachette, 1968), 437.]

15. [See Hans Blumenberg, *Shipwreck with Spectator: Paradigm of a Metaphor for Existence,* trans. Steven Rendall (Cambridge, MA: MIT Press, 1997).]

16. [This sardonic reference to Heidegger's fundamental ontology is developed further, with a sly nod to Hitchcock, in Hans Blumenberg, "Being—A MacGuffin: How to Preserve the Desire to Think," trans. David Adams, *Salmagundi* 90/91 (1991): 191–93.]

17. *tanta est potentia veritatis, ut seipsam, quamvis in rebus exiguis, sua claritate defendat. Div. inst.* III 1, 5. [*Ante-Nicene Fathers,* ed. Alexander Roberts and James Donaldson, trans. William Fletcher (Peabody, MA: Hendrikson Publishers, 2004), VII, 69.]

that will enable his client, the truth, to speak and give testimony for itself; for then "the simplicity of truth is set forth; its own worth sustains it; no ground remains for the least suspicion."[18] Here as elsewhere, a judicial metaphorics forms the frame and the stage upon which the triumph of truth is played out; the Scholastic disputation of the Middle Ages is informed to the last detail by the background idea of truth asserting itself in the medium of judicial proceedings. For this to occur, however, a suitably undistorted and receptive situation must be created. Thus Lactantius cites as evidence for monotheism that the Romans called upon neither Jupiter nor the gods in the emotional immediacy with which they swore their oaths, made wishes, and gave thanks, but simply "God": "so entirely does the truth of its own accord break forth by the force of nature even from unwilling breasts."[19] The prehistory of the scientific experiment likewise points toward this context, although the experiment was to become, in effect, the exemplar of precisely the opposite conception of truth, as we shall soon see. But the characteristic spirit of experimentation, the production of constellations from which knowledge all but 'jumps out', is originally embedded in a confidence in truth that believes it must do nothing more than provide the occasion for the verificational procedure. Nicolaus of Cusa, whom we should by no means picture as a real scientist working with various constructions under laboratory conditions (his "experiments with the scales" notwithstanding), nonetheless did a great deal to pave the way for experimental thinking by continually 'testing through' new constellations of ideas, never shying away from the boldness of a particular combination or procedure. He thereby created a *style* of 'experimental' thinking that was no longer so far removed from the experiment in the narrower sense of the term. And all this incipient courage to sail into uncharted waters reposes on a belief in the ease (*facilitas*) of knowledge[20] by virtue of the mightiness of truth: "The clearer truth is, the easier it is. I once thought that truth is better found amid the obscure. Truth is of great power."[21]

One thing should not be overlooked in this context: both the metaphor of the mightiness of truth and the topos of the ease of knowledge that flows from it overwhelmingly arise as characteristics of theological and moral concerns bearing on the issue of salvation. Classical Greek philosophy is certainly aware of hierarchical distinctions among the objects of theory, but it knows nothing of entire regions of objects that are to be excluded for having no eudaemonic value at all, or even for

---

18. *simplicitas veritatis in medio est; virtus illi sua adsistit; nihil suspicari licebit. Apolog.* 23, 7. [*Ante-Nicene Fathers,* trans. Fletcher, III, 37.]

19. *adeo ipsa veritas cogente natura, etiam ab invitis pectoribus erumpit. Div. inst.* II I, 7. [*Ante-Nicene Fathers,* trans. Fletcher, VII, 40.]

20. *Idiota de sapientia,* ed. Baur, II, 37: *O miranda facilitas difficilium!* [O marvelous ease of what is difficult!] On the inner coherence of Cusanus's thought, see my introduction to the anthology of his writings: *Die Kunst der Vermutung* (Bremen, 1957).

21. *Veritas quanto clarior, tanto facilior. Putabam ego aliquando ipsam in obscuro melius reperiri. Magnae potentiae veritas est. De apice theoriae* (1463/4). [Nicholas of Cusa: *Metaphysical Speculations,* trans. Jasper Hopkins (Minneapolis: Arthur J. Banning Press, 1997), 1: 6.]

placing that goal in jeopardy. It was left to the thinkers of the Hellenistic epoch, proceeding from the assumption, common to almost all the Hellenistic schools, of the *therapeutic* function of philosophy, to develop an economics of epistemic comportment. It is a still insufficiently heeded difference between Greek classicism and Hellenism that, whereas truth is conceived in the former as the consummating entelechy of spirit, for the latter it is a corrective with curative properties, a medicine (φάρμακον) to be administered in carefully measured doses. What matters now is that everything superfluous, contentious, and obscure in the theoretical field be excluded as a source of confusion, doubt, and dogmatic strife, that it be neutralized in the fundamental bearing of the ἐποχή. The fulfillment of existence is to be secured by *shielding* an inner space of subjectivity that now breaks away from the world, rather than by *enriching* one's stock of truth in interaction with the world. On the other hand, a specific set of statements is now pooled into a fund of truths deemed necessary for salvation, first and foremost the legacy of moral insights inherited from the Stoics. Teleology no longer signifies the universal concord of cosmos and logos for the fulfillment of human existence (εὐδαιμονία); instead, it guarantees the conspicuousness and penetrative force of those truths on which salvation depends, beside which all other truths sink back into the semidarkness of mere verisimilitude or the inaccessibility of *res obscurae.* Cicero, who represents the synthesis of Skeptical and Stoic elements I have just outlined, not just eclectically, but with an unerring instinct for the founding motivational unity of the Hellenistic schools, includes a preoccupation with the *res obscurae* and *non necessariae* in his catalog of offenses (*vitia*) against the ideality of wisdom (*sapientia*).[22] Practical reason thus regulates which truths are 'necessary' and which are not, and the murkiness and difficulty of many objects, particularly those pertaining to physics, is a teleological index of their salvational irrelevance: "That, perhaps, is one of Nature's hidden secrets. God has not willed me to know the cause, but only that I should use the means which he has given."[23] The patristic reception picked up this distinction between knowing (*scire*) and using (*uti*), honing it into the difference, so fundamental to the Middle Ages, between enjoying (*frui*) and using (*uti*).[24] Whereas Cicero, authorized by the tradition in which he stood, had still excluded the disciplines of

---

22. *De officiis* I 6, 18.

23. *Latet fortasse obscuritate involuta naturae. Non enim me deus ista scire, sed his tantummodo uti voluit. De divinatione* I 35. [Cicero, *De senectate, De amicitia, De divinatione,* trans. William Falconer (Cambridge, MA: Harvard University Press, 1971), 265.]

24. The traditional form of the dualism receives its most definitive formulation in the "Sentences" of Petrus Lombardus, I dist. I q. 2–3: *De rebus quibus fruendum est vel utendum.—Quia sit uti vel frui.* [Of those things which should be enjoyed or used.—The meaning of enjoying or using. Peter Lombard, *The Sentences,* trans. Guilio Silmo (Toronto: Pontifical Institute of Mediaeval Studies, 2007), I, 6; translation modified.] This was canonized as an object of the obligatory commentaries on the "Sentences" and became, in its sometimes very subtle modifications, one of the most important, still unwritten chapters in the conceptual prehistory of the modern age, an epoch for which the relationship between use and pleasure numbers among the most important preliminary decisions (and problems!). I hope to be able to present more on this in the future. I have ventured some initial remarks in *Studium Generale* IV (1951):

geometry and astronomy from his index of obscure and unnecessary things, the salvational absolutism of an Ambrosius goes a step further in its censure: all that lies hidden is the sole property of him to whom "nothing hidden is unknown."[25] With that, something quite unprecedented gets underway: entire domains of theoretical inquiry about the world are declared off-limits to human beings. They are associated with the sinful attitude of *curiositas,* which seeks to go beyond the limits of what God's salvational care has ordained.[26] Emphasis is placed on the insufficiency of whatever lies beyond these borders, so lending substantial support to the recalcitrance with which it withdraws from our sacrilegious attempts to explore and seize hold of it. This aspect had a profound and lasting impact on the epistemo-metaphysical position of *astronomy,* in particular, such that the greatest obstacle facing Copernicus was not so much a traditional celestial theory as the sanction placed upon *any* such theory. This sanction, which 'cleared' the heavens for research solely to the extent that such research was justified by the *utilitas* of calendar and feast-day calculations, stipulated that any hypothetical construction would do, so long as it satisfied this function. Cooperation with the calendar reform was the clandestine path taken by the theoretical interest. It follows that the type of research, speculation, and theorization specific to the early modern period is marked by its sojourn in a 'forbidden realm', and that truth, insofar as it is divorced from the salvational necessity of old and subordinated to a new ideal of human determination, still appears to bear the stamp of the seductive, the deviant, and the taboo. Here, the entire metaphorics of the might of truth is turned on its head in the idea of the violence that man must inflict upon the truth if he is to claim it for himself. Truth has completely forfeited what could be called its 'naturalness'; awareness of method and methodological reflection arise at the beginning of the

---

464–65. [Blumenberg's research in this area would culminate in *The Legitimacy of the Modern Age,* trans. Robert M. Wallace (Cambridge, MA: MIT Press, 1983).]

25. *De officiis ministrorum* I 26, 122–24.

26. Seneca had already subordinated this attitude to *intemperantia: Plus scire velle quam sit satis, intemperantiae genus est* (ad Luc. 88, 36) [To wish to know more than is sufficient is a kind of extravagance; Seneca, *Seventeen Letters,* trans. C. B. N. Costa (Warminster: Aris & Phillips, 1988), 83]. For an age that is no longer quite so sure that every truth—and even truth for its own sake—is good for mankind, a conceptual history of *curiositas* would be an urgent desideratum. A long and tortuous path leads from Augustine's authoritative definition (*Conf.* X, 35) *experiendi noscendique libido* [itch for gaining knowledge and experience] and *concupiscentia oculorum* [gratification of the eye] to the praise of curiosity as a "prescientific virtue" (E. Rothacker, *Studium Generale* XI [1958]: 144). As for the 'direction' of the boundary crossings, I quote—as an orienting model—a Talmudic text warning of the dangers of Gnosis: "For whomsoever investigates four things, it would have been better never to have been born: what is above and below, what came before, and what will come after." No Christian parallel for the severity of this verdict is known to me; and the degrees of intensity are all the more important the more a formulation becomes a topos that the author thinks he ought not to omit. Something new is often announced when objective reasons begin to flag, as when William of Ockham (in *Sent. Prol.* III 9 CC) only adduces a subjective economics of capacity for the negativity of *curiositas: intellectus vix sufficit ad illa quae sunt necessaria ad salutem* [The intellect is scarcely sufficient for those things that are necessary for salvation]. One sees here how the Scholastic hypertrophy of the 'salvationally necessary' has already led the principle *ad absurdum* as one of economy.

Modern Age from a profound sense of the forcefulness, caution, and circumspection required to establish a connection to truth. Truthful appearance is suspected of being only apparently true. All truth is earned and no longer freely given; from now on, knowledge assumes the character of *labor*.[27]

The master of the metaphorics of cunning, artfulness, and coercion in the acquisition of truth is Francis Bacon. In Bacon, the old metaphor of the world as theater and man as spectator is expressly revoked; the world becomes a tribunal, man the judge and convenor of the interrogation to which nature is to be subjected. From the account of "Poesy" given in the "Advancement of Learning" (II), Bacon nudges the reader on to the tribunal of the mind: "But it is not good to stay too long in the theatre. Let us now pass on to the judicial place or palace of the mind . . ." Bacon likes to speak of the "secrets" of nature, which it seems to want to conceal from us, and which we must prise from it through cunning. In "De augmentis scientiarum" (II, 2), the objection of illegitimate *curiositas* is briskly done away with: "Neither ought a man to make scruple of entering into the caves and hiding places of nature for inquisition of truth." The existing state of nature no longer enjoys metaphysical sanction; man is no longer just acting on nature's behalf, as in the Aristotelian conception of the relationship between nature and technology; he is no longer charged solely with the task of reproducing, improving, and completing what nature has left unfinished, without being able to change it, transform it, or refashion it from scratch. This, no less than the classical distinction between nature and technology itself, is an age-old error, which, as Bacon explicitly states, had led to "an overhasty discouragement of man in his endeavours." There is no need for man to confine himself to the repertory of eidetic types he finds in nature; to 'be able to do everything', he only has to know the constitutive rules and forces of natural processes. From this perspective, nature's resistance to the discovery of its truth can be recognized as a kind of self-protective reaction against man's will to technological transformation. The pursuit of knowledge becomes a well-organized expeditionary campaign. Bacon criticizes those who hold mechanical knowledge in contempt: "They be not the highest instances that give the securest information." The application of "History Mechanical" to causal research promises to shed new light on nature: "So nature exhibits herself more clearly under the trials and vexations of art than left to herself." The juristic "interrogate and prosecute with the utmost rigor" (*interrogare quam infestissime ac premere*) is the metaphorical formulation in which sheer mechanical force lays claim to institutional legitimacy, so to speak: in such metaphors, man banishes any doubts as to whether he is fit for this high office and whether he is justified in using all the means it places at his disposal. The rights exercised here are sovereign rights, and the unification of knowledge and power in a single hand, so fundamental for Bacon, has a pronounced

---

27. See my sketch "Technik und Wahrheit," in *Actes du Xième Congr. Int. de Philosophie* (Brussels, 1953), II, 113–20.

political-metaphorical background: "And so those twin objects, human knowledge and human power, do really meet in one."[28] The problem of the legitimacy of the claim to knowledge bequeathed by the medieval problematic of *curiositas* was of central importance to Bacon, as his metaphorics already indicates, although I cannot demonstrate this here in the requisite detail. But the arrogated sovereignty is manifested in the equipment: Bacon gave the theoretical instrumentarium its own dignity, even pathos. "Neither the naked hand nor the understanding left to itself can effect much. It is by instruments and helps that the work is done."[29] Bacon was decisively consolidated in this stance by the invention of the microscope and especially the telescope (which, in the seventeenth and eighteenth centuries, assumed metaphorical significance for the 'scope' of the human mind). In chapter 39 of book II of the "Novum Organum," Bacon praises Galileo's invention, "by the aid of which, as by boats or vessels, a nearer intercourse with the heavenly bodies can be opened and carried on." The metaphor betrays that a 'leap' has been made with the telescope, one that specifically already implies traffic in interstellar space. At the end of the chapter, Bacon, ever more inclined to devise plans than to execute them, and strangely uninterested in peering through the lens of a microscope or telescope himself, expresses his distrust in reports about the telescope. Tellingly, however, he does so not because they have anything incredibly new to impart, but "because the experiment stops with these few discoveries, and many other things equally worthy of investigation are not discovered by the same means."[30] Dilthey rightly identified Bacon's historical significance in his "scientific fantasy," in the "imagination of a head crammed full of facts," applying a Baconian metaphor to the man himself: "He constructs . . . his method like a gigantic machine designed to lift the weight of all experience."[31]

It is thus hardly surprising that in Bacon, the concepts of *labor* and *truth* appear together for the first time in the course of a *single* sentence. After more than two thousand years, truth's *splendid isolation*[32] from any hint of strain is brought to an end. Augustine could say of the relationship between activity and truth: ". . . The love of activity, which distracts from the truth, originates in pride, through which vice the soul chose to imitate God rather than to serve him."[33] This still seems to

28. *Instauratio Magna* I, 144. [Francis Bacon, *The New Organon and Related Writings,* ed. Fulton Anderson (trans. James Spedding, Robert Leslie Ellis, and Douglas Denon) (Indianapolis, IN: Bobbs-Merrill, 1960), 29.]

29. *Novum Organum* I, 2. [*The New Organon,* ed. Anderson (trans. Spedding, Ellis, and Denon), 39.]

30. [*The New Organon,* 206.]

31. *Weltanschaung und Analyse des Menschen seit Renaissance und Reformation* (Ges. Schr. II) (Leipzig, 1921), 261.

32. [English in original.]

33. *amor actionis, quae avertit a vero, a superbia proficiscitur, quo vitio deum imitari quam deo servire anima maluit. De musica* VI 40. [Augustine, *De musica liber VI,* trans. Martin Jacobsson (Stockholm: Amquist & Wiksell International, 2002), 87.]

conform to the ancient ideal of pure theory as the highest form of Being; yet it already hints at the genuinely Christian 'misunderstanding' of the Aristotelian definition of the divine as the *actus purus* in the direction of the *actio pura*, a reinterpretation irresistibly driven forward by the idea of creation and its consequences. Even if the fixed expression *actus purus* was to remain prevalent in rational theology throughout Scholasticism, the pseudomorphosis from 'pure reality' to 'pure activity' was a process that had been decided long ago, as we can see from the fact that the creator-god of the Bible had to be vigorously defended for resting on the seventh day. The god of Aristotelianism, who moves all the spheres while tarrying in self-contemplation, must now, by thinking *himself,* for that reason create from nothing; yet he must not create *what* he is thinking (otherwise he would once again posit himself, an operation already called on to explain the processes of the Trinity) but something else, a world whose truth he possesses by producing it. In this purportedly Aristotelian model, the conflation of truth and deed is prefigured: "Every thing is said to be true in the absolute sense because of its relation to a mind on which it depends."[34] In all consequence, the same idea applies to *homo faber* as well. A house depends "for its existence" on its builder, who alone can understand and evaluate the relationship between design and reality 'from within': "Man-made things are called true in relation to our mind."[35] That is a bold statement, albeit inconspicuous at the time, which contains the modern age *in nuce*—yet it is not quite thought through to its logical conclusion, since it does not dare to adjoin the *absolute* of the general proposition to the *verum*. But that is precisely what the modern age does in its technology, and still more emphatically in its art, or rather, that is what is done by the metaphysics implied in both. The medieval premise is pursued further: the more 'artificial' the object, the more 'truth' it has for mankind. While Baudelaire may have been the first to state this principle in so many words, it already resides in the modern industrial and artistic world as its otherwise incomprehensible tendency to ever 'purer' artificiality, to ever more radical synthetics, to the ever more resolute dissolution of natural ties. Take nothing for granted, produce everything and relate it to other products! Once we have freed our gaze from traditional theories about the receptive origin of mathematics (however that origin may be conceived), we can see the paradigm for what I have just described in the modern relationship between the natural sciences and mathematics, and we can understand at the same time the incomparable fascination that this nexus has exercised over all other intellectual domains.[36] Ultimately, it is always the conception

---

34. *unaquaeque res dicitur vera absolute secundum ordinem ad intellectum a quo dependet.* Thomas von Aquino, *Summa theol.* I q. 16a. I. [*Summa Theologiae* IV, trans. Thomas Gornall (London: Eyre & Spottiswoode, 1963), 77.]

35. *secundum suum esse . . . res artificiales dicuntur verae per ordinem ad intellectum nostrum.*

36. The *empirical* pathos of the modern attitude to knowledge easily obscures the structural fact that the simple question of *how the world appears,* together with its descriptive answer, can form only the prelude to active research (the "first vintage," in Bacon's terminology); the regulating question in

or 'preemption' [*Begriff oder 'Vorgriff'*] of truth dwelling within us that selects and regulates what can 'fascinate' us.

What we can now quite generally call the 'work character' of knowledge invested in the modern concept of truth has a pragmatic effect, not only in the manner of protention and experimental preparation, of methodic refinement and institutionalization (founding of institutes and societies to cope with the foreseen workload), but also in the way it functions as a selective criterion, placing under suspicion everything that 'capitulates' easily and immediately to interrogation. Descartes voices his distrust of ideas that fall to him out of the blue, as it were: "I have never set much store on the things that have first come to my mind."[37] He has a fondness for the martial metaphor of victory over difficulties and errors, which are not 'accidents'

---

the research process is then whether the world really appears the way it was modeled in the constructive, always preemptive act of rational investigation. The transformation of *phenomena* into *products* is the structure essential to the 'technicity' of the modern mind. Man, even empirical man, must already have 'his' world if 'the' world is to speak to him. That the genuine productivity of man also constitutes something like a world, that there is therefore a specifically 'human world', is a statement bearing an essential connection to the foundations of the modern age, and we really ought to know more about its history. That man is a microcosm is by no means synonymous with that statement; at most it may have helped launch it into the world. Here, as elsewhere, Nicolaus of Cusa points the way (*De coniecturis* I 3): "It must be the case that surmises originate from our minds, even as the real world originates from Infinite Divine Reason. For when, as best it can, the human mind (which is a lofty likeness of God) partakes of the fruitfulness of the Creating Nature, it produces from itself, qua image of the Omnipotent Form, rational entities, [which are made] in the likeness of real entities. Consequently, the human mind is the form of a surmised [rational] world, just as the Divine Mind is the Form of the real world" [Nicholas of Cusa, *Metaphysical Speculations,* trans. Hopkins, 2: 151]. What is general in the concept of a 'world' is the radical dependence of its immanent semantic structure upon its productive origin; the difference between the materiality of the real world and the intellectuality of its conjectural counterpart is only a *differentia specifica.* Cusanus continues: "Now, God works all things for His own sake, so that He is both the Intellectual Beginning and [Intellectual] End of all things. Similarly, the unfolding of a rational world—an unfolding that proceeds from our enfolding mind—exists for the sake of the producing mind" [151]. The semantic structure of the world is teleologically centered. Cusanus parallelizes two universal teleological circles: in the referential middle of the physical circle stands God; in that of the rational-conjectural circle stands man. Man's 'world' becomes the characteristic formula of a being that no longer seeks the signs of the absolute but posits its own signs instead, realizing itself in and through 'its' world. For Cusanus, this is so unproblematically 'attached' to the theologumenon of divine likeness that man must explicitly be exhorted to recognize *himself* in his world, in order thereby—through his productive imagination, that is!—to become all the more abundantly world-forming: "For the more subtly the mind contemplates itself in and through the world unfolded from itself, the more abundantly fruitful it is made within itself" [151]. Here, the seeing and knowing subject is subordinated to the active and productive subject (*mens fabricatrix*), thereby consolidating itself in the productive authenticity of its worldliness. The naïveté of the empiricist consists in thinking that he can step straight through 'his world' to the *mundus realis* and 'sound it out' for information; but "of all creatures that are there is none that has power to disclose himself to the knocker [at the door] and to show himself as he is . . ." Objects refuse all 'direct' claims upon them: "We can answer nothing, we can provide thee with no reply other than nothing . . . He who made us alone knows what we are, how we are and to what purpose. If thou wouldst know anything concerning us, seek it in our reason and cause, seek it not in us" (*De docta ignorantia* II 13) [Nicholas of Cusa, *Of Learned Ignorance,* trans. Germain Heron (London: Routledge, 1954), 121]. Although the inquirer is here still referred to God, "De coniecturis" already shows that he can equally be directed to his own reason.

37. *Je ne me fie quasi jamais aux premières pensées qui me viennent. Discours* VI, ed. Gilson, 68. [René Descartes, *Discourse on Method and the Meditations,* trans. F. E. Sutcliffe (Harmondsworth: Penguin, 1968), 77; translation modified.]

on the road to knowledge but represent the essential preamble to truth: "For he indeed fights battles who tries to overcome all the difficulties and errors that prevent him from arriving at the knowledge of truth . . ."[38] Descartes can thus characterize knowledge in procedural terms as an overcoming of obstacles, a clearing away of hindrances: "For myself, if I have already found any truths in the sciences . . . , I can say that they are only the results and consequences of five or six principal difficulties that I have overcome, and that I count as so many battles in which I had victory on my side."[39] Discovery (*découvrir*)—in the Latin version of the "Discours," *in apertum protrahere*—becomes the keyword of knowledge. For the historical self-understanding of the modern age, and particularly the Enlightenment, the assumption that truth 'shows itself' becomes precisely the error in which the Middle Ages' all too lax attitude to truth was rooted and the source of their self-incurred 'darkness'. For d'Alembert,[40] the postmedieval "regeneration of ideas" begins with the humanist revival of the lost truth, but the scholars of the Renaissance made things too easy for themselves by neglecting the most fundamental level, the "study of nature": for "it is far easier to read than to see."[41] A revealing turn of phrase! But to what should we attribute such complacency? A relic of medievalism persists here, the illusion that the beautiful and the true offer themselves unreservedly to mankind, whereas what is called for is a new attitude and activity, "one of those revolutions that give the earth a new face."[42]

In his inaugural address to the Academy of Bordeaux (1717), the twenty-eight-year-old Montesquieu unfurls the whole metaphorics of modern epistemic 'labor': "In short, we assail truth at the strongest point, and we seek it out in the murkiest depths to which it can withdraw."[43] The academician shoulders a heavy burden for the sciences to which he has dedicated himself, which seem "a means better suited to torment than to instruct us."[44] He continually drives himself to the point of exhaustion in pursuit of a truth that flees before him like the Proteus of legend, who

---

38. *Car c'est véritablement donner de batailles, que de tâcher à vaincre toutes les difficultés et les erreurs qui nous empêchent de parvenir à la connaissance de la vérité.* [Descartes, *Discourse on Method and the Meditations,* trans. Sutcliffe, 82.]

39. *Pour moi, si j'ai ci-devant trouvé quelques vérités dans les sciences . . . , je puis dire que ce ne sont que des suites et des dépendances de cinq ou six principales difficultés que j'ai surmontées, et que je compte pour autant de batailles où j'ai eu l'heur de mon côté.* [Descartes, *Discourse on Method and the Meditations,* trans. Sutcliffe, 82–83.]

40. *Discours préliminaire de l'Encyclopédie,* ed. E. Köhler, 110–16.

41. *régénérations des idées . . . étudier la nature . . . il est bien plus aisé de lire que de voir.*

42. *une de ces révolutions qui font prendre à la terre une face nouvelle.* The 'new face of the earth', as the most comprehensive expression for a human activity that trumps and transforms the activity of nature, has here already become a metaphor for a process in the history of the mind. Montesquieu, in the early "Projet d'une histoire physique de la terre" (1719), lists among other formative factors *des ouvrages faits de main d'homme qui ont donné une nouvelle face à la terre* [the works made by the human hand that have given a new face to the earth]. It would be interesting to learn more about this topos.

43. *on y attaque enfin la vérité par l'endroit le plus fort, et on la cherche dans les ténèbres les plus épaisses où elle puisse se retirer. Oeuvres complètes,* ed. Didot (Paris, 1846), 559.

44. *comme un moyen plus propre à nous tourmonter qu'à nous instruire.*

hid underneath a thousand forms and a thousand deceptive appearances.[45] And what does the researcher attain through his exertions? A summit where he can rest from his labors? No: "Through our labors we acquire only the right to further toil."[46] Ever since man so resolutely plunged into his work, the gods once again have the privilege of resting on Parnassus; was not Hercules in truth a scholar who cleansed philosophy of prejudices, those true monsters of the mind? To this image, which is by no means intended to be gloomy, Montesquieu now adds an element of historical self-interpretation: for him, the great triumphs in the scramble for knowledge seem already to lie in the past, the booty to have been largely plundered: "One could say that nature has acted like those virgins who for so long preserve what is most precious to them, only to allow themselves to be robbed, in an instant, of the treasure that they had guarded with such tenacity and defended with such steadfastness." At this point the motif of 'self-showing' reappears, but this time it is positively related to the heroic age of the scientific epoch and introduced as a backdrop to the strenuous exertions of the present, which considers itself doomed to scrape about in depleted shafts: "After having lain hidden for so many years, it (sc. nature) suddenly showed itself in the last century . . ."[47] Eight years later, Montesquieu spoke in another "Discours" of the considerations that ought to encourage us to take up scientific work;[48] here, the consciousness of epigonic exhaustion has given way to uncertainty as to where the human intellect currently finds itself on its path. But this uncertainty is assuaged by his admiration for the *method* guaranteeing that the whole path will eventually be traversed, no matter how long and arduous that path may prove to be. The greater the number of 'truths' brought to light by the new approach to knowledge, the less valuable these hard-earned rewards will seem in relation to the organon that made them possible, the method that has already seized possession of an indefinite, possibly infinite realm of knowledge, despite man not yet being in a position to make the most of this preemptive annexation. "What makes the discoveries of this age so astounding is not so much the truths that have been found as the methods for finding them; not the stones for the edifice but the tools and machines for building it as a whole. One man prides himself on owning gold; another on being able to make gold: the truly rich man would surely be the one who knew how to make gold."[49] The ever-expanding horizon of research tasks forces man to focus on the resources for undertaking them that

---

45. *Il semble que la Fable nous représentait la vérité sous le symbole de ce Protée qui se cachait sous mille figures et sous mille apparences trompeuses. Il faut la chercher dans l'obscurité même dont elle se couvre, il faut la prendre, il faut l'embrasser, il faut la saisir.* [It seems that the fable presents the truth to us under the symbol of Proteus, who hid himself beneath a thousand forms and a thousand deceptive appearances. One must seek it out even in the darkness in which it cloaks itself, one must take it, embrace it, seize it.]

46. *Nous n'acquérons par nos travaux que le droit de travailler davantage.*

47. *Après s'être cachée pendant tant d'années, elle (sc. la nature) se montra tout à coup dans le siècle passé.*

48. "Discours sur les motifs qui doivent nous encourager aux sciences" (*Oeuvres*, 579).

49. [*Ce qui rend les découvertes de se siècle si admirables, ce ne sont pas des vérités simples qu'on a trouvées, mais des méthodes pour les trouver; ce n'est pas une pierre pour l'édifice, mais les instruments et les machines*

stand at his disposal, and the 'enrichment' of these resources, their accommodation to the infinite demands placed upon him, assumes ever more central importance. The accumulation of nonspecific equipment for tackling exigencies of any type and any dimension, the stockpiling of 'pure' potentiality, arbitrarily transformable and transportable energies, omnipotent instruments: this will be the hallmark of the new phase of technicization that gets underway in the second half of the century. Supposedly historical causalities have long kept the true driving forces hidden from view; nonspecific equipment races ahead of real problems and requirements in a way that one fails to understand if one overlooks the attitude of mistrustfulness toward Being that stands behind every 'Enlightenment', an attitude that now places everything formerly entrusted to Nature or Providence in human hands. The theory of overpopulation is far older than the actual demographic explosions. To a considerable extent, technicization first *creates* the difficulties it was theoretically designed to remedy.

So diverse and far-reaching are the pragmatic consequences of the modern, deeply rooted sense of alienation from the truth, as this sense is conveyed in metaphorics of the domination and subjection of the truth. We will conclude by adjoining three famous testimonies to our documentation. The interrogation metaphor introduced by Kant in his foreword to the second edition of the "Critique of Pure Reason" is the first. He says there of the natural scientists of the modern age: "They comprehended that reason has insight only into what it itself produces according to its own design; that it must take the lead with principles for its judgments according to constant laws and compel nature to answer its questions, rather than letting nature guide its movements by keeping reason, as it were, in leading-strings . . . Reason, in order to be taught by nature, must approach nature with its principles in one hand, according to which alone the agreement among appearances can count as laws, and, in the other hand, the experiments thought out in accordance with these principles—yet in order to be instructed by nature not like a pupil, who has recited to him whatever the teacher wants to say, but like an appointed judge who compels witnesses to answer the questions he puts to them."[50] Then the oft-cited remark of George Cuvier: "The observer listens to nature; the experimenter interrogates it and forces it to unveil itself."[51] And finally, the most sensitive of them all to 'mood', to 'antipathy', to hectic dynamism, to possible circularity—Nietzsche notes around 1867/8: "Mistrust is now as limitless as trust was in the past, and doubt now seems ethical where faith was earlier . . . Through skepticism we undermine tradition, through the consequences of skepticism we drive the hidden truth from

---

pour le bâtir tout entier. Un homme se vante d'avoir de l'or; un autre se vante de savoir en faire: certainement le véritable riche seroit celui qui sauroit faire l'or.]

50. [Immanuel Kant, *Critique of Pure Reason,* trans. Paul Guyer and Allen Wood (Cambridge: Cambridge University Press, 1998), 109.]

51. *L'observateur écoute la nature; l'expérimentateur l'interroge et la force à se dévoiler.*

its cave, and we find perhaps that tradition was right even though it rested on un-sound foundations. A Hegelian might say that we have sought the truth through the negation of the negation."[52]

But the relationship to truth of the modern age also manifests itself in a resis-tance, in a refusal to perceive, most magnificently of all—precisely in the futility of one who otherwise did nothing in vain—in Goethe's Olympian rage against New-tonian physics. Goethe ventures, one last time, an existence of trust in Being; he was filled with the conviction that we only need to keep our eyes open to encounter the self-showing of truth. That this stance found its most subtle pragmatic exposition in the "Farbenlehre" [Theory of Color], *while at the same time* producing a docu-ment of a willful refusal to see, is itself proof of the radicality of the opposition that failed to be acknowledged here. That is why these testimonies could not simply be assimilated to the context of the metaphorics of the power of truth: here, the form and temporally determined function of the whole, the atmospheric turbulence, must be perceived in conjunction with the often crystalline purity of the individual statement if the historical meaning of the evidence is to be correctly grasped. What looks like immediate contact with nature nonetheless implies a protest against an essential factor in the semantic current of the age. In the midst of history there can be no more cosmocentric innocence, not even that of 'common sense'. The latter is presented as the higher tribunal to which truth, tormented by science, may appeal: "The phenomena must be freed once and for all from the grim torture chamber of empiricism, mechanism, and dogmatism; they must be brought before the jury

---

52. *Historisch-kritische Gesamtausgabe der Werke* III, 341–42. In his "Kritische Bemerkungen zu Heideggers Lehre von der Wahrheit" (*Kant-Studien* 48: 525–49), G. Ralfs brought this early Nietzsche aphorism into connection with certain remarks of Heidegger's, such as the following: "The un-hidden must be torn away from hiddenness and, as it were, robbed of its hiddenness" [Martin Heidegger, *The Essence of Truth,* trans. Ted Sadler (London: Continuum, 2002), 7; translation modified]. Tellingly, this sentence appears in Heidegger's interpretation of Plato's parable of the cave. It thereby gives rise to a further, surprising, and inverse parallel in connection with the Nietzsche quotation: whereas *there* the cave is the site of captivity and the exclusion of truth, *here* truth has secluded itself in the cave and must be dragged out into the open. But it is also striking how much the Heideggerian rhetoric of 'tearing' and 'robbing', guided less by the parable itself than by the dubious etymology of ἀλήθεια, 'modernizes' the Platonic concept of truth in order to make it responsible for the loss of the pre-Socratic ontologi-cal idyll. Nietzsche is then suddenly not so far off: "Plato's thinking follows the change in the essence of truth, a change that becomes the history of metaphysics, which in Nietzsche's thinking has entered upon its unconditioned fulfillment" (*Platons Lehre von der Wahrheit* [Bern, 1947], 50) [Martin Heide-gger, "Plato's Doctrine of Truth," trans. Thomas Sheehan, in *Pathmarks,* ed. W. McNeill (Cambridge: Cambridge University Press, 1998), 181]. A reading of the cave parable must not only interpret what it contains, but also account for what it does not; Neoplatonism can be understood in its genuine problem-atic as just such an attempt to reckon with what remains unaccounted for in the cave parable: how did the initial situation of captivity in the cave come about? This forced isolation from the daylight of truth was to be felt in all its unnaturalness and unessentiality. Neoplatonism consequentially interpreted the way out of the cave not as a first outing but as a volte-face and return; the parable itself thus becomes a guide to *metanoia,* redemption, rather than to *paideia.* This first gives the idea of truth contained therein its proper accent. [Blumenberg offers his own interpretation of the cave parable and its subsequent re-censions and mutations in the last book of his to be published in his lifetime, *Höhlenausgänge* (Frank-furt: Suhrkamp, 1989).]

of man's common sense."[53] Are we dealing here, to stick to the metaphor, with a revision of the original verdict, intended to bring *another,* purer truth to light, or with a pardon, which can ignore the question of truth with recourse to higher motives? To the torture chamber belong the instruments: "In reality, microscopes and telescopes confuse pure human feeling."[54] But Goethe is not like those philosophers at the university in Padua who refused to look through Galileo's telescope because their speculations had already taught them all they needed to know; Goethe shuns tools in order that the phenomenon itself may "appear in its entire simplicity, say where it comes from, and point to its conclusion."[55] Hypotheses and theories get in the way of the self-disclosure of the phenomena; in these operations, the intellect busies itself with its own constructs rather than opening itself to the given: "Theories are usually the rushed conclusions of an impatient mind, which would gladly be done with the phenomena and therefore inserts images, concepts, and often only words in their place."[56] The Goethean pragmatics of knowledge is determined by the belief that man does not force his way into nature as an intruder but always already enjoys the richest communion with truth from the midst of nature and by virtue of its favor. Mastery and subjugation, cunning and mechanics, infringe upon an almost theological sovereignty: "Nature reserved so much freedom for itself that we generally can neither get the better of it with knowledge and science nor drive it into a corner."[57] The intervention of technology leads to the point "where the instrument, instead of unfolding the mystery of nature, turns it into an insoluble riddle."[58] The truth is powerful; only to those who act as if they did not concede it any power does it show this power *as* resistance. Scarcely no other thinker has thought through and grounded his existence in so universally *teleological* a fashion. Three hundred years after Copernicus, two hundred years after Galileo, and a century after Newton, the attempt to live a cosmocentric existence was dared once again: "When man's nature functions soundly as a whole, when he feels that the world of which he is part is a huge, beautiful, admirable and worthy whole, when this harmony gives him pure and uninhibited delight, then the universe, if it were

---

53. *Die Phänomene müssen ein für allemal aus der düstern empirisch-mechanisch-dogmatischen Marterkammer vor die Jury des gemeinen Menschenverstanden gebracht werden. Maximen und Reflexionen, Aus den Heften zur Naturwissenschaft,* 430 (*Gedenkausgabe,* ed. E. Beutler, IX, 551). [Johann Wolfgang von Goethe, *Scientific Studies,* trans. Douglas Miller (New York: Suhrkamp, 1988), 309.]

54. *Mikroskope und Fernrohre verwirren eigentlich den reinen Menschensinn. Maximen und Reflexionen, Aus Wilhelm Meisters Wanderjahren,* 502 (IX, 564).

55. *in seiner ganzen Einfalt erscheinen, sein Herkunft aussprechen und auf die Folgerung hindeuten. Farbenlehre,* in *Vollst. Ausg. d. theoretischen Schriften* (Tübingen 1953), 574.

56. *Theorien sind gewöhnlich Übereilungen eines ungeduldigen Verstandes, der die Phänomene gern los sein möchte und an ihrer Stelle deswegen Bilder, Begriffe, ja oft nur Worte einschiebt. Aus den Heften zur Naturwissenschaft,* 428 (IX, 551).

57. *Die Natur hat sich soviel Freiheit vorbehalten, daß wir mit Wissen und Wissenschaft ihr nicht durchgängig beikommen oder sie in die Enge treiben können. Aus den Heften zur Naturwissenschaft,* 439 (IX, 553).

58. *wo das Instrument, statt das Geheimnis der Natur zu entwickeln, sie zum unauflöslichen Rätsel macht. Farbenlehre,* 576.

capable of emotion, would rejoice at having reached its goal and admire the crowning glory of its own being and becoming. For, what purpose would those countless suns and planets and moons serve, those stars and milky ways, comets and nebulae, those created and evolving worlds, if a happy human being did not ultimately emerge to enjoy existence?"[59]

---

59. *Wenn die gesunde Natur des Menschen als ein Ganzes wirkt, wenn er sich in der Welt als in einem großen, schönen, würdigen und werten Ganzen fühlt, wenn das harmonische Behagen ihm ein reines freies Entzücken gewährt, dann würde das Weltall, wenn es sich selbst empfinden könnte, als an sein Ziel gelangt aufjauchzen und den Gipfel des eigenen Werdens und Wesens bewundern. Denn wozu dient alle der Aufwand von Sonnen und Planeten und Monden, von Sternen und Milchstraßen, von Kometen und Nebelflecken, von gewordenen und werdenden Welten, wenn sich nicht zuletzt ein glücklicher Mensch unbewußt seines Daseins erfreut? Winckelmann und sein Jahrhundert* XIII, 417. ["Winckelmann and His Age," trans. Ellen von Nardroff and Ernest von Nardroff, in Goethe, *Essays in Art and Literature* (New York: Suhrkamp, 1986), 101; translation modified.] With regard to the trait that we have been explicating here, Goethe has often been compared to Montaigne. Closer inspection would be able to reveal the differences between their respective historical positions, particularly as far as the coloring of their related metaphors is concerned. What, in Montaigne, amounts to the repudiation of an interpretation of existence that he sees gaining ground around him, is for Goethe at bottom a resigned resistance to what already faces him as a 'system' in Newton. What Goethe sees represented in the levers and screws of scientific and technical equipment still assumes, in Montaigne, the form of the old metaphor of life as the conquest of a mountain. Montaigne opposes this metaphor: *Le monde . . . ne pense rien utile qui ne soit penible: la facilité luy est suspecte* (III 13) [The world . . . thinks that nothing does you good unless it hurts; pleasantness is suspect; Montaigne, *The Complete Essays,* trans. M. A. Screech (London: Penguin, 1991), 1233].

III

A Terminological and Metaphorological Cross Section of the Idea of Truth

In our investigations into truth metaphors, we have proceeded so far by placing *longitudinal sections,* or rather—to emphasize the deficiency of our material (which of course can only be measured against the inevitable deficiency of all historical material)—we have provided a series of points through which a curve may be drawn. Even if we disregard the factual density of the material offered in evidence, this procedure is as contestable as it is indispensable for the development of a metaphorology. But we want to illustrate what makes it contestable by seeking to satisfy the ideal postulate of a complementary method on at least one point of our longitudinal section. What leaps to the eye when selecting the appropriate metaphorical material needs for its part, before it can really be fixed on that curve, to be interpreted from the conceptual context in which it stands and functions, and from which it receives its contours and distinctive coloration. To stick with our first methodological image, we will need to place *cross sections,* ideally at each relevant point of our longitudinal section, in order to make completely comprehensible what the selected metaphors signify in each case. Seen for themselves, such cross sections can no longer be purely metaphorological; they must take concepts and metaphors, definitions and images, as the unity of the expressive sphere of a thinker or an age. Since complete availability of the material must be reconciled with the demands of space, my choice—about which I do not intend to argue with anyone—falls on Lactantius. Precisely the fact that he is not a thinker of the first order makes him a suitable case study for our investigations into epochal (not epoch-making) historical structures. Excellence calls for standards of singular immanence and cannot be regarded as mere expressive objectivization. Minds like Lactantius's have enough 'suction power' to soak up the nutrient solution of the historical current; yet because they also stand authentically in relation to the new crystallizations that, in the horizon of meaning of their age, correspond to its problems and needs, they can actively participate in the historical current without intervening to change its course.

Lactantius has a fondness for the metaphor of the force of truth (*vis veritatis*); two examples of this have already been cited. But this 'natural' characteristic of truth is not directly converted into potency; it is constrained by an order that comes to expression in a metaphorics of law superimposed on the metaphorics of force. Truth 'belongs' to God, "who has made everything," which for Lactantius must also be understood to mean "*because* he has made everything." This train of thought differs from the one we have encountered in Thomas Aquinas and Vico, where the absolute connection to truth is guaranteed by the creator's *insight* into the inner structure of his work; here, the legalistic idea of ownership by virtue of authorship predominates, and with it the sovereign right of the author to dispose his property as he pleases.[1] In the rhetorically fully orchestrated opening sentences of the "Divinae institutiones," Lactantius draws a sharp contrast between the strenuous exertions for truth of the

---

1. The property analogy quite obviously plays a fundamental motivating role in the modern foundational order of *labor* and truth. Late medieval nominalism, with its extreme theological idea of sovereignty, bequeathed the modern spirit a strong aversion to ideas of 'grace' and 'gift'. The origin of the modern age's acute methodological reflection thus essentially lies in the need not to have to accept and passively receive the truth, but to ground it *funditus denuo* [totally anew]—'ground' understood not just in the sense of coming up with grounds for a thesis, but of producing the thesis itself from its grounds. For *produced* truth is truth that is legitimately *one's own*. Here, too, we see a marked connection with the modern critique of teleology, whose robust aggressiveness stands in no relation to its purely *theoretical* significance, for instance in the contestation of the Aristotelian doctrine of the four causes. The principle of universal anthropocentric teleology makes a metaphysical foundation of private property impossible; that can be seen in the Stoic conception of *privata nulla natura* noted by Cicero, *De officiis* I 7, 21–22 [Cicero, *The Offices,* trans. Thomas Cockman (London: J. M. Dent & Sons, 1955), 10–11]. If nature looks after the basic needs of all human beings, then property is only possible through *occupatio,* and a layer of positive statutes is illegitimately superimposed on the state of nature. Once this teleological conception is dismantled, however, there arises the idea that nature is originally, constitutively, and chronically deficient with respect to human needs; labor now becomes the authentic property-founding act. Locke was the first to deploy this idea against neo-Stoic theories of the origin of property, and Rousseau became its most effective disseminator. Its crucial—and potentially revolutionary—characteristic can be found in its ever-present potential for critical application. (I remark in passing that the elimination of private property in communism rests at bottom on a restoration of Stoic teleology, only now as a teleology of society rather than one of nature.) Property's foundation in labor is thus implicit in the modern age's conception of truth before it gains the ascendancy in legal theory. Prior to that, however, it was a theologumenon that could be used to justify everything denied the human race by God. In both ancient and medieval metaphysics, God's exclusive right to property in the absolute sense is grounded in the fact that man, strictly speaking, cannot 'produce' anything at all. He is an agent mandated by nature or by God with the task of realizing what already lies before him.

epoch that is now drawing to a close and the free gift of this truth to a new epoch. The best minds of the past gave their all for the sake of truth: "Men of great and distinguished talent, when they had entirely devoted themselves to learning, holding in contempt all actions both private and public, applied to the pursuit of investigating the truth whatever labor could be bestowed upon it."[2] And these men were also quite worthy of knowing the truth: the existence of the Stoic sage who identifies virtue with happiness is presupposed in order that the ensuing 'but' may stand out in all its disheartening futility: "But they did not obtain the object of their wish, and at the same time lost their labor and industry; because the truth, that is the secret of the Most High God, who created all things, cannot be attained by our own ability and perceptions."[3] To accentuate truth's new character of grace, the leisure of ancient philosophical contemplation is retrospectively ascribed the character of 'labor'; compared with the light that is now breaking forth, the vaunted ontological brightness of the past was nothing but gloom. The further rationale given for God's concealment of the truth as an *arcanum dei* betrays its orientation toward the orientalized rulership model of the late imperial age: if human reflection could gain insight into the plans and decrees ordained by the eternal monarch, the difference between God and man would collapse. God's majesty would be imperiled if man could arrive at the truth without divine guidance. At the same time, however, God did not wish for him to err any longer, "and to wander through inextricable darkness without any result of his labor."[4] Here, it almost appears as if the combined efforts of the ancient philosophers, while doing nothing to alter the legal situation, nonetheless precipitated the act of grace, the final absolution from ignorance: "At length He opened his (sc. man's) eyes, and made the investigation of the truth His own gift."[5] God's gift accordingly consists in discharging the *vis veritatis* from His legitimate safekeeping.

Lactantius did not maintain this contrast throughout his entire work; otherwise he would have been unable to write much more than this introduction. The theological principle is incompatible with the scholarly plan he pursues thereafter. To keep the work flowing, more and more 'advances' from the *arcanum dei* had to be admitted into ancient philosophy, since the *arcanum dei* leaves no room for argument. Indeed, the specificity of a region of 'fideistic truths' is quite unknown to Lactantius; his central notion of a Christian comportment is accordingly not faith (*fides*) but righteousness (*iustitia*), whose legitimation is derived from Paul

---

2. *quicquid laboris poterat impendi, contemtis omnibus et privatis et publicis actionibus, ad inquirendae veritatis studium contulerunt* (I 1, 1). [*Ante-Nicene Fathers*, ed. Alexander Roberts and James Donaldson, trans. William Fletcher (Peabody, MA: Hendrikson Publishers, 2004), VII, 10.]

3. *Sed neque adepti sunt id, quod volebant, et operam simul atque industriam perdiderunt: quia veritas, id est arcanum summi dei, qui fecit omnia, ingenio ac propriis sensibus non potest comprehendi* (I 1, 5). [*Ante-Nicene Fathers*, trans. Fletcher, VII, 10.]

4. *ac sine ullo laboris effectu vagari per tenebras inextricabiles.* [*Ante-Nicene Fathers*, trans. Fletcher, VII, 10.]

5. *aperuit oculos eius (sc. hominis) aliquando et notionem veritatis munus suum fecit* (I 1, 6). [*Ante-Nicene Fathers*, trans. Fletcher, VII, 10; translation modified.]

and whose substance comes from Stoicism: Peter founded the church in Rome to "convert many to righteousness."[6] Truth is homogeneous, and if the 'philosophers' are to be conceded *any* truth at all, they must in principle be deemed capable of acquiring *all* of it. Lactantius's inconsistency with regard to the opening chapters of the "Divinae institutiones" is thus quite consequential when he later voices his astonishment that philosophy did not succeed in acquiring 'more' of the truth: "I wonder, therefore, that there was not a single philosopher who discovered the abode and dwelling place of the chief good."[7] Pagan philosophy's 'angle of vision' was skewed: Democritus said that truth lies sunk in a well so deep that it has no bottom, but that is a perfidiously false metaphor, "for the truth is not, as it were, sunk in a well to which it was permitted him to descend, or even to fall, but, as it were, placed on the highest peak of a lofty mountain, or in heaven, which is most true."[8] So long as neither alpinism nor astronautics had been invented, this means that the truth is absolutely unattainable, whereas one can always descend or fall into a well, and so 'hit upon' the truth hidden in its depths. Ancient philosophers did not even know in what direction they ought to look for the truth; they failed to heed the pointers given by nature in man's upright gait and in the elevation of his head; and they did so because God himself had somehow made his hints inscrutable to them: "They were turned away by Divine Providence, that they might not know the truth."[9] One sees how difficult it is to find a common denominator for the metaphorics of majesty and truth. For in book III, Lactantius grants that the Pythagoreans and Stoics had for their part 'perceived' the truth (*verum sentiunt*) with their doctrine of immortality, and here truth seems to be permitted, for once, to lie 'below', since "they tumbled upon the truth not by knowledge, but by accident."[10] The exact wording needs to be taken into account here: 'perception' (*sentire*) is meant in a clearly and distinctly derogatory way, in contrast to 'attainment' (*assequi*), 'discovery' (*invenire*), and so on. Smell and touch likewise appear as inferior forms for encountering the truth, which for that reason had not yet been properly 'verified': in many areas, philosophers groped their way in the dark toward correct opinion, "kept in touch by a sort of sniff of the truth, and touched upon the whole truth, and every secret of our holy religion," dispersed in particles among all the

---

6. *convertare ad iustitiam. De mort. persec.* II 5. [Lactantius, *De mortibus persecutorum,* trans. J. L. Creed (Oxford: Clarendon Press, 1984), 7.]

7. *Miror itaque, nullum omnino philosophorum exstitisse, qui sedem ac domicilium summi boni reperiret* (III 11, 5). [*Ante-Nicene Fathers,* trans. Fletcher, VII, 78; translation modified.]

8. *non enim tanquam in puteo demersa est veritas, quo vel descendere vel etiam cadere illi licebat; sed tanquam in summo monti excelsi vertice vel potius in coelo: quod est verissimum* (III 28, 14). [*Ante-Nicene Fathers,* trans. Fletcher, VII, 98; translation modified.]

9. *aversos esse arbitror divina providentia, ne scire possent veritatem* (IV 2, 5). [*Ante-Nicene Fathers,* trans. Fletcher, VII, 102; translation modified.]

10. *non scientia, sed casu inciderunt in veritatem* (III 17, 43). [*Ante-Nicene Fathers,* trans. Fletcher, VII, 88; translation modified.]

schools and sects.[11] Revelation thus does not impart any substantially *new* truths, only the certitude of discerning truth from falsehood, and with it the possibility of integrating the far-flung particles into a system. Lactantius rejects here the conclusion drawn by Academic Skepticism from the dogmatic differences separating the Hellenistic schools of philosophy; in order to defend the 'potency' of truth, however, he must distance himself considerably from his initial thesis. No sect was so misguided that it did not glimpse at least some of the truth,[12] and anyone who took the trouble to bring all of this together "assuredly would not disagree with us."[13] But this task could only be carried out by someone who already possessed the norm of verification, and this norm is first provided by the divine *testimonia*.[14] Lactantius makes this formal rather than material *novum* clear when comparing the Platonic with the Christian teaching on immortality: "We, therefore, are able to elicit the truth by more certain signs; for we have not collected it by doubtful surmise but have known it by divine instruction."[15] With that, the character of truth as *arcanum dei,* initially introduced in an undifferentiated fashion, is interpreted in such a way as to be made compatible with the light-seeking, light-claiming essence of truth: God did not withhold truth as such from the philosophers, only the criterion for its recognition, and hence the condition for its integration.

Another way of doing justice to the philosophical tradition in its supposed preliminary contribution, as well as securing its argumentative content for the consolidation of Christian doctrine, is to hypostasize untruth as a coeval counterworld to truth. This dualism is so deeply inscribed into the entire work of Lactantius that the passages in which it escalates into full-blown Gnosticism (and thus heresy),

---

11. *Quasi odore quodam veritatis retenti* (VI 12, 26), *totam igitur veritatem et omne divinae religionis arcanum . . . attigerunt* (VII 7, 14). [Lactantius, *Divine Institutes,* trans. Anthony Bowen and Peter Garnsey (Liverpool: Liverpool University Press, 2003), 358; *Ante-Nicene Fathers,* VII, 204.]

12. VII 7, 7. [*Ante-Nicene Fathers,* trans. Fletcher, VII, 204.]

13. *is profecto non dissentiret a nobis* (VII 7, 4). [*Ante-Nicene Fathers,* trans. Fletcher, VII, 204.]

14. Wherever the truth was 'known' in the absence of such *testimonia,* this was due to the fact that "the truth would explain itself by its own light" (*se ipsam veritas illustraret suo lumine;* VII 7, 5 [*Ante-Nicene Fathers,* trans. Fletcher, VII, 204]), but this occurs only 'by accident' (*casu*). The *testimonia divina* here have the same structural function that will later be accorded to 'method' by Descartes: any truths found only by accident are worthless so long as they have not been 'verified', whether by means of a revealed norm or a rationally constructed method. What distinguishes the Cartesian approach is that it is now no longer possible to justify that chance discovery by referring to the authentic radiance of truth. The parallel emerges even more clearly, perhaps, in the corresponding passage of the "Epitome" (6, 69 [*Ante-Nicene Fathers,* VII, 252]), where Plato is criticized for his teaching on immortality: he did not descend by regular gradations to that opinion (*non per gradus ad eam sententiam descendit*), he omitted the constitutive middle arguments (*amputatus mediis*), and he practically hurled himself upon the truth: "He rather fell into the truth, as though by some abrupt precipice" (*incidit potius in veritatem quasi per abruptum aliquod praecipitium*). As a result, he "found the truth by accident, and not by reason" (*casu, non ratione verum invenerat*). Metaphorically, the truth here once again lies 'below' for the philosopher, but the truth-seeker's approach must be 'methodically' appropriate in this direction, too; it must be *descensus* and not *praecipitium,* otherwise depth becomes an abyss: he still arrives at the truth, to be sure, but not without risking life and limb!

15. *Nos igitur certioribus signis eligere possumus veritatem, qui eam non ancipiti suspicione collegimus, sed divina traditione cognovimus* (VII 8, 3). [*Ante-Nicene Fathers,* trans. Fletcher, VII, 205.]

the so-called *additamenta dualistica,* can be taken away from the author only with great difficulty. When he writes in VI 22, 2: "Therefore God made all things to supply a contest between two things,"[16] this scarcely differs from what we read in the alleged interpolation II 8, where God appoints two sources of things (*duos fontes rerum*) and an inventor of evils (*malorum inventor*). Even if dualistic propositions are predominantly confined to the ethical sphere, they nonetheless encroach upon the relationship between truth and falsehood: false understanding (*falsum intelligere*) circumscribes the extent of human wisdom (*sapientia*); "to know the truth is the part of divine wisdom."[17] This is also the aspect in which the philosophers are to be regarded: "Thus philosophers have reached the height of human wisdom, so as to understand that which is not; but they have failed in attaining the power of saying that which really is."[18] Here, as in the text "De ira dei" (XI, 10), Lactantius refers to an interjection of Cicero's in "De natura deorum" (I 32, 91), where the philosopher exclaims that he only wishes he could discover the truth as easily as he can expose falsehood (albeit in what, for him, is a scandalous point). According to Lactantius, he did so "not with the dissimulation of an Academic," but honestly expressed his true opinion, since "that which the foresight of man was able to attain to, he attained to, that he might expose false things."[19] At this point, a highly characteristic interchange of the predicates of truth and falsehood takes place. It is no longer the case, as in the ancient tradition, that truth 'shows itself' and comes to light. Now falsehood is ascribed this mode of conspicuousness instead: "And thus he (sc. Cicero) himself testified that that which was false was evident; that the truth, however, lay concealed."[20] Only when the truth had been released by God from its provisional custody, so to speak, namely in Christian revelation, could it unleash its essential force (*vis*). This can be confirmed almost 'experimentally' by ascertaining that the number of Christians is continually increasing from the ranks of idolaters and never diminishing, not even under conditions of persecution; Lactantius concludes from this that even though men may commit sins and be defiled by sacrifices, "yet they cannot be turned away from God, for the truth prevails by its own

---

16. *itaque fecit omnia deus ad instruendum certamen rerum duarum.* [*Ante-Nicene Fathers,* trans. Fletcher, VII, 189.]

17. *verum autem scire divinae est sapientiae* (II 3, 23). [*Ante-Nicene Fathers,* trans. Fletcher, VII, 44.]

18. *Ita philosophi, quod summum fuit humanae sapientiae, assecuti sunt, ut intelligerent, quod non sit: illud assequi nequiverunt, ut dicerent, quid sit* (II 3, 24). [*Ante-Nicene Fathers,* trans. Fletcher, VII, 44.]

19. *non dissimulanter ut Academicus . . . quod adsequi valuit humana providentia, id adsecutus est, ut falsa detegeret.* [*Ante-Nicene Fathers,* trans. Fletcher, VII, 269.] It is a characteristic technique of the reception that aims to bring Cicero's authority on its side that Cicero's skepticism is made to appear as a kind of methodical tactic, or even pretense, by means of which he fulfilled the 'historical' task that fell to him from the Christian viewpoint, that of critically demolishing both the old religion and Epicurean dogmatism. The idea of 'methodical doubt' arises as an interpretation *ex eventu,* here no less than in Descartes, where doubter and interpreter are combined in a single person.

20. *adeo et ipse (sc. Cicero) testatus est falsum quidem apparere, veritatem tamen latere.* [*Ante-Nicene Fathers,* trans. Fletcher, VII, 269.]

power: no one departs from us, since the truth itself detains him."[21] Truth wields its power while itself remaining inviolable, and for that reason alone it cannot be connected in any way with the unpunished destructability of divine images: "Where, then, is truth? . . . Where nothing appears that can be injured."[22]

A final element in the complex of the idea of truth in Lactantius warrants consideration at this point, since it fundamentally determines the function of his metaphorics: the relationship between truth and *rhetoric*. Lactantius, himself a teacher of rhetoric by profession, finds himself in a tricky situation here. He is well aware of the disjunction, so acutely felt in early Christianity, between the stylistic demands of rhetoric and the peculiarity of the biblical textual universe. He knows that some people are carried away by hearing composed speeches (*compositae orationes*) and skillful disputations (*argutae disputationes*), and he therefore also knows that Christianity is at a disadvantage in this regard. Students of rhetoric will more than likely prove deaf to holy scripture: "They do not seek things that are true, but things that are pleasant; nay, to them those things appear to be most true that soothe the ears."[23] The philosophers have at their disposal the incredible force of eloquence (*incredibilis vis eloquentiae*); a power thus lies in the hands of people who are "pernicious and weighty for the disturbing of the truth."[24] Time and again, we see that the real conflict in Lactantius consists in the fact that he is dominated, on the one hand, by the idea of the *vis veritatis,* which he would like to think capable of doing everything on its own,[25] while on the other hand, his own familiarity with rhetorical technique, and his experience of its practical success, suggest to him that he should do a little (or a little more) to come to the aid of truth. He is continually casting around for compromise formulae. In the aforementioned programmatic opening chapter of book I of the "Divinae institutiones," he posits an opposition between oratorical rules and life rules: "Nor does he who imparts knowledge of speaking well deserve to do as well in human affairs as he who teaches men to live in piety and innocence."[26] He cites the Greeks, for whom the philosopher's fame

---

21. *averti autem non possunt a deo: valet enim vi sua veritas* (*Inst. div.* V 13, 1) [*Ante-Nicene Fathers,* trans. Fletcher, VII, 148]; *nemo discedit, ipsa veritate retinente* (V 19, 13) [*Ante-Nicene Fathers,* trans. Fletcher, VII, 156].

22. *ubi ergo veritas est? . . . ubi nihil, quod violari possit, apparet* (II 4, 7). [*Ante-Nicene Fathers,* trans. Fletcher, VII, 45; translation modified.]

23. *nec quaerunt vera sed dulcia: imo illis haec videntur esse verissima, quae auribus blandiuntur* (*Epitome* 52, 6–7). [*Ante-Nicene Fathers,* trans. Fletcher, VII, 248; translation modified.]

24. *ad perturbandam veritatem perniciosi et graves* (*De opif. Dei* 20, 2–3). [*Ante-Nicene Fathers,* trans. Fletcher, VII, 299.]

25. So also in the previously cited passage, where immediately after mentioning the philosophers' "incredible force of eloquence" he encouragingly brings up the *vis veritatis: cur desperemus, veritatem ipsam contra fallacem captiosamque facundiam sua propria vi et claritate valituram?* (*De opif. Dei* 20, 5) [Why should we despair that the truth itself will by its own peculiar force and clearness avail against deceitful and captious eloquence? *Ante-Nicene Fathers,* trans. Fletcher, VII, 299]. Something of the author's characteristic dualism is no doubt invested in this antagonism of powers.

26. *Nec tam de rebus humanis bene meretur, qui scientiam bene dicendi affert, quam qui pie atque innocenter docet vivere* (I 1, 9). [*Ante-Nicene Fathers,* trans. Fletcher, VII, 9; translation modified.]

surpassed that of the rhetor, as his authority. In other words, Lactantius reverts to the dissociation of philosophy and rhetoric directed by Plato against the Sophists, momentarily forgetting his reliance on the synthesis of the two brought about by Cicero, which had in fact determined his own 'solution' to the problem. The reasoning he offers—that to speak well (*bene dicere*) belongs only to a few, whereas to live well (*bene vivere*) belongs to all—is far from convincing. At bottom, he wants only to say that 'his' new truth has no need of all that, yet this, spoken in the ear of the emperor, sounds like the flattery of a courtier who hopes thereby to gain a free hand to pursue his own agenda: "for although the truth may be defended without eloquence, as it often has been defended by many, yet it needs to be explained, and in a measure discussed, with distinctness and elegance of speech, in order that it may flow with greater power into the minds of men, being both provided with its own force and adorned with the brilliancy of speech."[27] In the first chapter of book III, the problem is taken up once again in all its breadth and resolved in the sense of the 'amplification' formula, as much to defeat the opponent with his own weapons as "that men might more readily believe the truth when adorned with embellishments, since they even believe falsehood, being captivated by the adornment of speech and the enticement of words."[28] It is a topos of the rhetor Lactantius that he disparages his own eloquence in order to ascribe all the luster of his delivery to the cause he is espousing: ". . . I have never been eloquent, inasmuch as I never engaged in public speaking; but the goodness of the cause cannot fail of itself to make me eloquent, and for its clear and copious defense the knowledge of divinity and the truth itself are sufficient."[29] That is the perfect formula of union: rhetoric does not 'lend' itself to the truth, it is not an instrument but pure expression; the brilliance of the diction is the brilliance of truth itself, the direct self-translation of the 'matter' into language and its persuasive force.

Whoever thinks the problem of truth and rhetoric broached in these formulations is outdated should look for it again under the modern heading of "truth and style." Disregarding Cicero's influence on the form taken by this problem, it should not be forgotten that Lactantius figures among the authors reread by Petrarch (something that was to assume canonic significance), nor that Erasmus devoted to him one of his exemplary editions. It is not a question of adducing citable 'influences' here; but, after an interval of one and a half millennia, is not Lessing still striking much the same tune in his second polemic against Goeze? "How ridiculous

---

27. *Quae licet possit sine eloquentia defendi, ut est a multies saepe defensa; tamen claritate ac nitore sermonis illustranda et quodam modo disserenda est, ut potentius in animos influat, et vi sua instructa, et luce orationis ornata* (I 1, 10). [*Ante-Nicene Fathers,* trans. Fletcher, VII, 9–10.]

28. *quod magis possent credere homines ornatae veritati, qui etiam mendacio credunt, capti orationis ornatu . . .* (III 13, 12). [*Ante-Nicene Fathers,* trans. Fletcher, VII, 69.]

29. *eloquens nunquam fui, quippe qui forum ne attigerim quidem. Sed necesse est, ipsa me faciat causae bonitas eloquentem; ad quam diserte copioseque defendendam scientia divinitatis et ipsa veritas sufficit* (III 13, 12). [*Ante-Nicene Fathers,* trans. Fletcher, VII, 81–82.]

it is . . . to attribute the superiority over us that truth gives an opponent to his dazzling style! I know of no dazzling style that does not borrow its brilliance from the truth, more or less. Truth alone gives real brilliance; and it must underlie mockery and farce as well, at least as a foil."[30] Rhetoric can also furnish the model for a more comprehensive maxim, as when Vauvenargues writes: ". . . In itself, falsehood is weak and must carefully conceal itself; it takes a great deal of effort to hoodwink others with captivating speech. Yet one would be wrong to conclude that the art of eloquence consists solely therein. Does not this power of simple appearances of truth show how eloquent truth itself is, and how greatly superior to our own art! Only one who is adept at employing the truth and knows its power may consider himself clever."[31] A prudential maxim of this kind is the residue of a metaphysical axiom; metaphor outlives its vital function of expressing one of the ontological surmises underlying and governing all conduct, figuring henceforth only as a kind of pragmatic crutch.

---

30. *Wie lächerlich . . . die Überlegenheit, welche die Wahrheit einem Gegner über uns gibt, einem blendenden Stile desselben zuzuschreiben! Ich kenne keinen blendenden Stil, der seinen Glanz nicht von der Wahrheit mehr oder weniger entlehnet. Wahrheit allein gibt echten Glanz; und muß auch bei Spötterei und Posse, wenigstens als Folie, unterliegen.*

31. *Die französischen Moralisten,* ed. F. Schalk I, 112. [. . . *car le mensonge est faible par lui-même; il faut qu'il se cache avec soin; et s'il arrive qu'on persuade quelque chose par des discours captieux, ce n'est pas sans beacoup de peine. On aurait grand tort d'en conclure que ce soit en sela que consiste l'éloquence. Jugeons, au contraire, par ce pouvoir des simples apparences de la vérité, combien la vérité elle-même est éloquente et supérieure à notre art. Celui qui sait se servir avec adresse de la vérité et qui en connaît l'éloquence, peut seul se piquer d'être habile.* Vauvenargues, *Oeuvres complètes* (Paris: Hachette, 1968), II, 276.]

IV

Metaphorics of the 'Naked' Truth

While discussing the relationship between truth and rhetoric in the passage, cited in the previous section, from the first chapter of book III of the "Divinae institutiones," Lactantius comments on the 'natural' *nakedness of truth*. This divinely sanctioned nakedness is tarted up with rhetorical frippery in a manner that is characteristic precisely of the way in which lies manifest themselves: "But since God has willed this to be the nature of the case, that simple and undisguised truth should be more clear, because it has sufficient ornament of itself, and on this account it is corrupted when embellished with adornings from without, but that falsehood should please by means of a splendor not its own, because being corrupt of itself it vanishes and melts away, unless it is set off and polished with decoration sought from another source . . ."[1] That brings us to a new field of metaphors in which a quite particular aspect of historical representations of truth comes to light.

---

1. *Sed quoniam deus hanc voluit rei esse naturam, ut simplex et nuda veritas esset luculentior, quia satis ornata per se est, ideoque ornamentis extrinsecus additis fucata corrumpitur; mendacium vero specie placet aliena, quia per se corruptum vanescit ac diffluit, nisi aliunde ornatu quaesito circumlitum fuerit ac politum* . . . (III 1, 3). [*Ante-Nicene Fathers,* ed. Alexander Roberts and James Donaldson, trans. William Fletcher (Peabody, MA: Hendrikson Publishers, 2004), VII, 69.]

The reader will surely agree that it is tautologous to speak of the 'naked truth', since we are always dealing with truth "when a thing lies naked before us."[2] But this metaphor does not mean to bring anything into the *concept* of truth; it projects conjectures and evaluations of a very complex kind over the top of the concept, as it were. The metaphor is intimately linked with the import and importance of *clothing,* considered as guise or disguise, in relation to which nakedness likewise splits into unmasking, into the uncovering of a deception, on the one hand, and shameless unveiling, the violation of a sacred mystery, on the other. Truth can have its 'culture' in its clothing, just as mankind's cultural history is essentially identical to that of its apparel, since man is the creature that dresses itself and refuses to expose itself precisely in its 'naturalness'. Is truth—insofar as it may be imagined, as truth *for* man, to show any consideration for him at all—even compatible, in its 'natural' openness and insistence, with a 'clothed' being? An aggressive aphorism from Franz Werfel's "Theologumena" will perhaps make clearer what is intended here: "The naked truth, the 'nuda veritas', is the whorish bride of the barbarian. Culture begins at the exact moment when something is to be hidden, in other words, with an awareness of original sin (Adam's fig leaf is the first document of culture). Regression into barbarism, however, begins at the exact moment when what is hidden begins to be uncovered, that is to say, with psychology." Kierkegaard expressed a similar thought in a far more subtle manner in a journal entry from 29 October 1838: "There is always a great tendency among ecstatic factions, expressed with a curious ironic consistency, to reveal themselves outwardly in the negligee in which their train of thought always emerges: the Adamites thought that in order to be perfectly free one had to go stark naked, and presumably regarded this as the specific difference between man's state in paradise and his later condition. The sansculottes are well known—the attempt of bare-necked persons to reestablish the Nordic spirit is just now in full swing."[3] In the long entry from 1 August 1835, to which we will have occasion to turn a little later in this section, the problematic of the 'naked truth' is grasped by Kierkegaard in an even more radical sense.

Nakedness originally appears to be the sole mode in which creatures can submit themselves before God and be 'suffered' by him. "O Lord, the depths of man's conscience lie bare before your eyes,"[4] Augustine exclaims, in order that this na-

---

2. Ortega y Gasset, "Über das Denken," in *Vergangenheit und Zukunft im heutigen Menschen* (Stuttgart, 1955), 126. ["Notes on Thinking," in *Concord and Liberty*, trans. Helene Weyl (New York: W. W. Norton, 1963), 59.]

3. [Søren Kierkegaard, *Kierkegaard's Journals and Notebooks,* trans. N. J. Cappelørn et al., (Princeton: Princeton University Press, 2007), 1: 257.] I find a somewhat different and, in this context, highly apposite interpretation of the nakedness of these sectarians cited in a review by E. Voegelin (in *Philosophische Rundschau* I, 34): "When Adamitic sectarians were informed by their conscience that God's naked truth would best be symbolized if they walked down the streets without any clothes, even a Roger Williams was forced to throw the naked symbols of truth into prison."

4. *Domine, cuius oculis nuda est abyssus humanae conscientiae. Confessiones* X 2, 2. [Augustine, *Confessions,* trans. R. S. Pine-Coffin (London: Penguin, 1961), 207.]

kedness, which already exists in an essential sense, may for its part be accepted in the manner of *confessio,* appropriated, but also testified as a literary work.[5] In his exposition of the Psalms (134, 16), he writes: "A good heart is hidden, and a bad heart is hidden; there is an abyss in the good heart and in the bad heart too, but both are naked to the eyes of God . . ."[6] That is also how Rousseau still stylizes the opening of his "Confessions": he wants to appear before his fellows in the naturalness of his truth, a truth that can hold its own even before the transcendent situation of the Last Judgment, since it believes it can bear comparison with the view of man's bared soul to which the Eternal Being itself is privy. The pentitent's contemporaries are again cited as witnesses, but in such a way that his self-accusation now only provides the model that they are all expected to follow when presenting themselves before the divine tribunal: "But let each one of them reveal his heart at the foot of Thy throne with equal sincerity, and may any man who dares, say, 'I was a better man than he.'"[7] The imagined courtroom scene of naked human truth is the stylistic means by which a social outcast can appeal to solidarity in nakedness. Man's nudity at the hypothetical end of his history corresponds, in Rousseau, to his assumed nudity at its beginning, which he reconstructs "by stripping this being, thus constituted, of all the supernatural gifts he could have received and of all the artificial faculties he could have acquired only by long progress, by considering him, in a word, as he must have come from the hands of nature."[8] From the individualistic point of departure, human society has evolved as an elaborate system of disguises that the critic of its actual state tears away one by one, as if the tribunal had already convened before which we will all have to reappear naked. As soon as clothing begins to be understood *as* a disguise to be cast aside, ripped off, or seen through, the existing state of society loses its quality of self-evidence. A hundred years before the great revolution, President Miron of the Third Estate had proclaimed at the assembly of the Estates General: "If Your Majesty does not take action"—against the oppression of the people by the nobility, that is—"then one day the scales could fall from the eyes of the poor, and they will see that a soldier is nothing more than a

---

5. *Conf.* X 1, 1: *Volo eam (sc. veritatem) facere in corde meo coram te in confessione, in stilo autem meo coram multis testibus* [I wish to act in truth, making my confession both in my heart before you and in this book before the many who will read it; Augustine, *Confessions,* trans. Pine-Coffin, 207]. The reader's function consists solely in bearing witness to such self-exposure and is therefore intended to rule out *curiositas.* Only thus does a human relationship to the other's nakedness become possible, not as a 'psychological interest'.

6. *Latet cur bonum, latet cor malum, abyssus est in corde bono et in corde malo. Sed haec nuda sunt deo, quem nihil latet . . .* [Augustine, *Expositions of the Psalms 121–150,* trans. Maria Boulding (Hyde Park, NY: New City Press, 2004), 204.]

7. [Jean-Jacques Rousseau, *The Confessions,* trans. J. M. Cohen (Harmondsworth: Penguin, 1979), 17.]

8. *En dépouillant cet être ainsi constitué de tous les dons surnaturels qu'il a pu recevoir, et de toutes les facultés artificielles qu'il n'a pu acquérir que par de longs progrès: en le considérant, en un mot, tel qu'il a dû sortir de la nature . . . Discours sur l'inegalité* 1 (Phil. Bibl. 243, 84). [Jean-Jacques Rousseau, *Rousseau's Political Writings,* ed. Alan Ritter and Julia Conaway Bondanella, trans. Julia Conaway Bondanella (New York: W. W. Norton & Company, 1988), 11.]

peasant with a weapon in his hand . . ."[9] In the modern age, talk of the 'naked truth' has mainly figured in bourgeois diatribes against the sartorial world of the First and Second Estates, but it could equally be adopted by every up-and-coming class that thought itself naked and wanted to strip others of their vestments as so many disguises. The "Communist Manifesto" spells out the pioneering achievement of the bourgeoisie in this regard with all desirable clarity: "The bourgeoisie, wherever it has got the upper hand, has put an end to all feudal, patriarchal, idyllic relations. It has pitilessly torn asunder the motley feudal ties that bound man to his 'natural superiors', and has left remaining no other nexus between man and man than *naked self-interest,* than callous 'cash payment' . . . The bourgeoisie has *stripped of its halo* every occupation hitherto honoured and looked up to with reverent awe. It has converted the physician, the lawyer, the priest, the poet, the man of science, into its paid wage-labourers."[10] Rousseau had believed that true and natural man would come to light once this socially disguised being had been stripped of its clothing; Marx discovers that after this disrobement, all that remains are the *commodity* and the *interest* shown in it, hence a new functional concealment that must be stripped away in turn if man is at last to be seen for who he really is, in his naked truth. Thus the ever-shifting backdrop against which the modern age carries out its interminable quest for 'natural nature'.

Pascal had already seen through this dialectic of social dissimulation and 'naked truth'. For him, disguises express the facticity of all self-institutions of human togetherness, the inessentiality of all laws and statutes as mere rules of play.[11] He had read chapter 42 of book I of Montaigne's "Essais," in which the author voices his astonishment that we do not appraise a man in the same way as when we haggle over a horse: "You examine it naked and bare." Instead, we judge a man by everything he is not, by his suite of attendants, his palace, his influence, his income—"all that may surround him but it is not in him." Our view of him is blocked by his pictures, clothing, decorations, and furnishings; he appears before us shrouded in impropriety, in the literal sense of the term. "Why do you judge a man when he is wrapped up like a parcel? He is letting us see only such attributes as do not belong to him while hiding the only ones which enable us to judge his real worth." In effect, Montaigne is calling on his reader to insist on the naked truth of man, even if he stops a little short of that: "Let him . . . show us himself in his shimmy."[12] Pascal vehemently and repeatedly opposes this thought: "This really is to be won-

9. Cited in Carl J. Burckhardt, *Richelieu*, 12th ed. (Munich, 1947), 65.

10. [Karl Marx and Friedrich Engels, *The Communist Manifesto* (London: Penguin, 2002), 222.]

11. See Hans Blumenberg, "Das Recht des Scheins in den menschlichen Ordnungen bei Pascal," *Philosophisches Jahrbuch* 57 (1947): 413–30.

12. *vous le veoyez nud et à descouvert . . . tout cela est autour de luy, non en luy . . . Pourquoy estimant un homme, l'estimez vous tout enveloppé et compacqueté? Il ne nous faict monstre que des parties qui ne sont aulcunement siennes, et nous cache celles par lesquelles seules on peut vrayement iuger de son estimation . . . qu'il se presente en chemise.* [Michel de Montaigne, *The Complete Essays,* trans. M. A. Screech (London: Penguin, 1991), 289.]

dered at: I am supposed not to bow to a man in brocade clothing followed by seven or eight lackeys! . . . His clothes are his power."[13] To Pascal, it seems ridiculous that Montaigne should demand a cause for the distance that is in play here, that he should appeal to reason (*d'en demander la raison*). The imagination has helped human beings come to terms with the practical impossibility of their equality while simultaneously acknowledging their inability to infer any essential hierarchy: "Obedience—from imagination." Pascal finds the people's habit of judging from appearances salutary, since no other rational option is open to them: "Cannibals laugh at an infant king."[14] Fragment 82, a lengthy text entitled "Imagination," is devoted to illustrations of the facticity of the human world, the collection of social figurines among which—mercifully—we have been placed. What will later be attempted by the Enlightenment is here characterized as futile: "Reason never entirely overcomes the imagination, whereas the imagination often completely drives reason from its throne." The red gowns of the judges, the ermine skins they wear, the courts where they pass judgment, their fleurs-de-lis, "this whole impressive accoutrement," all of it betrays their knowledge of the secret of disguise. If doctors had really mastered the art of healing, why would they need to show off in their square caps and oversized gowns? Princes practice the same technique with other means, never appearing without a complement of trumpeters, drummers, and guards. "Imagination orders everything. It is the spring of beauty, justice, and happiness which is the be-all and end-all of the world."[15] Justice and truth are matters too delicate to be arrived at by the crude means placed at our disposal. But human beings have the good fortune to be so constituted "that they have no exact principle of truth, and many excellent ones of falsehood."[16] From this position, Pascal viewed with skepticism the increasing tendency to apply reason indiscriminately, to insist on the 'naked truth' without any thought for the cost: ". . . when a private soldier takes the square cap off a first president and throws it out the window . . ."

The relationship to truth in our tradition proves far more ambiguous in the medium of metaphorics than it would ever appear if subjected to a systematic, terminological analysis. In the Skeptical tradition, to be sure, all the arguments that might lead us to despair of ever taking possession of the whole truth, or even a fraction of the truth, had been assembled, and the contentment to be gained by renouncing the immoderate demands of theory seemed preferable to a quest for

---

13. *Cela est admirable: on ne veut pas que j'honore un homme vêtu de brocatelle et suivi de sept ou huit laquais! . . . cet habit, c'est une force.* [Blaise Pascal, *Pensées and Other Writings,* trans. Honor Levi (Oxford: Oxford University Press, 1995), 31.]

14. *Obéissance—de fantaisie . . . cannibales se rient d'un enfant roi.* [Pascal, *Pensées and Other Writings,* trans. Levi, 34.]

15. *jamais la raison ne surmonte l'imagination alors que l'imagination démonte souvent tout à fait la raison de son siège . . . tout ce appareil auguste . . . L'imagination dispose de tout; elle fait la beauté, la justice et le bonheur, qui est le tout du monde.* [Pascal, *Pensées and Other Writings,* trans. Levi, 19.]

16. *qu'il n'a aucun principe de vrai et plusieurs excellents du faux.* [Pascal, *Pensées and Other Writings,* trans. Levi, 20.]

the impossible. But whether truth, considered as hypothetically attainable, could really constitute or consummate human happiness is another of those imponderable, potentially futile questions that have only ever arrived at answers by means of metaphor. In the manner of composition of its sacred texts, the Christian epoch had given a certain hint that the self-revealed truth could be no less intolerable for man than his own nakedness: in these texts, after all, images serve to protect man. Thomas of Aquinas directly poses the question of the necessity of figurative speech in the Bible,[17] and he concludes: "Holy Scripture delivers spiritual things to us beneath metaphors taken from bodily things."[18] This "beneath" (*sub*) has a double meaning: it signifies both the 'vehicle' and the 'screen' of revelation ("thereby divine matters are more effectively screened against those unworthy of them").[19] This metaphorical didactics finds support in Aristotelian epistemology: "Now we are of the kind to reach the intelligible realm through the sensible realm . . ."[20] It seems that the vehicle can become dispensable, and hence that, for Thomas, this biblical metaphorics is not absolute: ". . . The beam of divine revelation is not extinguished by the sense imagery that veils it and its truth does not flicker out, since the minds of those given the revelation are not allowed to remain arrested with the images but are lifted up to their meaning."[21] That is why something said metaphorically (*sub metaphoris*) in one passage of holy scripture can be stated explicitly (*expressius*) in another, so that we were dealing on the first occasion with nothing more than a useful figurative disguise (*occultatio figurarum utilis*). Yet Aquinas also speaks of a necessity (*necessitas*) that goes beyond the poetic use of metaphors (*propter repraesentationem*): "their indispensable usefulness."[22] But that remains without further justification and reflection; the Aristotelian premises did not leave much room for exploring the 'linguistic' problem of divine revelation. It is accordingly Aristotelians of the strictest Averroistic persuasion whom we encounter as "lovers of the naked truth,"[23] in

---

17. *Summa theol.* 1 q. 1 a. 9: *Utrum sacra scriptura debeat uti metaphoris.*

18. *in sacra scriptura traduntur nobis spiritualia sub metaphoris corporalium.* |*Summa theologiae* I/1, trans. Thomas Gilby (London: Eyre & Spottiswoode, 1964), 35.|

19. *per huiusmodi divina magis occultantur indignis.* |*Summa theologiae* I/1, 37.|

20. *est autem naturale homini ut per sensibilia ad intelligibila veniat . . .* |*Summa theologiae* I/1, 33; translation modified.|

21. *radius divinae revelationis non destruitur propter figuras sensibiles, quibus circumvelatur . . . sed remanet in sua veritate, ut mentes, quibus fit revelatio, non permittat in similitudinibus permanere, sed elevat eas ad cognitionem intelligibilium.* |*Summa theologiae* I/1, 35.|

22. *propter necessitatem et utilitatem.* |*Summa theologiae* I/1, 35.|

23. Richard d'Angerville von Bury (1265–1345), *Philobiblion,* cited by G. Toffanin, *Geschichte des Humanismus* (1941), 437: *Omnia genera machinarum, quibus poetas solius nudae veritatis amatores obiiciunt, duplici refelluntur umbone: quia vel in obscena materia gratus cultus sermonis addiscitur, vel, ubi ficta vel honesta sententia tractatur, naturalis vel historialis veritas indagatur sub eloquio typicae fictionis.* |All the types of machines with which the lovers of the naked truth do battle against the poets are refuted with a double defense: because (a) the fine art of discourse is learned even via obscene material, and (b) when a contrived or sincere word of wisdom is employed, a natural or historical truth is discernible under the fancy words of a work figured as fiction.| Note the metaphor of mechanical force used to characterize those who oppose the poetic dissimulation of truth. It is remarkable how comparatively inoffensive the 'scan-

the parlance of early humanism, and this in the sense that, on the side of the contested veils and disguises of truth, the poetic images of the ancient authors *and* the sacred images of the Bible coalesce into a single homogeneous sphere that is to be defended against the importunate demands of the new will to truth. The humanist concept of *sapientia* refers to this sphere in its opposition to *scientia,* an opposition that would not be overcome until Descartes. Yet it is in this dissociation of 'wisdom' and 'science' (the latter by no means yet understood in the modern sense of the term), of humanism and Aristotelianism, that the pathos of the 'naked truth' emerges as the stylistic characteristic of a new, uncompromising will to knowledge. This consequence is almost palpable in Petrarch's "Invectivae contra medicum"; Giovanni Pico della Mirandola, in his famous letter to Ermolao Barbaro from 1485, explicates it in relation to both positions by reckoning with the six years he had squandered in Aristotelian-Averroistic studies.[24] He confronts his addressee with a fictitious Schoolman who gives a speech in defense of the 'naked truth', couched in a deliberately 'barbaric' and plain idiom, even if the defendant does not eschew figurative language altogether: "Who will not condemn synthetic beauty, or rouge, in a reputable maiden?" Can there be any affinity, the Schoolman asks, between the philosopher and the orator, whose magic arts give "the things themselves . . . whatever face and costume he pleases," and who knows how "to give falsehood the semblance of truth and to dupe his audience into mistaking fictions for realities"?[25] On this head, reference is made to the stylistic shortcomings of the Bible, a source of considerable anxiety to the fathers of the church. "A speech with long locks is always wanton. Wherefore we prefer ours shaggy . . ."[26] The deep suspicion of the modern age is here directed for the first time toward language, not so much as the vehicle of truth than as its dress: if Pythagoras had been able to communicate his thoughts through some other medium than speech, for example by looks, no words would ever have passed his lips; we thus "do not want our style delightful, adorned, and graceful; we want it useful, grave, something to be respected." But the truth is not meant for everyone, only for those who are able to endure the sight of the exposed 'inner side of things': "The bitter rind of our words prevented the plebs from sullying our thoughts. Those who wish to conceal treasure are wont to cover it with refuse or rubbish, so that only those passers-by may take it who are considered worthy of such a gift. A like endeavor, to wit, that of philosophers to hide their business, were fitting for people who not only do not appreciate but also do not even understand them."[27] Here, too, the naked truth is still reserved for the

dalous' subject of the poets appears in relation to the ambivalence of those 'lovers of truth' who do not wish to see their beloved other than naked.

24. [Trans. Quirinus Breen, in "Giovanni Pico della Mirandola and the Conflict of Philosophy and Rhetoric," *Journal of the History of Ideas* 13.3 (1952): 384–412.] Cf. also G. Toffanin, 308 ff.

25. [Breen, "Giovanni Pico della Mirandola," 395–96; translation modified.]

26. [Breen, "Giovanni Pico della Mirandola," 396.]

27. [Breen, "Giovanni Pico della Mirandola," 397; translation modified.]

initiated. This reserve has been taken out of God's hands and placed under 'expert' management; science has begun to exercise what once were divine rights. But will it be able to keep them for itself?

Under the normative concept of 'objectivity', the modern age relinquishes every exclusive claim to ownership of the truth: once it has been wrested from the object, truth becomes in principle the common property of the human race, accessible in equal measure to all. For the professional researcher of the modern age, to know and to 'publish' is practically the same thing, and barbarous nakedness remains the characteristic stylistic feature of such 'publications'. Bacon had already written in his first essay: "Truth is a naked and open day-light that doth not shew the masks and mummeries and triumphs of the world." The new knowledge likes to contrast its approach with that of earlier epochs through its determination to expose and unveil: "Is not Aristotle unjustly lauded / To whom Nature never showed herself undistorted?" the young Lessing rhymes.[28] Truth is only naked so long as the vigilance of the 'enlightened' intellect compels it to remain so by frustrating the ploys that would obfuscate and obscure it: the "spirit of examination" must be kept alive by the clash of viewpoints so that it may "stop painted untruth from establishing itself in place of truth," Lessing writes in his foreword to "Wie die Alten den Tod gebildet" [How the Ancients Depicted Death]. And in the same passage, we find another highly significant statement about the modern age's concept of truth: what counts is the formal quality of the unveiled truth as such, not whatever degree of 'importance' attaches to the material content of this truth, since "as a disposition of our knowledge . . . one truth is as important as any other."[29] Knowledge is not justified by what it allows us to know, but essentially the self-confirmation of the human intellect; hence reason's insistence on the *unconditional surrender* of the naked truth.[30] Religion, too, is normed through this 'type' of truth. In Toland's "Christianity not mysterious" (1702), the historical merit of Jesus is seen in his having "stripp'd the Truth" so as to make it "easy and obvious to the meanest capacities."

The metaphor of the 'naked truth' pertains to the self-awareness of enlightened reason and its claim to mastery.[31] More subtle aesthetic distinctions in the layers to be stripped away are generally ignored; where they are made, however, a different, historically sensitized meaning can already be discerned, as in the distinction

---

28. *Wird Aristoteles nicht ohne Grund gepriesen, / Dem nie sich die Natur, als unterm Flor gewiesen?* Aus einem Gedichte an den Herrn M** (*Werke*, ed. Rilla, I, 189).

29. *die geschminkte Unwahrheit verhindert, sich an der Stelle der Wahrheit festzusetzen . . . als Beschaffenheit unserer Erkenntnis ist . . . eine Wahrheit so wichtig als die andere* (V, 672).

30. [English in original.]

31. Perhaps I may be permitted to illustrate this connection by citing a modern literary example: in his Joseph novel, Thomas Mann lets Jacob say to Eliezer: "Pure was I, but God hath drenched me over and over in filth, and such people find it reasonable, for knowing naught of pious palliation they let the truth go naked." [Thomas Mann, *Joseph and His Brothers*, trans. Helen Lowe-Porter (Harmondsworth: Penguin, 1978), 433; translation modified.]

between 'covering' (*Verhüllung*) and 'disguise' (*Verkleidung*) introduced by Winck-elmann in his "Versuch einer Allegorie" [Attempt at an Allegory] from 1766: ". . . Finally, when wisdom began to grow more human among the Greeks and wanted to impart itself to a greater number, it cast aside the cloak under which it had been difficult to recognize. It nonetheless remained disguised, yet uncovered, so that it could be detected by those who sought it out and examined it, and in this form it appears among the well-known poets . . ."[32] The discovery of *history* within the Enlightenment and against its semantic current is the discovery of the illusion of the 'naked truth' or the illusoriness of nakedness. It is at once the negation of the metaphor and its renewal in a different direction: the 'disguises' of truth now no longer issue from the poetic imagination and the need for rhetorical ornamenta-tion—they do not represent fashion accessories, so to speak, that could be cast off without further ado—but are themselves constitutive of the way in which truth manifests itself. It almost sounds like an Enlightenment anachronism when Ranke writes in his critique of Guicciardini: "We for our part have a different idea of his-tory. Naked truth without any decoration . . ."[33] It is exemplary that the clothing metaphor recurs precisely where the early and high modern age thought to have reached through to the bare core of Being-in-itself, in the mathematical knowledge of nature: what looked like nakedness turns out to be a "well-fitting *garb of ideas*" whose measurements are taken in the geometrical and natural-scientific mathema-tization of the lifeworld—so Edmund Husserl in his interpretation of Galileo.[34] A supposedly merely aesthetic phenomenon[35] has become a fundamental characteris-tic of historical life itself; the veiledness of truth seems to guarantee our continuing viability. "Truth is death," the elderly Fontane writes to his daughter Martha on 24 August 1893. "One must be dead to see things naked," a modern mystic notes.[36]

The last two quotations lead us to the insight that a new form of skepticism, one that is utterly without precedent in prior intellectual history, emerges from within the modern age: a doubt, not primarily concerning the attainability of truth, but the human meaning of its attainment, the human supportability of the demand for the 'naked truth'. At issue here is not just a superficial 'digestibility' of truth, as Breitinger claims when justifying a metaphorical 'sugar coating': "Just as

---

32. . . . *endlich, da unter den Griechen die Weisheit anfing menschlicher zu werden und sich mehreren mit-teilen wollte, tat sie die Decke hinweg, unter welcher sie schwer zu erkennen war, sie blieb aber verkleidet, doch ohne Verhüllung, so daß sie denen, welche sie suchten und betrachteten, kenntlich war, und in dieser Gestalt er-scheint sie bei den bekannten Dichtern . . .*

33. Cited in E. Kessel, "Rankes Geschichtsauffassung," *Universitas* 11 (1947): 920.

34. *Die Krisis der europäischen Wissenschaften und die transzendentale Phänomenologie,* Husserliana VI (The Hague, 1954), 51. [Edmund Husserl, *The Crisis of European Sciences and Transcendental Phenome-nology,* trans. David Carr (Evanston, IL: Northwestern University Press, 1970), 51.]

35. The limits of the aesthetic are marked in one of La Rochefoucauld's aphorisms (in Schalk, *Die französischen Moralisten,* I, 35): "There are disguised untruths that so naturally feign truth that to be de-ceived by them implies a lack of judgment."

36. Simone Weil, *La pesanteur et la grace,* German ed. (Munich, 1952), 144.

a clever physician gilds or sweetens a bitter pill, so those who want to use the truth as an aid for the furthering of human happiness must proceed in the same way."[37] Rather, the very fittingness of this 'aid' to its purpose, the 'furthering of human happiness', is called into question. Lessing's *Wenn Gott in seiner Rechten . . .* is all too familiar,[38] but the lines that immediately precede this oft-quoted passage and provide it with its rationale should be read as well: "Not the truth which someone possesses or believes to possess, but the honest effort he has made to get at the truth, constitutes a human being's worth. For it is not through the possession of truth, but through its pursuit, that his powers are enlarged, and it is in this alone that his ever-growing perfection lies. Possession makes us inactive, lazy, and proud—."[39] One needs to pay close attention to these lines to see that their overarching logical subject is not truth but human worth. It is not the intrinsic value of a truth that determines the measure in which it is to be given to us, but its capacity to motivate and provoke human self-development, self-realization, and self-assertion. The modern character of truth as labor, the 'honest effort' to be expended on it, is here reevaluated and appropriated in an entirely positive way—so much so that the result, the 'naked truth', is devalued and estranged by the process: ". . . Pure truth is for you alone!" Lessing cries to God at the end of the same celebrated passage. The problem of the human relation to truth preoccupied Lessing throughout his life; it is already very clearly evident in his early comedy "Der Freigeist" [The Freethinker] (act IV, scene 3): "ADRASTUS: . . . I can never believe that truth can be common, any more than I could believe daylight to exist throughout the world at the same moment. That which under the form of truth passes current amongst all people, and is acknowledged as such by the most weak-minded, is assuredly no truth, and it requires but courage to lay hands on it, and divest it of its covering, when the most frightful errors stand naked before us.—JULIA: What wretched creatures are men, and how unjust their Creator, if you are right, Adrastus, in what you say. Either there must be no such thing as truth, or else it must be of that

---

37. *Gleichwie ein kluger Arzt die bitteren Pillen vergüldet oder verzucket: also müssen diejenigen, welche die Wahrheit als ein Hilfsmittel zur Beförderung der menschlichen Glückseligkeit gebrauchen wollen, gleicherweise verfahren. Critische Dichtkunst* (Zurich, 1740), 166. Breitinger's more specialized "Kritische Abhandlung von der Natur, den Absichten und dem Gebrauche der Gleichnisse" [Critical Treatise on the Nature, Intentions, and Use of Parables] (Zurich, 1740) is also pertinent to a metaphorology.

38. [Perhaps not to anglophone readers. The reference is to "A rejoinder": "If God held fast in his right hand the whole of truth and in his left hand only the ever-active quest for truth, albeit with the proviso that I should constantly and eternally err, and said to me: 'Choose!', I would humbly fall upon his left hand and say: 'Father, give! For pure truth is for you alone!'" Gotthold Ephraim Lessing, *Philosophical and Theological Writings,* trans. H. B. Nisbet (Cambridge: Cambridge University Press, 2005), 98.]

39. *Nicht die Wahrheit, in deren Besitz irgendein Mensch ist, oder zu sein vermeinet, sondern die aufrichtige Mühe, die er angewandt hat, hinter die Wahrheit zu kommen, macht den Wert des Menschen. Denn nicht durch den Besitz, sondern durch die Nachforschung der Wahrheit erweitern sich seine Kräfte, worin allein seine immer wachsende Vollkommenheit bestehet. Der Besitz macht ruhig, träge, stolz—. Eine Duplik* (*Werke,* ed. Rilla, VIII, 27). [Lessing, *Philosophical and Theological Writings,* trans. Nisbet, 98; translation modified.]

nature, that it may be perceived by the majority, indeed by all, at least in matters of consequence.—ADRASTUS: It is not the fault of truth, that it cannot be received, but of men.—We are to live happily in the world; for that purpose we are created; for that purpose alone. As often as truth is opposed to this great end, it is obliged to be set aside; for few minds can find their happiness in truth itself."[40]

In his critique of science, Rousseau likewise entertains serious misgivings as to the essentiality of our need for truth. For him, truth's hiddenness at the bottom of the well (in Democritus's metaphor) is not an incentive to 'honest effort', but—in teleological explication—a reference to the yawning inhumanity of the concealed truth: "Are we destined then to die fixed to the edge of the well where the truth has hidden?"[41] According to an age-old legend handed down by the Egyptians to the Greeks, the inventor of the sciences was a god hostile to the tranquillity of mankind (*un dieu ennemi du repos des hommes*). Here, in contrast to Lessing's conception, the process is seen to be even more dangerous than the result: in probabilistic terms, those who seek the truth find themselves at a hopeless disadvantage, since falsehood permits an infinity of combinations and permutations, whereas truth exists in one form alone. "How many errors, a thousand times more dangerous than the truth is useful, must be surmounted in order to reach the truth?" And finally, the weightiest objection of them all: "If by luck we finally find it, who among us will know how to make good use of the truth?"[42] Rousseau's pragmatic refunctioning of the 'truth in the well' metaphor is, in short, to leave the truth undisturbed. The depth of the well protects us from the problematic of its nakedness.

Kierkegaard's lengthy journal entry from 1 August 1835 shows the metaphor of the 'naked truth' in its most radical aspect: the indifference of objective truth to this one life, its unresponsiveness to the question of his life's 'purpose' that is gnawing away at him. What matters is "to find a truth that is a truth *for me,* to find

---

40. *ADRAST: . . . Es ist mir unmöglich zu glauben, daß die Wahrheit gemein sein könne; eben so unmöglich, als zu glauben, daß in der ganzen Welt auf einmal Tag sein könne. Das, was unter der Gestalt der Wahrheit unter allen Völkern herumschleicht, und auch von den Blödsinnigsten angenommen wird, ist gewiß keine Wahrheit, und man darf nur getrost die Hand, sie zu entkleiden, anlegen, so wird man den scheußlichsten Irrtum nackend vor sich stehen sehen.—JULIANE: Wie elend sind die Menschen, und wie ungerecht ihr Schöpfer, wenn Sie Recht haben, Adrast! Es muß entweder gar keine Wahrheit sein, oder sie muß von der Beschaffenheit sein, daß sie von den meisten, ja von allen, wenigsten im Wesentlichen, empfunden werden kann.—ADRAST: Es liegt nicht an der Wahrheit, daß sie es nicht werden kann; sondern an den Menschen.— Wir sollen glücklich in der Welt leben; dazu sind wir erschaffen; dazu sind wir einzig und allein erschaffen. So oft die Wahrheit diesem großen Endzwecke hinderlich ist, so oft ist man verbunden, sie beiseite zu setzen; denn nur wenig Geister können in der Wahrheit selbst ihr Glück finden . . .* [G. Lessing, *Three Comedies,* trans. J. J. Holroyd (Colchester: Totham, 1838), 67.]

41. *Sommes-nous donc faits pour mourir attachés sur les bords du puits où la verité s'est retirée? Discours sur les sciences et les arts* II (Philos. Bibl. 243, 28 f.). [Jean-Jacques Rousseau, *The First and Second Discourses,* trans. Roger Masters and Judith Masters (New York: St Martin's Press, 1964), 48; translation modified.]

42. *Par combien d'erreur, mille fois plus dangereuses que la vérité n'est utile, ne faut-il point passer pour arriver à elle? . . . si par bonheur nous la trouvons à la fin, qui de nous en saura faire un bon usage?* [Rousseau, *The First and Second Discourses,* trans. Masters and Masters, 49.]

the idea for which I am willing to live and die. And what use here would it be to me if I were to discover a so-called objective truth . . . or were able to construct a world which, again, I myself did not inhabit but merely held up for others to see? . . . to explain many separate facts, if it had no deeper meaning *for myself* and *my life?* . . . What use would it be to me if truth were to stand there before me, *cold and naked,* not caring whether I acknowledged it or not, and inducing an anxious shudder rather than trusting devotion? . . . That is what I lack, and this is why I am like a man who has collected furniture and rented rooms but still hasn't found the beloved with whom to share his life's ups and downs."[43] Whereas the metaphor of nakedness presupposes a voyeuristic relationship of exteriority, Kierkegaard is searching for a truth *in which* he can live. His learning to that point had brought him satisfaction only in the moment of cognition and had failed to leave behind any deeper mark. "It seems to me that I have not drunk from the cup of wisdom but have fallen into it."[44] In the sermon "De Ultimatum" that concludes "Either/Or," it is said of this concept of truth: ". . . One can recognize a thing many times and acknowledge it, one can want a thing many times and attempt it, yet only the deep inner movement, only the indescribable motions of the heart, only these convince you that what you have recognized 'belongs unto you', that no power can take it from you; for only the truth that edifies is the truth for you."[45]

---

43. [Søren Kierkegaard, *Papers and Journals: A Selection,* trans. Alastair Hannay (London: Penguin, 1996), 32–33; translation modified.]

44. [Kierkegaard, *Papers and Journals,* trans. Hannay, 34.]

45. [Søren Kierkegaard, *Either/Or,* trans. Alastair Hannay (London: Penguin, 1992), 608–9.]

V

Terra Incognita and 'Incomplete Universe' as Metaphors of the Modern Relationship to the World

I would like now to provide further evidence of the pragmatic function of absolute metaphors in relation to two very specific examples, the *terra incognita* metaphor and the metaphorics of the *'incomplete universe'*. It is characteristic of both that they originate in quite specific historical 'experiences': the first gives a metaphorical gloss to the age of discovery's conclusion that the 'known world', which for millennia was relatively constant and appeared to have certain zones of unfamiliarity only at its edges, proves in retrospect to have taken up only a small corner of the earth's surface; the other views the universe as analogous to a workpiece and draws from the newly emerging idea of evolutionary cosmogony the metaphorical conclusion that man is faced with the 'task' of bringing the workpiece to completion. 'Evolution' is transformed via the metaphor into a *transitive* idea: everything that nature has already effected becomes the framework for future human achievement.

The 'America' metaphor enjoys widespread popularity in the seventeenth century. In the foreword to his "Pseudodoxia," Thomas Browne speaks of the "America and untravelled parts of Truth," the new world of a truth that has expanded beyond all expectation. Joseph Glanvill gives a similar account in "The Vanity of Dogmatizing" (1661): "And that there is an America of secrets, and unknown Peru of Nature, whose discovery would richly advance them, is more than conjecture." Abraham Cowley, whose epic "Davideis" (1656) grafts a Newtonian history of creation on a foundation that remains firmly Ptolemaic, apostrophizes Thomas Hobbes in a poem:

> The Baltick, Euxine, and the Caspian,
> And slender-limbed Mediterranean,
> Seem narrow creeks to thee, and onely fit,
> For the poor wretched fisher-boats of wit.
> Thy nobler vessel the vast ocean tries,
>   And nothing sees but seas and skies,
>   Till *unknown regions it descries;*
>
> Thou great *Columbus* of the golden lands of new philosophies,
>   Thy task was harder much than his,
>   For thy *learned America* is
> Not onely found out first by thee,
> And rudely left to future industrie;
> But thy eloquence and thy wit
> Has planted, peopled, built, and civiliz'd it.[1]

The feeling or intimation that the most important landmasses of truth have yet to be discovered, or have only been dimly perceived in their outlines, gives rise to an *attentio animi* |attentiveness of the soul|, conditioning the mind to see, in each new finding, only the headlands and outlying islands of unexplored continents. It is again Thomas Browne who integrates the discovery of the *terra incognita* of human interiority into this metaphorics: "I could never content my contemplation with those generall pieces of wonders, the flux and reflux of the sea, the encrease of Nile, the conversion of the Needle to the North, and have studied to match and parallel those in the more obvious and neglected pieces of Nature, which without travell I can doe in the Cosmography of my selfe; we carry with us the wonders we seeke without us: There is all *Africa,* and her prodigies in us . . ."[2] Montesquieu, who complains in his previously cited 1717 address to the Academy of Bordeaux that nature's stock of mysteries appears to be nearing exhaustion, compares this process with the discovery of a 'new world' in the age that had just drawn to a close. The discoverers had taken their pick of the accumulated spoils, leaving only

---

1. Thomas Hobbes, *Opera philosophica quae latine scripsit omnia,* ed. Molesworth, vol. 1 (London, 1839), V. I thank G. Gawlick for this reference.

2. |Thomas Browne, *Religio Medici* (1643), in *The Major Works* (Harmondsworth: Penguin, 1977), 78.|

savages and wildernesses for those who came after them. But this image is merely the somber rhetorical foil for the words of encouragement that follow: "Nonetheless, messieurs, let us not lose heart: what do we know of what lies in store for us? Perhaps there are a thousand secrets still awaiting discovery: when the geographers have reached the end of their learning, they put vast seas and wild climes in their maps; but perhaps there are even more riches in these seas and in these climes than we currently possess."[3] In the aesthetic realm, we find a parallel to this metaphorical opening of the horizon of expectations in Lessing's discussion of a *wretched novel,* whose author had lamented in his foreword that "there is nothing new any more, everything has been used up besides the thirst for novelty." The reviewer believes this excuse to be unwarranted: "In the world of poetry a genius will still find a country that seemed to have been waiting for his discoveries."[4] We notice just how characteristic the *terra incognita* metaphorics is for the kind of 'intentionality' of consciousness that marked the early modern period when we reencounter it in our own century as an expression of scholarly self-assertiveness. When Husserl, for example, compares the first steps of his phenomenological method with a coastal landing in a 'new country' on which we must now gain a firm footing,[5] or when, in his late "Crisis" treatise, he characterizes the methodical *epochē* as "the gate of entry through which one must pass in order to discover the new world of pure subjectivity,"[6] this strikes us as indicating a curiously anachronistic self-confidence that would be more at home at the beginning of our epoch. An investigation of Husserl's self-intepretation, in which he repeatedly places himself in Descartes' position, would confirm this in the most astonishing manner.

Needless to say, no isolated metaphorological investigation can suffice to articulate the specific feeling for the ratio of the known to the unknown, the old to the incipiently new, that distinguishes the first centuries of the modern age. An investigation of this kind can convey only a sense of the pretheoretical, nervously expectant, premonitory quality of a relation to the world that imagines itself to be standing on the threshold of an immeasurable increase in knowledge, and that converts this awareness into perseverance, labor, method, and energy. Metaphors stake out the terrain within which terminological investigations would have to supply

---

3. *Cependant, Messieurs, ne perdons point courage: que savons-nous ce qui nous est reservé? peut-être y a-t-il encore mille secrets cachés: quand les géographes sont parvenus au terme de leurs connaissances, ils placent dans leurs cartes des mers immenses et des climats sauvages; mais peut-être que dans ces mers et dans ces climats il y a encore plus de richesses que nous n'en avons. Oeuvres compl.,* ed. Didot, 560.

4. *erbärmlichen Roman . . . es gäbe nichts Neues mehr, es sei alles abgenutzt, außer der Neugierigkeit . . . In der Welt der Erdichtungen wird ein Genie noch immer ein Land finden, das seinen Entdeckungen aufbehalten zu sein schien. Berlinische Privilegierte Zeitung* (1753), 13. Stück (*Werke,* ed. Rilla, III, 85).

5. *Die Idee der Phänomenologie,* Husserliana II (The Hague, 1950), 45–46. [Edmund Husserl, *The Idea of Phenomenology,* trans. Lee Hardy (Dordrecht: Kluwer Academic Publishers, 1999), 35.]

6. *das Eingangstor, mit dessen Durchschreiten die neue Welt der reinen Subjektivität entdeckt werden kann.* Husserliana VI (The Hague, 1954), 260. [Edmund Husserl, *The Crisis of European Sciences and Transcendental Phenomenology,* trans. David Carr (Evanston, IL: Northwestern University Press, 1970), 257.]

the details. One need only think of the transvaluation undergone by the concepts of the *new* and *novelty,* beginning perhaps with the negative appraisal we find in Petrarch, who reassures his reader that he has nothing new (*nihil novum*) to say, and who voices the opinion (to Charles IV) that novelty must in all cases arouse suspicion (*Epist. fam.* VI, 2; X, 1). This is a huge field.[7] It includes the naturalization of the concepts of the *miracle* and the *miraculous,* which are now assigned to the same nature whose interruption and transcendence had previously established the miracle's theological character as divine testimony. The reevaluation of *mirabilia* and *meraviglia*—directed against the morphological invariance of Aristotelianism, with its claim that a definitive compendium of worldly things would be possible—considerably broadens the empirical horizon and the attendant attitude of *curiositas.* A seismic shift in expectations accompanies the process by which the principle of *nihil impossibile, nihil incredibile* is transformed from a theological axiom hanging over mankind as an ultimate, all-threatening uncertainty into a postulate of knowledge about the world, stimulating and challenging the human mind by imposing upon it a new and productive restlessness. The growing partiality for *plural* 'worlds' belongs in this context, as does a new genealogy of the concept of cosmological *infinity,* viewed not so much in the aspect of its theoretical as that of its pragmatic function: the infinite universe is above all a universe of new modes of comportment and deportment. The *imagination* becomes an organ of quite unprecedented positivity when, in the open horizon of the not-impossible, the unexpected has become precisely what can be expected at all times. All this can be sketched here only in broad outline.

The idea of completing the incomplete by means of human ingenuity already contains within it the Aristotelian definition of τέχνη, which either brings to an end what nature cannot complete or imitates nature.[8] But what is here presupposed as the incomplete work of productive nature is still only ever the concrete world-piece, which, as an 'example' of its kind, can be halted and put to one side in the process of becoming what it 'ought to be', but whose form and purpose have been insurpassably fixed in the eternal state of nature. What the world is and can be in its entirety, as cosmos, has been determined once and for all; completing the incomplete thus requires nothing more than mimesis, and human 'technique' can only act on nature's behalf. We can easily see how deeply and unquestioningly the idea of a world's invariable quintessence is rooted in our metaphysical tradition by recalling that, even in the mechanistic-atomistic cosmogony of Democritus and Epicurus, only one and the same cosmic pattern ever emerges from chaos and the vortex of chance. 'World' in the plural, already present here in a grammatical sense, still offers no incentive for the imagination, for free variation, for plasticity in imagining what

---

7. [Blumenberg would more thoroughly explore this field in part 2 of *The Legitimacy of the Modern Age,* "The Process of Theoretical Curiosity."]

8. *Physics* II 8; 199a15–17.

might yet be. Even in Descartes and the tradition that followed him, cosmogonic evolution still appears—despite the explicit disavowal of teleological principles—to have terminated in precisely the state and condition of the world as we actually find it. It was by no means so easy as it appears *post festum* to think the idea of 'nature abandoned to itself' to its utmost consequence, or to gain distance from whatever eidetic typicality has crystallized in our conception of the 'world' by understanding it as the product of a *factual* cut at an unremarkable point in the total process of nature. Becoming only unconditionally explains Being if the current state of what has become is equivalent to all others, past and future—in other words, if Being is neither 'finished' nor 'finishable'. Kant, who draws on the *terra incognita* metaphor in his "Allgemeine Naturgeschichte und Theorie des Himmels" |Universal Natural History and Theory of the Heavens| ("I have ventured, on the basis of a slight conjecture, to undertake a dangerous expedition; and already I discern the promontories of new lands"), evokes the idea of the *incomplete universe* in the great cosmological speculation that concludes that work: "The creation is never finished or complete. It has indeed once begun, but it will never cease. It is always busy producing new scenes of nature, new objects, and new worlds."[9] Curiously enough, however, mankind has been excluded from this process and takes no part in it. The entire infinite outlay of a 'world of worlds' is referred exclusively to divine omnipotence, of which it is conceived as the fitting self-demonstration. But this means that the cosmic sphere in which man has his seat has attained its "proper perfection" (a concept that betrays Kant's continuing debt to the static cosmos-eidos of antiquity), a telos of the mechanistic self-production of matter beyond which there lies only decay. Indeed, the very existence of man, "who seems to be the masterpiece of creation," goes to show that the part of the whole he occupies represents a "world that has been brought to completion," poised between worlds that are still in the process of becoming and those that are already in decline.[10] Furthermore, man's relation to the entirety of the infinite self-production process of nature is an essentially contemplative one: the immortal mind beholds the eternal demonstration of worlds at God's side, so to speak.[11] A critical examination of these ideas would be able to show

---

9. *Ich habe auf eine geringe Vermutung eine gefährliche Reise gewagt und erblicke schon die Vorgebirge neuer Länder . . . Die Schöpfung ist niemals vollendet. Sie hat zwar einmal angefangen, aber sie wird niemals aufhören. Sie ist immer geschäftig, mehr Auftritte der Natur, neue Dinge und neue Welten hervorzubringen. Zweiter Teil, Siebentes Hauptstück, Von der Schöpfung im ganzen Umfange ihrer Unendlichkeit sowohl dem Raume als der Zeit nach (Werke,* ed. Cassirer, I, 309–25). |Immanuel Kant, *Kant's Cosmogony,* trans. W. Hastie (New York: Johnson Reprint Corporation, 1970), 17, 145–46.|

10. *gehörige Vollkommenheit . . . der das Meisterstück der Schöpfung zu sein scheinet . . . zur Vollkommenheit gebrachtes Weltgebäude.* |*Kant's Cosmogony,* trans. Hastie, 144, 150, 148; translation modified.|

11. *Die ganze Natur, welche eine allgemeine harmonische Beziehung zu dem Wohlgefallen der Gottheit hat, kann diejenige vernünftige Kreatur nicht anders als mit immerwährender Zufriedenheit erfüllen, die sich mit dieser Urquelle aller Vollkommenheit vereint befindet. Die Natur, von diesem Mittelpunkte aus gesehen, wird von allen Seiten lauter Sicherheit, lauter Wohlanständigkeit zeigen* (op. cit., 324). |All nature, which involves a universal harmonious relation to the self-satisfaction of the Deity, cannot but fill the rational creature with an everlasting satisfaction, when it finds itself united with this Primary Source

that here, Kant's reference to an incomplete universe is by no means metaphorical; it is the terminological articulation of a realistic cosmology. There can therefore be no question of ascribing a pragmatic significance to these expressions, since the idea of man's cosmic position cannot be tied to the idea of the universe's unfinished state. 'World' is not yet seen as a dimension of properly human tasks; a foundational relationship is first produced by the regulative function of this concept in relation to 'experience'.

We can get an almost tangible sense of how the cosmological idea of totality mutates into an idealist metaphor by turning to Friedrich Schlegel's "Transcendental Philosophy," which contains a valuable fragment on the thesis 'that the universe is still incomplete': "This principle, that this universe is still incomplete, is of the utmost importance for everything. If we think of the universe as complete, then all our actions are in vain. But if we know the universe to be incomplete, then we are probably destined to work toward its completion. Empiricism is thereby given infinite scope. Were the universe complete, there would only be knowledge of it, but no action."[12] Schlegel, certainly no systematic thinker of the first rank, had a sure feeling for the vital subterranean current of his age, and in this respect there are still discoveries to be made in his work. At a time when systematic claims to finality were practically *de rigueur,* he had the courage to advocate a 'provisional philosophy',[13] and this preference for preemptive and presumptive thought is what, among other things, makes his metaphorical language so indicative. He had the courage to convert his intuitions directly into assertions, a position he defended very consciously against the "formalities of professional philosophy" (*Förmlichkeiten der Kunstphilosophie*): "But the main point is always to know something or say some-

---

of all perfection. Nature, seen from this center, will show on all sides utter security, complete adaptation; *Kant's Cosmogony,* trans. Hastie, 155–56]. One sees here for how long *pre-Copernican* thinking remained in force after Copernicus, albeit in highly opaque transformations and transcendent projections. Kant only brought his thinking to its *Copernican consequences* when he was compelled by the antinomy of pure reason to idealize the concept of 'world' as a totality inaccessible to all experience, yet still given to experience as a task. One need only compare Kant's cosmological text from 1755 with a note to the chapter on "the transcendental ideal" in book II of the Dialectic of the "Critique of Pure Reason" (*Werke* III, 399–400): "The observations and calculations of astronomers have taught us much that is worthy of admiration, but most important, probably, is that they have exposed for us the abyss of ignorance, which without this information human reason could never have imagined to be so great" [Immanuel Kant, *Critique of Pure Reason,* trans. Paul Guyer and Allen Wood (Cambridge: Cambridge University Press, 1998), 555; translation modified]. A comparison of the metaphors alone—"promontories of new lands" here, "abyss of ignorance" there—tells us a great deal about the structure of the soil in which Kant's ideas are rooted.

12. *Dieser Satz, daß die Welt noch unvollendet ist, ist außerordentlich wichtig für alles. Denken wir uns die Welt als vollendet, so ist alles unser Thun nichts. Wissen wir aber, daß die Welt unvollendet ist, so ist unsere Bestimmung wohl, an der Vollendung derselben mitzuarbeiten. Der Empirie wird dadurch ein unendlicher Spielraum gegeben. Wäre die Welt vollendet, so gäbe es dann nur ein Wissen derselben aber kein Handeln.* "Transcendentalphilosophie, 1. Teil: Theorie der Welt," in *Neue Philosophische Schriften,* ed. J. Körner (Frankfurt, 1935), 156.

13. Athenaeum fragment 266. [Friedrich Schlegel, *Philosophical Fragments,* trans. Peter Firchow (Minneapolis: University of Minnesota Press, 1991), 55.]

thing. To want to prove or even explain it is in most cases wholly unnecessary."[14] This 'subterranean' dimension of his thought allows us to understand his ability to grasp the 'practical force' (as Kant would put it) of the idea of the incomplete universe. For him, this idea was no longer amenable, nor ought it to be amenable, to any kind of theoretical justification; instead, it projects the image of an unfinished workpiece—its challenging inadequacy, its mute appeal to constructive conjecture, to an intervention that would 'redeem' it by bringing it to completion—as an absolute metaphor for the nonobjectifiable, nonapprehensible totality of Being. The 'incomplete universe' legitimates the demiurgic will of mankind and thus belongs in the history of those elements of consciousness on which the technological age was founded. This is not to claim, overestimating the role played by a marginal and all-but-ignored thinker, that Schlegel created this legitimation; he merely isolated and detached it from its context in a particular mental structure. Schlegel resolutely held fast to the idea of the incomplete universe. In his "Philosophy of Life," he writes: "Man is free, but nature, or the sensuous world and material creation, is still quite unfinished, anything but complete."[15] The metaphor is similarly linked to the idea of freedom in the "Philosophical Lectures from the Years 1804 to 1806": "Only if the world is conceived as caught in the throes of becoming, as perfecting itself in continual evolution, is freedom possible."[16] It is remarkable that, for Schlegel, precisely the *organic* specification of the metaphor seems to allow latitude for human activity: "Predestination is unavoidable once the universe is conceived as a series of necessary laws. Things are quite different, according to our theory, where the world is an organism, a nature. We wish, after all, for our actions to be crowned with success, for them to bear fruit, for everything not to be already over and done with; but that is precluded in the mechanical system. Our view also brings out the importance of the moment, and indeed the present as such."[17] Here a flaw appears in the logic of Schlegel's argument: by regarding the given as provisional, in the sense of the challenge described above, man reduces it to mere 'material' for his intervention; organic metaphors, however, indicate precisely a resistance to the materialization of nature and the corresponding absolutization of 'labor'. In his eagerness to attack the deterministic metaphysics of the 'mechanism', Schlegel dis-

---

14. *Die Hauptsache . . . bleibt doch immer, daß man etwas weiß und daß man es sagt. Es beweisen oder gar erklären wollen, ist in den meisten Fällen herzlich überflüssig* (Athenaeum fragment 82). [Schlegel, *Philosophical Fragments*, trans. Firchow, 28; translation modified.]

15. *Frei ist der Mensch, ganz unfertig aber, durchaus unvollendet noch ist die Natur oder die Sinnenwelt und materielle Schöpfung. Sämtliche Werke*, 2nd ed. (Vienna, 1846), XII, 149.

16. *Nur wenn die Welt als werdend gedacht wird, als in steigender Entwickelung sich ihrer Vollendung nähernd, ist die Freiheit möglich.* Ed. C. J. H. Windischmann (Bonn, 1837), II, 201.

17. *Wird die Welt gedacht als eine Reihe nothwendiger Gesetze, so ist die Prädestination unvermeidlich. Ganz anders ist es nach unserer Theorie, wo die Welt ein Organismus, eine Natur ist. Wir wollen doch, daß unser Handeln einen Erfolg habe, daß etwas dabey herauskomme, daß nicht schon alles abgeschlossen sey; aber das fällt bey dem System des Mechanismus weg. Aus unserer Ansicht geht auch die Wichtigkeit des Augenblicks und überhaupt der Gegenwart hervor.* "Transcendentalphilosophie, II. Teil: Theorie des Menschen," ed. Körner, 187.

regards the fact that the organic, understood as the ontological state of the universe, denies man the freedom accorded him by the nonbinding character of mechanistically conceived objectivity.[18] With that, we have already arrived at the topic of our next section. In the lectures from 1804/6 cited above, Schlegel attempted to defuse the chronic indeterminacy inherent in the metaphor of the 'incomplete universe' by anchoring that metaphor in a metaphysical, teleological order: "Even if the end of human history, like its beginning, is supernatural and mystical, it nonetheless remains philosophically certain that the fortitude and active collaboration of mankind will be instrumental to the true completion of the universe."[19] Ten years before this domestication of the metaphor, Schlegel had jotted down an anthropological thesis that represents the exact correlate to the metaphor of the 'incomplete universe': "Man is almighty and all-knowing and all-loving; yet he is not altogether there in the individual, only in bits and pieces . . ."[20]

The last part of the Schlegel fragment I have just quoted raises the question of how 'almighty man' could be integrated, and his powers thereby rendered adequate to the task of finishing an 'incomplete universe'. The modern age came up with two solutions to this problem: the idea of method and the idea of the collective. It was Pascal who, in his "Traité du vide," first saw the meaning of the Cartesian idea of method in the possibility it offered of uniting exertions scattered over time and space into a *single* concerted human effort that, since it would not have to begin anew with the passing of each individual and each generation, might finally prove equal to the task of a being "who is formed only for infinity." Human reason realizes itself precisely by allowing the plurality of individuals to function as a single subject (*cet homme universel*): "Thence it is that . . . not only does each man advance from day to day in the sciences, but all mankind together makes continual progress

---

18. Mechanistically conceived reality structures are of a nonbinding character because the same act of destruction that wipes out the organic as such frees up the machinal for a new act of construction. This can be verified with recourse to social history: whereas organic 'images' of society are propagated by conservative theories or lead to such theories, mechanical social metaphors predispose to revolution. Historical experience has so accustomed us to this that we tend to take it for granted, even though it contains the 'practical force' of antithetical metaphors.—I find the metaphor of the 'incomplete universe' in its sociological dimension in so perceptive an observer of immanent social processes as Marcel Proust. In the sixth volume of "À la recherche du temps perdu," he remarks of the permanent self-constitution of society: "The creation of the world did not occur at the beginning of time, it occurs every day." [Marcel Proust, *The Sweet Cheat Gone*, trans. C. Scott Moncrieff (London: Chatto & Windus, 1968), 348.]

19. *Wenn auch das Ende wie der Anfang der Menschengeschichte übernatürlich und mystisch ist, so bleibt doch philosophisch gewiß, daß für die wahre Vollendung der Welt auf die Kraft und die tätige Mitwirkung des Menschen mitgerechnet ist.* Ed. Windischmann, II, 235.

20. *Der Mensch ist allmächtig und allwissend und allgütig; nur ist der Mensch in dem Einzelnen nicht ganz, sondern nur stückweise da . . .* "Fragmente aus dem Nachlaß," ed. A. Dempf, *Merkur* 10 (1956): 1176. That is likewise metaphorical: theological attributes are *transferred* onto man, who thereby himself becomes an object of faith. For it is impossible to *know* that one is almighty; for that, one would have to be omniscient, but in the potentiated form of an omniscience that would include itself in the totality of its knowledge. Yet that would give rise to an infinite iteration of acts of knowledge. Necessarily, even God can only *believe* that he is almighty; in this respect, Schlegel's almighty and all-knowing man is no different from God.

in proportion as the world grows older, since the same thing happens in the succession of men as in the different ages of single individuals. So that the whole succession of men, during the course of many ages, should be considered as a single man who subsists forever . . ."[21] To the always 'incomplete universe', which still lies hidden and undeveloped beneath the metaphor of the aging universe, corresponds the ever-unfinished *homme universel,* who here passes directly from the Platonic *universale* of *humanitas* to the regulative ideal of humanity as a collective labor force.[22] The achievement of *knowledge,* understood as being tied to a specific qualification of the functionaries it is expected to integrate, is homogenized through the encompassing rule of 'method'; yet if human achievement—provoked by a world that seems ever less incomprehensible, yet ever more incomplete—is understood essentially as *labor,* if the quantative problem of energy thus appears with at least equal justice alongside the theoretical preconditions for mastering the world, then the 'collective' now suggests itself as the aggregate state adequate to man's situation. I only hint at this connection here in order to place in its foundational nexus the pivotal role played by the idea of the 'incomplete universe' in the pathos of communism. Nikolai Berdiajev reports the comments of a young Russian communist who had spent several months in France and denied that freedom was possible there, since true freedom was to be found only in the Soviet Union: "Here, every young person feels a bit like an architect of the universe, a universe that has suddenly been freed up and can be shaped into forms that no eye has ever seen. That's what the young find more enchanting than anything else . . . Freedom is understood here not as the freedom of choice but as the active transformation of everything . . . Freedom

---

21. *qui n'est produit que pour l'infinité . . . De là vient que . . . non seulement chacun des hommes s'avance de jour en jour dans les sciences, mais que tous les hommes ensemble y font un progrès à mesure que l'univers vieillit, parce que la même chose arrive dans la succession des hommes que dans les âges différents d'un particulier. De sorte que toute la suite des hommes, pendant le cours de tant de siècles, doit être considérée comme un même homme qui subsiste toujours . . .* [Blaise Pascal, *Thoughts, Letters, and Minor Works,* trans. Charles W. Eliot (New York: Folcroft Library Editions, 1910), 449.]

22. In its paradigmatic character, the Platonic idea is directed principally at nature, although in biographical terms it was originally discovered as an ethical norm. The ethical is read off the model of rectitude manifested in nature's continually reproducing itself true to form. The intermediate term between this understanding of universal *humanitas* and the methodical integration of Pascal's *homme universel* is the humanist idea of 'education', understood as an ethical formative process that is no longer natural, or naturally guaranteed, or the 'continuation' of nature with pedagogic means, but rather an imprinting operation [*Prägeleistung*] that is codified in historical paradigmatics and must be reproduced in activity of a specific kind. We find the proximity and difference of this intermediate stage to Pascal's formula in a passage from Fontenelle's "Digression sur les anciens et les modernes" (1688), written some time after Pascal's "Traité" and to a superficial reading, at least, practically indistinguishable from it: *Un bon esprit cultivé est, pour ainsi dire, composé de tous les esprits des siècles précédents; ce n'est qu'un même esprit, qui s'est cultivé pendant tout ce temps-la.* [A cultivated mind is composed, so to speak, of all the minds of preceding centuries; one mind has lived from the beginning of the world to the present day; Bernard Le Bovier de Fontenelle, "A Digression on the Ancients and the Moderns," trans. Donald Schier, in *The Continental Model: Selected French Critical Essays of the Seventeenth Century,* ed. Scott Elledge and Donald Schier (Minneapolis: University of Minnesota Press, 1960), 366.] The stasis of the humanist canon has been overcome here, but the enlargement of the mind, conceived as an individual unity, is imagined as its inner cultivation, not as its objectivized cognitive or ergonomic achievement.

has to be understood as a creative energy, a means for reshaping the world."[23] The idea of the 'incomplete universe' undergoes a modification here as its presuppositions are detached from historical or metaphysical factors: the world is not so much *still* uncompleted as made incomplete *again,* released from a stasis that was quite unmerited in view of its imperfections, rematerialized through revolution. Freedom, according to the same demiurgic interpretation we have already encountered in Friedrich Schlegel, requires a plastic substrate; it is all the greater the more the world, as nature, can be regarded as mere *hylē,* a heap of raw material to be exploited at will, the most nonbinding preformation of future transformations. But this interpretation can only proceed 'back to front', as it were, from an awareness of the unlimited quantity of labor still awaiting deployment. Creating this consciousness is the chief function of the social collectivity.

---

23. Cited in R. E. Skonietzki, "Der neue Mensch: Ein Versuch über Sowjetpädagogik," *Hochland* 50 (1957): 97.

VI

ORGANIC AND MECHANICAL
BACKGROUND METAPHORICS

Metaphorics can also be in play where exclusively terminological propositions appear, but where these cannot be understood in their higher-order semantic unity without taking into account the guiding idea from which they are induced and 'read off'. Statements referring to data of observation presuppose that what is intended can, in each case, be brought to mind only within the parameters of a descriptive typology: the reports that will one day be transmitted to us by the first voyagers to the moon may well require us to engage in a more thorough study of American or Russian geography if we are to grasp the selective typicality of these reports, corresponding to the eyewitnesses' (anticipated) background.[1] Faced with an artificial structure of speculative statements, the interpretation will only 'dawn' on us once we have succeeded in entering into the author's imaginative horizon and reconstructing his 'translation'. What preserves genuine thinkers from the crabbed

---

1. [*Paradigms* was published nine years before the first moon landing. Blumenberg's fascination with the implications of space travel for human self-understanding, jocularly conveyed in his application to university authorities for seed funding to establish a new discipline called "astronoetics," is most fully in evidence in the posthumously published volume *Die Vollzähligkeit der Sterne* (Frankfurt: Suhrkamp, 1997).]

scholasticism of their imitators and successors is that they keep their 'systems' in vital orientation, whereas academic routine uproots concepts and suspends them in an idiosyncratic atomism. In undertaking an interpretive reconstruction, we will succeed in reviving such translations, which we propose to call 'background met-aphorics', only within the parameters of a certain typology, and this is most likely to occur where a prior decision between *opposed* kinds of metaphors—between *or-ganic* and *mechanical* guiding ideas, for example—has been made. It is not just lan-guage that thinks ahead of us and 'backs us up', as it were, in our view of the world; we are determined even more compellingly by the supply of images available for selection and the images we select, which 'channel' what can offer itself for experi-ence in the first place. Therein would lie the significance of a metaphorological *sys-tematics*, on the possibility of which, however, I will refrain from speculating here.

In his book "The Americans," Geoffrey Gorer claims that European metaphors are organic whereas American metaphors are mechanical.[2] Whether the observa-tion is accurate need not concern us here; what interests me instead is the method-ological import of the attempt to trace stylistic differences of a *way of life*[3] back to a layer of elementary ideas that always shows itself most clearly where the 'supply of images' has been tapped. Yet before we rush to identify, in this antithesis of organic and mechanical metaphors, at least one subdivision of a secure metaphoro-logical 'systematics', we should ask ourselves to what extent this dualism reflects our own, historically conditioned perspective. When, for example, we come across the term *machina* (or one of its cognates: *machine, macchina,* and so forth) in a his-torical text, it can be very difficult for us to avoid superimposing our modern un-derstanding of what a 'machine' is on the far less specific content signified by the older word. When, moreover, we first encounter the expression *machina mundi* in an author like Lucretius, our initial association seems to have been fully confirmed. But *machina* is a 'machine' only in part and among other things. It refers more broadly to a contrivance that is both complex and purposeful, without that purpose being immediately transparent to the untrained eye; likewise to an occurrence of this kind: a cunning maneuver or 'machination', a deceitful trick, a startling effect. Machines in the narrower sense (for transporting goods or laying siege) fall into this category by virtue of their ability to astonish the unknowing spectator; that is why the expression has accrued so much of its history in the theater, where the effect on the spectator is no longer incidental. So far as I am aware, there is no precedent in Greek for the composite term *machina mundi*. Indeed, it is difficult to see how 'cosmos' could be assimilated to this semantic field: as *machina,* the world is 'art-fully contrived' rather than 'cosmic', and the expression *machina mundi* pertains to a theology which either—as in Lucretius—is directed against the Stoic metaphysics

---

2. [Geoffrey Gorer, *The Americans: A Study in National Character* (London: The Cresset Press, 1948), 116.]

3. [English in original.]

of providence (*pronoia*) or in which God hides behind his work rather than manifesting himself in it. Above all, the expression must not be contaminated with those connotations that would first flow to it from modern Deism, where it designates the automatic 'functioning', guaranteed by its immanent perfection, of a world that has no need of divine intervention. The nondescript and unspecific expression *machina mundi* is first endowed with a momentous specificity by the *clockwork metaphor,* suggesting the idea of a spring mechanism that, having once been wound up, can be relied on to tick smoothly and continuously until the end of time. We get a sense of just how little our 'machine' has in common with the meaning of *machina* when we recall that the Middle Ages could isolate precisely these 'mechanical' components in *ingenium,* the basis for the corresponding early forms in the Romance languages (Spanish: *engenno;* French: *engin*).[4] Even in classical French, the meaning of 'universe' predominates in *machina,* whereas what we now call 'machine' goes by the name of *engin.* I therefore think it not out of the question that precisely the added cosmological implication of *machina,* revitalized in an age of newfangled technical constructions, predisposed it to designate the technical phenomenon of the 'machine'. Only now can 'machine' become the programmatic byword for a particular interpretation of the world, a metaphor that contests the 'organic' in its spiritually determined self-sufficiency and self-evidence. The history of the concept, initially quite untouched by metaphysical considerations, becomes virulent in the materialism of the French Enlightenment: *la machine de l'univers, la machine du corps humain*—these are now no longer blandly descriptive denominations (akin to our 'construction'); they are already *interpretations.* The expression enters the German language in the seventeenth century as a purely technical term for the tools used in siege warfare and fortress construction.[5]

The dualism of the organic and the mechanical is thus not something with which we can operate unreflectively in the history of thought. In Plato, generative and constructive metaphors are interconnected and even built into each other.[6] The construction of the universe presented to the reader of the "Timaeus" seems to have been derived from the so-called armillary sphere, a mechanical model of the revolutions of the firmament; yet what the demiurge ultimately brings into being is a 'life-form', an organic unity. This can be explained by the fact that the problem of constructing the celestial orbits to account for all constellational phenomena was directly juxtaposed with the problem of the kinetic energy driving the heavenly bodies on their rounds. Whereas the former was a question of mechanical engineering, the latter necessarily entailed a spiritual factor, since the soul was conceived as the capacity for primary autokinesis; motion was thus an essentially

---

4. Cf. A. Rehmann, "Die Geschichte der technischen Begriffe *fabrica* und *machina* in den romanischen Sprachen" (Diss., Münster, 1935), 54.

5. Ibid., 109.

6. E.g., *Symp.* 209A, *Soph.* 266B, *Tim.* 28C.

organic phenomenon. The mechanical orientation of its attempts to make sense of the world failed to deter classical antiquity from its commitment to archetypal representations of an organic kind; as an 'imitation' of the natural state of affairs, the artificial model was regarded from the outset as an inferior makeshift. To compare the cosmic order with a clock was not to claim that the cosmos was clocklike, only that the main predicates of a clock, at least, pertained to it as well: "If then the products of nature are better than those of art, and if art produces nothing without reason, nature too cannot be deemed to be without reason."[7] As innerworldly products, works of artistic and technical craftsmanship cannot attain to the dignity of the cosmic order as a whole: ". . . How then can it be consistent to suppose that the world, which includes both the works of art in question, the craftsmen who made them, and everything else besides, can be devoid of purpose and of reason?"[8] Archimedes' famous orrery, the *Sphaera,* is not meant to suggest the mechanical nature of the celestial motions, but to prompt the conclusion: if even this imitation of the cosmos is *perfecta ratione,* then how much more so—and more reliably so—must be the original on which it is modeled?[9] It is interesting that precisely the example of the Archimedean sphere, this marvel of ancient technology, permits us to see how Christian theological motives realigned the model's interpretive function toward the cosmological mechanism. Lactantius also cites Archimedes' *figura mundi,* but now with the intention of refuting the idea of a stellar *motus voluntarius:* if even Archimedes was able to construct such a well-functioning model without having to resort to animated bodies, how much more so could God dispense with voluntary motion (and hence celestial intelligences) altogether? Here, a motif appears that would first come to full flower in Deism: the organic character of the cosmos is denied in order that the cracks through which transcendence can leak into the universe—including the universe's capacity for autokinesis, in the sense of the Platonic idea of the soul—may be reduced to a bare minimum. In hindsight, we can easily see that it took the discovery of the principle of inertia to satisfy this demand completely and to deprive organic metaphors, given a new lease of life at the beginning of the modern age by the resurgent Stoic tradition, of their legitimacy. But let us not get too far ahead of ourselves. The model of the Archimedean sphere (which he probably only knew secondhand from Cicero, unless it was still standing in the temple of Virtue in Rome, where Marcellus had put it on display as a trophy[10]) first opened Lactantius's eyes to the perfection proper to mechanical creation,

---

7. *Si igitur meliora sunt ea quae natura, quam illa quae arte perfecta sunt, nec ars efficit quicquam sine ratione, ne natura quidem rationis expers est habenda.* Cicero, *De natura deorum* II 34, 87 [Cicero, *De natura deorum,* trans. H. Rackham (Cambridge, MA: Harvard University Press, 2005), 217]. Archimedes' sphere was, as Cicero suggests (II 38, 97), moved by machinery and set in motion like a clock, probably through a hydraulic mechanism.

8. . . . *mundum autem, qui et has ipsas artes et earum artifices et cuncta complectatur, consilii et rationis esse expertem putare?* [Cicero, *De natura deorum,* trans. Rackham, 217.]

9. Cicero, *De natura deorum* II 34, 88.

10. Cicero, *De re publ.* I, 14. It had previously been housed in Syracuse (Ovid, *Fasti* VI, 279).

which depends on its author in an altogether different sense than the engendered organism, and which therefore, as the reified execution of his will, testifies far more directly to its maker: "Therefore the motion of the stars is not voluntary, but of necessity, because they obey the laws appointed for them."[11] We see that here, too, the notion of physical 'laws' has its basis in a theological 'interest'. Lactantius admonishes those who still refuse to believe that God had manifested his absolute sovereignty over the world in the manner befitting his authorship: "Was it then impossible for God to plan and create the originals, when the skill of man was able to represent them by imitation?"[12] Either the mechanism is the wholly material property of its artificer, *or* (and this option is not yet up for discussion) it belongs to whoever has gained insight into its laws of operation and knows how to turn such insight to good use. Here, in Lactantius, the relationship is still quite straightforward: "In the stars there is therefore design, adapted to the accomplishment of their courses; but it is the design of God, who both made and governs all things, not of the stars themselves, which are thus moved."[13] Lactantius even explicitly plays his own, mechanical model of the world off against the organic alternative proposed by the Stoics: "Therefore the world is neither god, nor living, if it has been made: for a living creature is not made, but born; and if it has been built, it has been built as a house or ship is built. Therefore there is a builder of the world, even God; and the world which has been made is distinct from Him who made it."[14] The mechanism metaphor guarantees God a 'clear' transcendence, as it were. Made, not begotten, the world cannot be of one being with the Father. It is purely and simply an 'object of practical use': "For as a house, made for the purpose of being inhabited, has no sensibility by itself, and is subject to the master who built or inhabits it; so the world, having no sensibility of itself, is subject to God its Maker, who made it for His own use."[15]

---

11. *non est igitur astrorum motus voluntarius, sed necessarius: quia praestitutis legibus officiisque deserviunt. Div. inst.* II 5, 13. [*Ante-Nicene Fathers,* ed. Alexander Roberts and James Donaldson, trans. William Fletcher (Peabody, MA: Hendrikson Publishers, 2004), VII, 48.]

12. *Deus ergo illa vera non potuit machinari et efficere, quae potuit sollertia hominis imitatione simulare?* Ibid., 5, 18 [*Ante-Nicene Fathers,* trans. Fletcher, VII, 48]. Compare the roughly contemporary *genetic* metaphorics of origin in Plotinus, who uses the word 'father' in a purely metaphorical sense devoid of all emotional or religious shades of meaning (*Enn.* VI 9, 9). This type of metaphor establishes a radically different relationship to the universe than the mechanical: it makes all the difference whether the world 'descends' from the divine father or has been 'thought out' by the ingenuity of an artificer (*artificis ingenio*), possibly selected as one design among infinitely many.

13. *Inest ergo sideribus ratio ad peragendos meatus suos apta: sed dei est illa ratio, qui et fecit et regit omnia, non ipsorum siderum, quae moventur* (II 5, 19). [*Ante-Nicene Fathers,* trans. Fletcher, VII, 48; translation modified.]

14. *(mundus) nec animans, si constructus est, animans enim non construitur, sed nascitur: et si est aedificatus, sic utique tanquam domus, tanquam navis est. Ergo aliqius artifex mundi deus: et seorsum erit mundus, qui factus est, seorsum ille, qui fecit* (II 5, 37). [*Ante-Nicene Fathers,* trans. Fletcher, VII, 49.]

15. *Sicut enim domus in usum habitandi facta per se nihil sentit, dominoque subiecta est, qui eam fecit aut incolit; ita mundus per se nihil sentiens factori deo subiacet, qui eum in usum sui fecit* (5, 42). [*Ante-Nicene Fathers,* trans. Fletcher, VII, 49.]

We reencounter the sphere, this time ascribed to Ptolemy, in Nicolaus of Cusa, but here it is no longer cited as an *imitative* representation of the firmament, but as evidence for the *inventive* power of the human mind.[16] The concept of hypothesis, which had become entrenched in astronomy along with the Ptolemaic system, precluded any knowledge that would be adequate to its object, any mimetic representation of the real structure of the stellar paths. The sole criterion for astronomical hypotheses was their phoronomic verifiability. In setting up a *model,* the human mind thus had to rely on its original constructive capacity; that is why this achievement assumes exemplary significance for Cusanus's understanding of the human mind, which he believes to be just as creative, in the realm of rational and artistic entities, as God in the realm of real and natural entities.[17] With that, the mechanical construction succeeds in holding its own against the natural phenomenon, which we are powerless to fathom unless the product of the human mind can somehow be installed *in place* of the product of the divine mind. And this very possibility is derived from the functioning of the astronomical model: the model is *projected* in place of what seemed essentially impervious to the theoretical demand for objectivity. The structure of this process is already intimately familiar to us: it is the structure of 'absolute metaphor'. The modern cosmological mechanism is the elaboration of an absolute metaphor that presupposed a new conception of what the human mind was capable of achieving. The traditional Aristotelian view of technology as mimesis lent itself to an organic metaphorics of the mechanical, as the following passage from Leon Battista Alberti's treatise "On the Art of Building" (1452) attests: ". . . Here we need only consider the machine as a form of extremely strong animal with hands, an animal that can move weights in almost the same way as we do ourselves. These machines must therefore have the same extensions of member and muscle that we use when pressing, pushing, pulling, and carrying."[18] The *direction* of the metaphor here follows a particular metaphysical theory about art's descent from nature, a premise to which the *pragmatic* meaning of the organic metaphor also remains bound. 'Pragmatic', in this context, means that theoretical attention is

---

16. *De ludo globi* II: *Creat anima sua inventione nova instrumenta, ut discernat et noscat: ut Ptolemaeus astrolabium et Orpheus lyram et ita de multis. Neque ex aliquo extrinseco inventores crearunt illa, sed ex propria mente. Explicarunt enim in sensibili materia conceptum.* [The soul by its own inventiveness creates new instruments in order to discern and to know. For example, Ptolemy invented the astrolabe, and Orpheus invented the lyre, and so on. (These) inventors created these instruments not from something extrinsic but from their own minds. For they unfolded their conceptions in a perceptible material; Nicholas of Cusa, *Metaphysical Speculations,* trans. Jasper Hopkins (Minneapolis: Arthur J. Banning Press, 2000, 2: 303.]

17. *De beryllo* VI: *Nam sicut deus est creator entium realium et naturalium formarum: ita homo rationalium entium et formarum artificialium.* [For just as God is the Creator of real beings and of natural forms, so man is the creator of conceptual beings and of artificial forms; Nicholas of Cusa, *Metaphysical Speculations,* trans. Hopkins, 47.]

18. *De re aedificatoria,* cited in F. Klemm, *Technik: Eine Geschichte ihrer Probleme* (Freiburg/Munich, 1954), 119. [Leon Battista Alberti, *On the Art of Building,* trans. Joseph Rykwert, Neil Leach, and Robert Tavernor (Cambridge, MA: MIT Press, 1994), 175.]

drawn in the counterdirection of metaphorization. There is perhaps no more striking example of such optical guidance by metaphorics than the history of the idea of
human flight, from the sketches of Leonardo to Lilienthal's "Vogelflug als Grund-
lage der Fliegekunst" [Bird Flight as the Basis of Aviation]; only with the Wright
brothers does the boyishly wistful sight of the birds winging their way across the
horizon become a mere topos obscuring the bare mechanics of the solution to the
problem.[19] A comparable case with respect to its pragmatic durability might be
the *ut pictura poesis* metaphor that held sway in eighteenth-century aesthetics, with
its voguish talk of 'poetic paintings'. When the dominance of that metaphor was
finally broken by Lessing's "Laokoon" (1766), a whole battery of criteria was invalidated that had initially been suggested and sanctioned by the metaphorical model.
Baumgarten saw this supposedly systematic theory for the metaphor that it was[20]—
but this only as an excursus on the phenomenon of metaphorical optics!

The reference to the exemplariness of the astronomical model for Cusanus
could shed light on the metaphysical assumptions upon which the nascent rule of
mechanical metaphorics depended. It would be instructive to combine this with an
investigation into the history of the idea of the 'hypothesis', which could show, for
example, how the hypothetical and the metaphorical are structurally interlinked in
the Cartesian theory of organisms as automata. For Descartes, the theoretical situation in which the researcher finds himself in relation to the organism is in principle identical to his situation in relation to the starry sky: confined to an outsider's
perspective (as if Vesalius had never lived!), he sees only effects and symptoms but
nothing of the 'inner' causal structure. This situation of theoretical occlusion and
obscurity is what provokes the 'transference'—provided, of course, that the pious
or skeptical attitude of resignation before the claims of theory has first been overcome. Man puts what he 'can do' (or 'could do') *in place of* the unknown, supposedly unknowable product of the divine *potentia absoluta*. For Descartes, however,
the highest quintessence of what man 'can do' is the machine. As a purposeful
structure put together entirely from insight, the machine now becomes a coun-
terconcept to 'nature', which the modern age strictly forbids itself from interpreting teleologically. Toward the end of the fourth part of the "Principia," Descartes
reflects on the structure of knowledge realized in the preceding sections: "I have
described the earth and indeed the whole visible universe as if it were a machine."[21]
The phenomenon is grasped as a product whose direct explanation—direct because guided by the product as its purpose—is the machine: "So it is no less natural

---

19. See my study "'Nachahmung der Natur': Zur Vorgeschichte der Idee des schöpferischen Menschen," *Studium Generale* X (1957): 269. [Reprinted in Hans Blumenberg, *Ästhetische und metaphorologische Schriften*, ed. Anselm Haverkamp (Frankfurt am Main: Suhrkamp, 2001), 9–46.]

20. See E. Cassirer, *Die Philosophie der Aufklärung* (Tübingen, 1932), 470.

21. *hactenus hanc terram, totumque adeo hunc mundum aspectabilem, instar machinae descripsi* (IV,
188). [René Descartes, *The Philosophical Writings of Descartes*, trans. John Cottingham, (Cambridge:
Cambridge University Press, 1985), 1: 279.]

for a clock constructed with this or that set of wheels to tell the time than it is for a tree which grew from this or that seed to produce the appropriate fruit."[22] Here, the metaphorical relationship is concealed through a very skillful sleight of hand: whereas the machine is represented by the 'phenomenon' (the purpose of the clock is unproductively exhausted in its self-display, in its 'telling the time'), nature is represented by the 'product' (which, to be sure, can benefit man only from the disallowed teleological perspective that goes beyond the purpose of preserving the species). The 'transference' can thus be forgotten all the more readily, and nature and art 'reveal' their homogenous ontological structure: "In this matter I was greatly helped by considering artefacts. For I do not recognize any difference between artefacts and natural bodies except that the operations of artefacts are for the most part performed by mechanisms which are large enough to be easily perceivable by the senses—as indeed must be the case if they are to be capable of being manufactured by human beings."[23] The difference between the organic and the mechanical is purely quantitative, and therefore only accidentally optical. Having concealed the metaphorical character of the universal mechanism in this way, Descartes finds the problem of 'transference' reappearing elsewhere, this time under the concept of *hypothesis* in the proper sense; for the fact that nature is *generally* interpreted as a totality of mechanical aggregates does not yet explain which *specific* construction the mechanisms have been given. If we take this to be the authentic realm of 'hypotheses', then it follows that there is a clear founding relationship between the universal 'transference' and the hypotheses it necessitates only as types, and whose verifiable 'extent', limited to the phenomenal realm, will never completely reach and cover the universal metaphorical basis (if I may put it this way). In the realm that hypotheses are supposed to illuminate, one and the same phenomenon may have been brought about through various constructions: "So the supreme craftsman of the real world could undoubtedly have produced all that we see in several different ways."[24] In deciding among these possibilities, the researcher is guided solely by considerations of economy; yet this is not perceived as a defect—and here the *pragmatic* function of the founding metaphor becomes evident—because the *interest* that guides us when we examine a machine is *not purely theoretical*. Having emerged from an originally theoretical demand, the metaphor now retroactively modifies this initial stance: a researcher studies a machine in order to appropriate its effect; to that end, however, any constructive solution producing the same effect

---

22. *nec minus naturale est horologio, ex his vel illis rotis composito, ut horas indicet, quam arbori ex hoc vel illo semine ortae, ut tales fructus producat* (IV, 203). [Descartes, *Philosophical Writings*, trans. Cottingham, 1: 288.]

23. *atque ad hoc arte facta non parum me adiuverunt: nullum enim aliud inter ipsa et corpora naturalia discrimen agnosco, nisi quod arte factorum operationes, ut plurimum peraguntur instrumentis adeo magnis, ut sensu facile percipi possint: hoc enim requiritur, ut ab hominibus fabricari queant* (IV, 203). [Descartes, *Philosophical Writings*, trans. Cottingham, 1: 288.]

24. *non dubium est, quin summus rerum opifex omnia illa quae videmus, pluribus diversis modis potuerit efficere* (IV, 204). [Descartes, *Philosophical Writings*, trans. Cottingham, 1: 289.]

will do; indeed, in the event that a given hypothetical solution proves to be more economical than its real counterpart (which must remain undecidable), it would be the 'more correct' one in the sense of the overriding cognitive interest. A purely theoretical attitude that demands to know how things are made 'in reality' (*revera factae*) is characterized by the machine metaphor as presumptuous. The stance that is here metaphorically induced rests content with moral certainty (*certitudo moralis*); in other words, it feels no compulsion to advance beyond the point where solutions have "sufficient certainty for application to ordinary life, even though they may be uncertain in relation to the absolute power of God."[25] Tellingly, absolute truth is here linked not to the divine intellect (*intellectus divinus*), but to divine power (*potentia divina*), thereby betraying the essential relation of truth to *potentia* presupposed by the entire chain of reflections.

Immediately following our last quotation, Descartes cites the example of someone who wanted to decipher a letter written in code: whoever obtains a legible meaning with the help of a particular key can only ever presume to know (*sola coniectura cognoscat*) that this was the same code used by the author, but the more sense the plaintext seems to make, the greater the likelihood that it is identical to the original message: "it would hardly have been possible for so many items to fit into a coherent pattern if the original principles had been false."[26] What interests me here is not the reference to the functional context of hypothesis and system, but the use of a quite different metaphorical background: script, letter, book. The 'encrypted' text, the 'cipher',[27] distorts an entirely heterogeneous metaphorical tradition, the metaphorics of the *book of nature,* to accommodate it to the nominalistic

---

25. *hoc est quantum sufficit ad usum vitae, quamvis si ad absolutam dei potentiam referantur, sint incerta* (IV, 205). [Descartes, *Philosophical Writings*, trans. Cottingham, 1: 289–90.]

26. *vix potuisse contingere, ut tam multa simul cohaererent, si false essent.* [Descartes, *Philosophical Writings*, trans. Cottingham, 1: 290.]

27. See also in Descartes the *Regulae* X: . . . *ut si legere scripturam ignotis characteribus velatam, nullus quidem ordo hic apparet, sed tamen aliquem fingimus, tum ad examinanda omnia praejudicia, quae circa singulas notas, aut verba, aut sententias haberi possunt, tum etiam ad illa ita disponenda, ut per enumerationem congoscamus quidquid ex illis potest deduci* [. . . Say we want to read something written in an unfamiliar cipher which lacks any apparent order: what we shall do is to invent an order, so as to test every conjecture we can make about individual letters, words, or sentences, and to arrange the characters in such a way that by enumeration we may discover what can be deduced from them; Descartes, *Philosophical Writings*, trans. Dugald Murdoch, 1: 35–36. The analogy serves here as an exhortation to methodic consequentiality: a code only has value if it is rigorously adhered to: "The method usually consists simply in constantly following an order, whether it is actually present in the matter in question or is ingeniously read into it" [1: 35]. The revision given the basic metaphor by Galileo, in a letter to Fortunio Liceti in Bologna, January 1641, deviates characteristically from the 'secret code' metaphor (ed. Albèri, VII, 352): "If philosophy is that which is contained in Aristotle's books, you would be the best philosopher in the world, such is your familiarity with all possible passages of the same. But I really think that the book of philosophy is that which is perpetually open to our eyes. But being written in characters different from those of our alphabet, it cannot be read by everyone" [trans. Carla Rita Palmerino in her essay "The Mathematical Characters of Galilei's Book of Nature," in *The Book of Nature in Early Modern and Modern History*, ed. Klaas van Berkel and Arjo Vanderjagt (Groningen: Peeters, 2006), 30]. Legibility is guaranteed for all those who are fluent in the language in which the book is written: the language of mathematics is nature's 'mother tongue', as it were, and must be learned by man.

conception. This metaphor will not be subjected to renewed scrutiny here;[28] I introduce it only as a contrast to help bring out the specificity of mechanical metaphorics, with which it can most readily be compared in the form of the metaphor of the clockwork universe. The fact that a book, even one written in secret code and composed with only potential readability in mind, has a communicable content is inseparable from the basic idea that the author has something he wants to communicate, if only to the initiated. In order to do so, he needs readers who are interested in what he has to say and keen to read about it. As a device for measuring and telling the time, a clock likewise has an informative function; but the metaphor refers to this function only incidentally. Its main interest lies in the automaticity and regularity of the mechanism: the clockwork universe is a timepiece without a dial and a face.[29] The meaning of this timepiece consists solely in the fact that it *functions,* and this by virtue of the immanent constitution that has been given it once and for all. As the consequences of Deism were to show, the clockwork metaphor consolidates the theologumenon of creation at the cost of other theologumena such as the *concursus divinus generalis.* According to this doctrine, which enjoyed increasing popularity toward the end of the Middle Ages, the course of nature is continuously and substantially linked to a divine sovereign act; in the clockwork metaphor, by contrast, the fiat by which nature was established amounts to a definitive self-limitation of God's omnipotence. This idea of the divine kinetic function

---

28. See E. R. Curtius, *Europäische Literatur und lateinisches Mittelalter* (Bern, 1948), 321 ff. [*European Literature and the Latin Middle Ages,* trans. Willard Trask (Princeton: Princeton University Press, 1953), 323–29], as well as the literature cited there. An unpublished work on "The Book of Nature" is listed in the bibliography of E. Rothacker (*Mensch und Geschichte* [Bonn, 1950], 238). [Blumenberg would devote a major work to this topos, *Die Lesbarkeit der Welt* (Frankfurt: Suhrkamp, 1983).]

29. It is therefore difficult to believe that the mechanistic clockwork metaphorics is derived from the cosmic clock in the "Timaeus" (39 BC), for what matters most in Plato is the 'readability' of the chronometric units and the foundational production of time through the stellar motions. Precisely because the cosmic clock is so difficult to read in most of its units (the largest of which is the great cosmic year, 39D), the demiurge is mindful of providing a clear measure (μέτρον ἐναργές) that will make the temporal character of the celestial phenomena especially evident: the alternation of night and day as the smallest 'natural' chronometric division. Whether the "human beings" mentioned in 39C are the addressees of this arrangement, outlined in 39B, depends on whether one emends the text, with Archer-Hind, to read καθ᾽ ἃ or sticks, with Taylor, to καὶ τὰ, which links the sun's function to the relative velocities of the other stars and the brightness of their orbits. [See Plato, *Timaeus,* trans. R. G. Bury (Cambridge, MA: Harvard University Press, 2005), 80–81.] If καὶ τὰ is a corruption, it is one that attests to a distinctive Plato interpretation on the part of the scribe: man cannot be the teleological reference point of the cosmic installation; that is a Stoic conception, or one thought along the lines of the Stoic-patristic interpretation of Deuteronomy 4, 19. Cornford, who opts in his commentary for Archer-Hind's reading (see p. 115 n. 4), thereby conflicts with the assumption guiding his interpretation of the fact that, in the design of the cosmos, so little consideration was shown to mankind that the clock's display side, so to speak, is not even accessible to him, while the last and most perfect unit of time, the 'Great Year', remains completely hidden from view. Perhaps a connection can be made from here to the clockwork metaphor in nominalism: just as Plato's cosmic clock is turned toward the divine stars and reserved for them alone, so too the 'meaning' of the cosmic clockwork is only apparent to its creator. (These remarks do not intend to add anything to the debate about the thorny passage in the "Timaeus," which cannot be thematized as such here; in my opinion, that would have to occur in the context of a discussion of Plato's views on teleology.)

depositing itself, so to speak, in the mechanics of the universe—at once the terminal form of the Aristotelian *motor immobilis* and the embryonic form of the principle of inertia—is already contained in the early formulation that Nicolaus of Oresme gives the clockwork metaphor in his "Traicté du ciel et du monde" [Treatise of the Sky and the World] (1377). Nicolaus still quite naïvely builds the already redundant spherical intelligences into his cosmology: ". . . When God created the heavens, He put into them motive qualities and powers just as He put weight and resistance against these motive powers in earthly things . . . The powers against the resistances are moderated in such a way, so tempered, and so harmonized that the movements are made without violence; thus, violence excepted, the situation is much like that of a man making a clock and letting it run and continue its own motion by itself. In this manner did God allow the heavens to be moved continually according to the proportions of the motive powers to the resistances . . ."[30]

Whereas the book metaphor implies that man, as the book's 'intended reader', does not himself appear as an element of the cosmic volume laid out before him, the clock metaphor assimilates man to the machine as one of its functioning components. In Voltaire's "Traité de métaphysique" (1734), the human passions are legitimized as so many cogs in a world machine that still seems to require supervision by God, newly promoted from 'geometer' to the rank of 'mechanic': "These passions, which do the truth so much harm when abused, are in effect the principal cause of the order we see today on earth . . . It is with this mechanism that God, whom Plato calls the eternal geometer, and whom I here call the eternal mechanic, has driven and embellished nature: the passions are the wheels which keep all these machines in motion."[31] In justifying the previously misrecognized passions, even a teleological viewpoint is deemed acceptable; characteristically, however, it requires that human labor be deployed as a 'transformer' of raw instinctive energy: "And it is very probable that God only gave us these needs, these passions in order that they might be turned to our advantage through our industry."[32] By virtue of his reason, man, the microcosmic analog of the clockwork universe, is now seen as a clock

---

30. . . . *quand Dieu créa (sc. les corps célestes), il mit en eux qualités et vertus motives aussi comme il mit pesanteur és choses terrestres et mit en eus résistances contre les vertus motives . . . Et sont ces vertus contre ces résistances tellement modérées, attrempées et accordées que les mouvements sont faits sans violence. Et excepté la violence c'est aucunement semblable quand un homme a fait une horloge et la laisse aller et être mûe par soi; ainsi laissa Dieu les cieux être mûs continuellement selon les proportions que les vertus motives ont aux résistances . . .* (II, 2). [Nicole Oresme, *Le livre du ciel et du monde,* trans. Albert D. Menut (Madison: University of Wisconsin Press, 1968), 289.] P. Duhem, *Le système du monde* IV (Paris, 1916), 163–64, credited the author of the "Traicté" with an all too 'far-sighted' interpretation and, in consequence, bestowed upon him a not entirely justified renown.

31. *Ces passions dont l'abus fait à la vérité tant de mal, sont en effet la principal cause de l'ordre que nous voyons aujourd'hui sur la terre . . . C'est avec ce ressort que Dieu, appelé par Platon l'éternel géomètre, et que j'appelle ici l'éternel machiniste, a animé et embelli la nature: les passions sont les roues qui font aller toutes ces machines* (ch. 8).

32. *et il est très vraisemblable que Dieu nous a donné ces besoins, ces passions qu'afin que notre industrie les tournât à notre avantage.*

with a dial and a face; in his "Introduction à la connaissance de l'esprit humain" [Introduction to the Knowledge of the Human Mind] (1746), Vauvenargues draws on this metaphorological model when interpreting the relationship between affective depth and rational surface, showing that reason is no longer the 'substance' of man but only the agency that converts his essential motor forces into signs, systems, and meanings. Beneath a layer of significations, the clock face conceals the true mechanism that keeps human existence ticking, and this layer imposes upon the inwardly driven dial a code that regulates its 'translation' of the genuine driving forces. The metaphor's enduring modular function is here particularly tangible: the entire French moralist tradition, in this respect one of the chief forerunners of the psychology to come, is dominated by the 'schema' of this model, which transposes inner impulses into social 'significations' without ever bridging the gap between inside and outside, existence and 'world' (*le monde,* in Pascal's sense). 'Reason' is unmasked as the systematic justification to the 'world' of what we really want, or rather—already anticipating the modern notion of the 'subconscious'—of what 'it wants with us' as it rises up from the hidden mechanism (hidden to ourselves as well) of that instinctive sphere. Everything that Marx was to draw on for his schema of 'substructure' and 'superstructure' is already contained in this metaphor, even if Marx was unable to view the double-storeyed mechanism with quite the same ironic detachment as the moralists, for whom "being able to observe man's true nature with a cheerful and contemplative eye and without the slightest prejudice" afforded satisfaction enough. The philosopher of the "Encyclopédie," applying the mechanical metaphor to his own person, had a little more to do: "The philosopher is a human machine just like every other human being; but he is a machine that, owing to the way it is constructed, reflects on its own motion . . . He is a periodically self-winding clock, as it were."[33]

It is remarkable that the clockwork universe is introduced by H. S. Reimarus at precisely the point where he oversteps the bounds of the metaphor, in his critique of the biblical story of God bringing the sun to a halt: "For by and by, even the theologians begin to feel ashamed of such monstrosities, which turn all of nature on its head. No doubt they understand that there is a little more at stake in the revolutions of the great cosmic bodies than if someone were to let the pendulum of his clock stop swinging for a day, and that it would mean the death of everything that lives and breathes should this *perpetuum mobile* come to rest for even a split second."[34] Reimarus sees something in the clock that is not quite in keeping with the new understanding of nature: we may certainly rest assured that it will remain

---

33. Cited in Paul Hazard, *Die Herrschaft der Vernunft* (German edition of *La pensée européenne au XVIIIème siècle de Montesquieu à Lessing*) (Hamburg, 1949), 379–80.

34. *Denn nachgerade fangen auch die Herren Theologi selbst an, sich solcher Ungeheuer, welche die ganze Natur umkehren, zu schämen. Sie begreifen wohl, daß es mit der gesammten Bewegung der großen Weltkörper ein wenig mehr zu bedeuten habe, als wenn einer den Perpendikel seiner Uhr einen Tag wollte ruhen lassen, und daß es Allem, was Odem hat, das Leben kosten würde, wofern dieses* perpetuum mobile *nur eine*

in good working order if it is not interfered with, but only on the condition *that* it is not interfered with. A clock can be a toy as well, and this idea had been transposed on to the universe by a theology that left the universe at the mercy of an arbitrary and despotic clock-maker. Reimarus does not invoke Copernicus in presenting the solar standstill as a fable; he has a more fundamental critique in mind. Yet this more fundamental concern has been emotionally actualized since Copernicus: the world has outgrown the dimensions of a divine 'plaything'; capricious interference with its integrity and regularity redounds on the creator and reveals him to be a 'monster'. We touch here on the emotional core of Deism, the new self-consciousness of a worldliness that is no longer prepared to tolerate being abandoned to a transcendent power, and that seeks, even in its metaphors, to ward off the cosmocrat's willful encroachments.

Were our chief concern to make our 'supporting evidence' as ample and imposingly representative as possible, a detailed discussion of Julien Offroy de Lamettrie and his "L'homme machine" (1748) would have to follow at this point. We will instead make a (hopefully elegant) bypass around this zone of greatest congestion by showing the master of mechanical metaphysics from the distance of ironic metaphorical reflection. In the forty-ninth of his "Kritische Nachrichten aus dem Reiche der Gelehrsamkeit" |Critical Dispatches from the Realm of Scholarship|, dated 19 November 1751, Lessing regales his readers with news of Monsieur Lamettrie, whom Frederick the Great had recently appointed court reader: "No doubt they expect him to have once again committed some trifling and amusing act of folly. And they would not be mistaken; no indeed: if only it had not had such all too grave consequences for his person. He is dead . . . His *Animula vagula, blandula,* / *Hospes comesque corporis* has up and left its dwelling place, and it grew despondent for no other reason than because the clockwork of its life got stuck before it had run down. One sees that we are speaking here half in his concepts, half in our own . . ."[35] The premature death of the man posthumously commended by Lessing for his "considerable insight into that science by which he would assuredly have kept himself alive, had it been useful for physicians to remain immortal," represents an ironic affront to the precision that had been the hallmark of Lamettrie's mechanical metaphors.[36]

Augenblick ruhete. Apologie I 4, 1, according to the manuscript cited by D. F. Strauss, *Hermann Reimarus und seine Schutzschrift für die vernünftigen Verehrer Gottes* (Ges. Schr. V), 305.

35. *Ohne Zweifel vermuten sie eine kleine witzige Torheit, die er schon wieder begangen hat. Es ist so was; ja: wenn sie nur nicht auf seiner Seite etwas allzuernsthaft ausgefallen wäre. Er ist gestorben . . . Seine* Animula vagula, blandula, / Hospes comesque corporis *hat ihre Wohnung ganz anständig verlassen, und sie hat sich über nichts betrübt, als daß das Uhrwerk ihres Lebens ins Stecken geraten, ehe es noch abgelaufen war. Man sieht wohl, daß wir hier halb nach seinem, halb nach unserm Lehrbegriffe reden . . . Gesammelte Werke,* ed. Rilla, III, 37.

36. *eine ansehnliche Einsicht in diejenige Wissenschaft, durch die er sich gewiß bei dem Leben würde erhalten haben, wenn es nützlich wäre, daß die Ärzte unsterblich blieben.* Another ironic reflection of "L'homme machine," which can only be recommended here rather than discussed in detail, is to be

To conclude this section, we will round out our confrontation of mechanical and scriptural metaphors with a latter-day paradigm in which they are developed further and transformed in a highly characteristic way. These metaphors now no longer refer to the sense and structure of the world as reality, but to the sense and structure of the world as *science*. That is hardly fortuitous when one considers how the gains yielded by scientific inquiry have intruded more and more between the subject and its world; this world 'is' ever more identical to the aggregate of all the theoretical propositions that can be made about it (which is not to claim that something like an 'immediate' and pure experience of the world has ever existed). Now for our metaphors, both of which appear in the posthumously published "Crisis" volume of Husserl's works. The first is entirely in keeping with Husserl's view that the mathematization of the natural sciences through Galileo caused theoretical accomplishment and the perceptible relation to meaning in research to part ways, a structural split that, so far as its methodological implications are concerned, already anticipates the process of 'technicization' by which formalized operations are transferred to machines. This process is initially made possible through a 'disguising' of truth: "It is through the garb of ideas that we take for true being what is actually a method . . . It is because of the disguise of ideas that the true meaning of the method, the formulae, the 'theories', remained unintelligible and, in the naïve formulation of the method, was never understood."[37] Highly significant, in our context, is the way in which the disguise metaphor makes way for the mechanism metaphor. The mechanical is regarded as a sphere isolated from the vitally relevant consummation of meaning, and this isolation is seen to have been brought about through a 'disguise' that, in deflecting tiresomely insistent questions of meaningfulness, first unleashes the potential for scientific achievement: "Are science and its method not like a machine, reliable in accomplishing obviously very useful things, a machine everyone can learn to operate correctly without in the least understanding the inner possibility and necessity of this sort of accomplishment?"[38] In Husserl, the book metaphor is likewise closely connected to the problem of the idea and

---

found in the penultimate section of Jean Paul's "Auswahl aus des Teufels Papieren" [Selection from the Devil's Papers]. Hidden here amid a welter of scurrilities stands the most compromised formulation ever given to the mechanistic formative claim on mankind: *Nichts sein und Alles können* [To be nothing and be able to do everything]. And it is a stroke of genius to allow the story to be written for *Leute auf dem Monde, auf dem Saturn, auf dessen Trabanten, auf dessen Ringe* [people on the moon, on Saturn, on its satellites, on its rings], only to have the reader brought back to earth with a thud in the final sentence: *denn Ihr Saturnianer allzumal merkt doch wohl beim Henker, der Leser ist ja eben—Maschinenmann selbst* [for you Saturnians will have remarked, by the devil, that the reader is—the machine-man himself].

37. *Das Ideenkleid macht es, daß wir für wahres Sein nehmen, was eine Methode ist . . . die Ideenverkleidung macht es, daß der eigentliche Sinn der Methode, der Formeln, der 'Theorien' unverständlich blieb und bei der naiven Entstehung der Methode niemals verstanden wurde.* Husserl, *Die Krisis der europäischen Wissenschaften und die transzendentale Phänomenologie,* Husserliana VI (The Hague, 1954), 52. [Edmund Husserl, *The Crisis of the European Sciences and Transcendental Phenomenology,* trans. David Carr (Evanston, IL: Northwestern University Press, 1970), 51–52.]

38. *Gleicht die Wissenschaft und ihre Methode nicht einer offenbar sehr Nützliches leistenden und darin verläßlichen Maschine, die jedermann lernen kann, richtig zu handhaben, ohne im mindesten die innere Mög-*

integration of science. In an addendum to the "Crisis" treatise from winter 1936/7, he writes of the peculiarity of the scientist's 'horizon of interests' within the life-world. This "goal-directed life which is the scientist's life-vocation" is determined by an immanent teleology that makes each advance in knowledge the premise for further achievement, such "that all the works of science [come together] in a coherent total work, the theoretical system (the theory contained in an ideal textbook)."[39] The 'ideal textbook' as the goal and integral of the infinite exertions of science—this is a truly ironic transcription of the "Book of Nature" originally composed by the Author-God.

---

lichkeit und Notwendigkeit so gearteter Leistungen zu verstehen? [Husserl, *Crisis of the European Sciences,* trans. Carr, 52.]

39. *lebensberufliche Zweckleben der Wissenschaftler . . . daß alle Werke der Wissenschaft zu einem einheitlichen Gesamtwerk, dem theoretischen System (der Lehre des idealen Lehrbuches) zusammengeschlossen werden.* [Husserl, *Crisis of the European Sciences,* trans. Carr, 380; translation modified.]

VII

MYTH AND METAPHORICS

If we attempt now to elaborate and set out a *typology of metaphor histories* with the help of paradigms, this does not imply that the thematic goal and ideal of the metaphorology we have in mind would consist in such a typology. In carrying out this task, we should recall that metaphorology—as a subbranch of conceptual history, and like the latter itself considered as a whole—must always be an auxiliary discipline to philosophy as it seeks to understand itself from its history and to bring that history to living presence. Our typology of metaphor histories must accordingly endeavor to distinguish and work through particular aspects—new aspects, perhaps—of philosophy's historical self-understanding. In the process, it is above all the *transitions* that will allow the specificity of each metaphor and its expressive forms to appear in sharper focus.

One such phenomenon of 'transition' arises from the relationship between *myth* and *metaphorics*. From this perspective, the 'myths' of Plato by no means prove to be homogeneous means of expression; we can see also that the schema that posits a dualism of mythos and logos, or a transition from one to the other, fails to grasp their functional differences in an adequate fashion.[1] The allegorical exegesis

---

1. [This will be a major theme of Hans Blumenberg, *Work on Myth,* trans. Robert M. Wallace (Cambridge, MA: MIT Press, 1985).]

of myth, as practiced first by the Sophists and then, above all, by the Stoics, took mythos to be a 'preliminary form' of logos, grasping it as an essentially convertible utterance. This schema has its correlate in an interpretation of myth that still holds sway today. Myth is regarded as a 'prelogical' phenomenon and assigned to a primitive form of mental 'development' that has been superseded and supplanted by more exact forms of understanding. But what has emerged from our reflections under the heading of 'absolute metaphor' has, in its indissoluble alogicality, given us reason to believe that such Cartesianism *avant la lettre* brings an inappropriate norm to the historical findings. In myth, too, questions are kept alive that refuse to yield to theoretical answers without thereby becoming obsolete. The difference between myth and 'absolute metaphor' would here be a purely genetic one: myth bears the sanction of its primordial, unfathomable origin, its divine or inspirative ordination, whereas metaphor can present itself as a figment of the imagination, needing only to disclose a possibility of understanding in order for it to establish its credentials. The Platonic Socrates qualifies the myth of the judgment of the dead in the "Gorgias" by asserting that what Callicles will regard as a "fable" (*muthos*), he himself holds to be an "actual account" (*logos*).[2] This myth arises in the dialogue from a deep sense of discomfort concerning the need to find an answer to the question of final justice. Socrates has tried, using all the argumentative means at his disposal, to cling to the idea of a justice immanent to history. All too often, the Athenian polis has condemned its finest men and so committed what appears to be a gross injustice; but Socrates dares to claim that here a crucial dereliction of duty has come back to haunt the statesman, his failure to improve the citizens under his rule to such an extent that they would no longer be capable of unjustly condemning so excellent a statesman as himself—just as the Sophists, when cheated by their students of their fees, were confronted with proof of the hollowness of their own moral teachings. Yet had not Socrates earlier been unable to respond to Callicles' prophetic suggestion that he might one day be unjustly tried and found guilty by the polis (486AB)? The philosopher may well stand up for the truth, but the truth does not stand up for him: it would therefore not be at all surprising should he one day be forced to lay down his life for it (521D). It should not be forgotten that, for both the author and the reader of the "Gorgias," this aporia had already been realized in the death of Socrates. That is reflected in the conversational situation: the last judgment myth arises as the 'final word' from an unshakable postulate, a deep-seated confidence that the skillfulness of the Sophists and the haplessness of the philosophers before the court of the polis *cannot* represent the final allocation of roles but will be reversed before a higher tribunal. The myth stands ready to assure us of this; but what confidence would it merit were it not grounded in the need of one who was prepared to die for the truth? Mythos is not logos, nor does Socrates

---

2. [Plato, *Gorgias,* trans. W. R. M. Lamb (Cambridge, MA: Harvard University Press, 1996), 519.]

ignore the differences between the two; we would be in a position to disparage myth, he says, if only we could find what we are looking for, the better and more truthful discourse for which we would gladly relinquish it (527A). The thinker's situation in relation to myth coincides here with his situation in relation to 'absolute metaphor': it fails to satisfy his requirements, yet for want of an alternative it will have to do.

The myth of the cave from book VII of the "Republic" is situated in another region of the 'twilight zone' between mythos and logos. The cave as the setting of a primordial event is grounded in the mythic tradition and authorized by that tradition.[3] For Plato himself, the exodus from subterranean darkness 'into the light' is *the* elemental process of human history. This can already be seen in the Prometheus myth of the "Protagoras" (321C), where the transition from earth to light is connected with the gift of "wisdom in the arts together with fire," hence an endowment that goes beyond the form of existence 'foreseen' for mankind.[4] In the cosmological myth of the "Phaedo," too (108 sqq.), man 'naturally' finds himself plunged in cavernous gloom, languishing in a dreary confinement from which only the transcendent gift of mathematical and astronomical speculation can release him. The formal ground plan of the cave myth, upon which an escape route of human self-fulfillment, indeed self-transcendence, has been overlaid, is thus rooted in a primeval mythic vision while at the same time having the function of an absolute metaphor. But the 'interior design' of the cave, the properties with which it has been fitted out, shows that very different specific tasks can be transferred to this instrument: the myth functions as a *model*. Such a model can even inform the exposition of what, at first glance, may appear to be completely unrelated ideas. Plato's portrayal of his antihero in the "Sophist" betrays clear links to the cave scenario:[5] he is the one who, having taken refuge in the concealing darkness of the nonexistent, now imitates the existent in images devoid of being, the machinator of the shadow-play apparatus, the conjurer seeking to beguile his audience with mere semblance.[6] The cave first 'explains' the possibility of a phenomenon like the Sophist. What we have called 'background metaphorics', the implied use of a metaphor, is here once more in evidence. It was not until Neoplatonism that this myth was fully taken as an 'absolute metaphor', in part drawing on Empedocles and Plato, in part on the nymph grotto in Homer, which had advanced to cosmic significance in Homeric

---

3. Traces in Empedocles (Diels B 120) and Pherecydes of Syros (Diels B 6). The cosmos-cave metaphor in Plotinus, *Enn.* IV 8, I, 5 refers explicitly to Empedocles, as does Porphyry, *De antro nymph.* 8. Erwin Rohde had already defended the adequacy of this Empedocles interpretation against Wilamowitz. Cf. now R. Harder's commentary on Plotinus 1b (Hamburg, 1956), 445.

4. ἐξιέναι ἐκ γῆς εἰς φῶς [Plato, *Protagoras,* trans. W. R. M. Lamb (Cambridge, MA: Harvard University Press, 2006), 133. See also Hans Blumenberg, *Höhlenausgänge* (Frankfurt am Main: Suhrkamp, 1989).]

5. A view shared by F. M. Cornford in his "Sophist" commentary, in "Plato's Theory of Knowledge," 195.

6. The interpretation collocates *Soph.* 233C–235A with 254A.

allegoresis, as Porphyry's treatise "De antro nympharum" |On the Cave of the Nymphs| demonstrates. Now the cosmos is a 'cave', cut off from a realm of sheer transcendence that can no longer be reached by paideutic means. The absolute metaphor had been materialized in the 'architecture' of cultic lore.[7] The church fathers and Gnostics reappropriated it as the site of the soteriological event, which breaks in upon creation as a 'light in the cave'. In each case, the cave metaphor expresses and explicates a particular feeling about the world.

A different quality again comes to expression in the myth of the demiurge in the "Timaeus." Here everything pivots on the explanatory function (as Plotinus already noted, *Enn.* IV 8, 4), an ad-hoc construction dressed up in the stylistic garb of myth. Individual qualities of the demiurge, his 'goodness' for example, serve only as premises from which the required theoretical propositions, such as the completeness of the transposition of the ideal cosmos into the real cosmos, may be derived. In essence, the myth is here nothing more than the model for the exposition of a cosmogonic 'hypothesis'. No specific differences can be adduced when one compares this fictitious myth with the cosmological model outlined by Descartes in the "Principia" (III, 43 sqq.). In both cases, the dynamic model is called on to explain the static condition of the universe; what matters is that the universe *might* have arisen in this way, so that Descartes—in contradistinction to Plato—can even insist that it did *not* arise in this way, something he need not have written simply to keep the Inquisition at bay. Stoic exegesis first transformed the "Timaeus" into the hallowed ur-myth that it stylistically purports to be, while the patristic technique of inversion claimed the myth's descent from the story of Genesis. That left Augustine with the problem, given added urgency by Gnosticism, of squaring the biblical account of creation through the divine *mouth* with demiurgic creation through the divine *hand*. These were two distinct metaphors of origin: whereas the word of command neither explains nor seeks to explain anything, disdaining rationality and compelling submission, the step-by-step constructive labor of the demiurge seeks to explain everything, to dispel the mystery of what exists by granting insight into its becoming. One sees how for centuries heterogeneous elements were distorted and constrained into a false compatibility for the sake of the 'summation' of the traditional authorities. Examining such heterogeneities with an eye to the founding metaphors helps bring out their shades of difference.

---

7. F. Creuzer, *Symbolik und Mythologie der alten Völker* (Leipzig, 1836), 1: 246–47 (on the scenario of the Mithras cult): "According to Eubulos, Zoroaster had set up such a Mithras cave as a depiction of the universe. Everything in it was significant: the half-light, as the transition from darkness to light, was symbolic, the rock was matter, and in its innermost recesses all cosmic relations and forms were represented, the zones, the fixed stars, the planets, the signs of the zodiac, the elements, etc. At the entrance to this cosmic grotto appears Mithras . . ."

VIII

TERMINOLOGIZATION OF A METAPHOR: FROM 'VERISIMILITUDE' TO 'PROBABILITY'

In keeping with what was announced in the title to these studies, we have not set out to provide an exhaustive account of the relationship between myth, metaphor, and logos; we purport only to exemplify a particular manner of questioning, a particular analytic approach. This admission of the modesty of our enterprise is even more pertinent, perhaps, to the complex field of *transitions from metaphors to concepts,* which we will now attempt to contour with reference to the paradigm of 'verisimilitude', 'truthlikeness', or 'probability' [*Wahrscheinlichkeit*].[1] In this case, the metaphor has been absorbed by the word; although it has been flattened out by the terminological expression [i.e., *Wahrscheinlichkeit* in the conventional sense of 'probability'], it can always be foregrounded again through a shift in focus: *Wahrscheinlichkeit* denotes the semblance [*Schein*] of truth [*Wahrheit*], whereby semblance has the double meaning of reflection, irradiation, aura, translucence, of representative and apophantic shining, on the one hand, and empty glitz, chimerical deception,

---

1. [*Wahrscheinlichkeit* literally means "verisimilitude" or "truthlikeness" but today has the primary meaning of "probability"; the difference is that between the *likeness* and *likelihood* of truth. My translation of the term varies depending on context. I have modified the title of this section accordingly. In German, it reads: "Terminologisierung einer Metapher: Wahrscheinlichkeit."]

illegitimate simulation, of fakery and forgery, on the other. The metaphor here takes the word at its word, not as the name for a defined rule governing a body of facts. To illustrate with an example how, and at what point in its history, the word's metaphorical aspect is no longer perceived, I quote a passage from the "System of Stoic Philosophy" by Dieterich Tiedemann (Leipzig, 1776), I 22, where Cicero's purposive determination of logic in "De finibus" (III 21, 72) is described as follows: "It is meant to make us withhold our approbation from a false proposition, and to prevent us ever being taken in by a fraudulent semblance of probability [*betrüglichen Schein der Wahrscheinlichkeit*] . . ."[2]

The metaphor doubtless has its roots in the ambivalence of ancient rhetoric: the orator can cause truth to 'appear' in its rightful splendor, but he can also make falsehood 'look' true; how his ability is better invested will depend on a basic predisposition that we have already discussed in relation to the metaphor of the 'mightiness of truth', and that we must constantly bear in mind here. Precisely this question of man's 'natural' relationship to truth was positively settled by Aristotle in a passage toward the beginning of his "Rhetoric" (1355a14), where, drawing on Plato's definition of likelihood (εἰκός) in the "Phaedrus" (273D) as δι' ὁμοιότητα τοῦ ἀληθοῦ ἐγγιγνόμενον,[3] he coined the expression 'truthlikeness' (τὸ ὅμοιον τῷ ἀληθεῖ), later translated and popularized by Cicero as *verisimile*. A Platonic element, reinforced by Academic Skepticism, is in play here. We should not be too hasty to dismiss Cicero's self-understanding as a Platonist, even if he belongs 'only' to the supposedly degraded form of Academic Skepticism. The latter is more consistently 'Platonic' than it may appear at first glance; more than a revolt in the doctrinal history of Platonism, it is equally a response to the heightening of the transcendence character of truth we find in the late Plato. The anecdote related by Sextus Empiricus about the school head Arcesilaus, according to which he continued to teach Platonic orthodoxy to a select group of students even as he exoterically professed to Skepticism,[4] has never been taken all that seriously; it nonetheless provides an illuminating pointer to this context. The situation of the hopeless unattainability of truth had been vividly brought home to his readers by the late Plato. At the beginning of the second part of the "Timaeus" (48D), the εἰκός, that which looks to be true, is introduced as a way out of disorienting and disconcerting confusion; God is called upon "to see us through a strange and unusual argument to a likely conclusion."[5] Likelihood is the graciously conferred 'representative' of truth; it will guide the errant seeker to salvation, provided that

---

2. *sie soll uns hindern, einem falschen Satz Beyfall zu geben, und uns nie von einem betrüglichen Scheine der Wahrscheinlichkeit hintergehen (zu) lassen . . .*

3. [Tisias, some time ago, before you came along, we were saying that this probability of yours was accepted by the people because of its likeness to truth; Plato, *Phaedrus*, trans. W. R. M. Lamb (Cambridge, MA: Harvard University Press, 2005), 559.]

4. *Pyrrh. hyp.* I 33, 234.

5. ἐξ ἀτόπου καὶ ἀήθους διηγήσεως πρὸς τὸ τῶν εἰκότων δόγμα διασώζειν. [Plato, *Timaeus and Critias*, trans. Desmond Lee (London: Penguin, 2008), 39.]

he is willing to 'stay the course' (56A). Truth is invested with an almost 'theological' dignity: the certitude that arises from grasping the truth can be bestowed on man only by divine confirmation (θεοῦ ξυμφήσαντος), whereas the seemingly true befits him even in his current state (καὶ νῦν, 72D). In the "Critias" (107D), the slight resemblance to truth manifested by the celestial and the divine as the objects of our worship is contrasted with the precision of our investigations into perishable and human things; the distance of transcendence permits us to perceive only the faintest afterglow of truth. Significantly, this distinction determines the degree of certainty in inverse fashion to its later determination in the Christian tradition, where certitude of faith towers over the mere 'verisimilitude' of our knowledge of nature. This inversion was destined to have a profound effect on how verisimilitude (or probability) would be represented.

The role of the verisimilar in Academic Skepticism, as the rock on which man, cast adrift in a sea of uncertainty, can stake his life-conduct and his claim to fortune, can be understood only if one perceives the 'Platonic residue' in this conception. Cicero—the thinker who effortlessly, and by no means just in eclectic, piecemeal fashion, brought together those irreconcilable adversaries, Academy and Stoicism, equally blind to all they had in common—could interpret the distinction between practical evidence and theoretical obscurity in Stoic terms, as a teleological economy for the fulfillment of true human needs. From this, a comportment arises that betrays no trace of resignation in the ἐποχή: dogmatists may well trade blows on behalf of 'their' truth, but the Skeptics are quite sure of the path they have to take, even if they will never be able to prove it: "Nor is there any difference between ourselves and those who think that they have positive knowledge except that they have no doubt that their tenets are true, whereas we hold many doctrines as probable, which we can easily act upon but can scarcely advance as certain."[6] In its efficacy and orienting reliability, the probable (*probabile*) inspires and merits confidence to the extent that man needs it to get by in this world; as soon as he oversteps this restriction, the probable is neutralized and quickly degenerates into specious probability (*captiosa probabilitas*).[7] This idea that the character of probability differentiates itself within an anthropocentrically oriented 'field' became important for the patristic line of tradition influenced by Cicero in the same measure that it was understood and misunderstood by that tradition. It is closely connected to the metaphor of *verisimile*, with which Cicero both translates and reinterprets the Academic πιθανόν. The latter is already characterized in its specificity by the fact that it designates first and foremost the 'persuasive' effect and personal allure of speakers, then that of their oratory, and finally that of the argumentative means

---

6. *nec inter nos et eos qui se scire arbitrantur quicquam interest nisi quod illi non dubitant quin ea vera sint quae defendunt, nos probabilia multa habemus, quae sequi facile, adfirmare vix possumus. Lucullus* prooem. 8. [Cicero, *Academica*, trans. H. Rackham (Cambridge, MA: Harvard University Press, 2005), 475.]

7. *De fin.* III 21, 72. [Cicero, *De finibus bonorum et malorum*, trans. H. Rackham (Cambridge, MA: Harvard University Press, 2006), 293.]

they use to prosecute their case. The *verisimile* is primarily a quality of the matter itself in its relation to the faculty of knowledge; even when the expression spills into the rhetorical domain, where the πιθανόν had traditionally been located,[8] it does not signify the persuasive force bound up with the person of the speaker and his technique, but the representative truthfulness lent him by his 'cause'. In the 'interspace' between truth and falsehood, the probable stands very close to the truth (*prope verum*),[9] partaking of its appearance *because* it partakes of its being—that is why the metaphorical *verisimile* can decisively amplify the terminological *probabile*: "The narrative will be probable if it seems to embody characteristics which are accustomed to appear in real life . . . ; verisimilitude can be secured by following these principles."[10] Cicero thus wants the *veri simile* to be taken 'literally', as he makes clear elsewhere by prefacing it with a *quasi*.[11] But the reliability of what looks to be true is only ever confined to the economically circumscribed sphere of the human need for orientation in the world, a sufficiency that stands in sharp contrast to the evidence typical of the ethical consciousness of norms. Therein lies the key difference to the economics of the verisimilar in Epicureanism; when Epicurus, for example, interprets celestial phenomena in such a way as to neutralize their religious, mythical, and astrological significations, the forced admission that such theories are only seemingly true[12] serves to guarantee peace of mind (ἀταραξία) by demonstrating the affective equivalence of every extant doxographical opinion on the matter in question, since to insist on any one interpretation to the exclusion of all others would be to fall back into myth. In this respect, Epicurus (or one of his early pupils) is far more circumspect with the probable than his successor Lucretius, who often conflates physical and poetically striking probability, as when he proclaims it unlikely that only *one* world came into being without considering how improbable it is *that* a world should have come into being at all in the infinite shower of atoms.[13] That a 'cosmos' of the same type will always spring forth whenever and wherever something emerges from the chance interplay of atoms is a covert metaphysical-

8. See Plato, *Phaedrus* 272DE. On the entire complex of the *verisimile* in Cicero, see G. Gawlick, "Untersuchungen zu Ciceros philosophischer Methode" (Diss., Kiel, 1956), 69–70.

9. *De oratore* I 240. [Cicero, *De oratore*, trans. E. W. Sutton (Cambridge, MA: Harvard University Press, 2001), 175.]

10. *probabilis erit narratio, si in ea videbuntur inesse ea, quae solent apparere in veritate . . .; ac veri quidem similis ex his rationibus esse poterit. De inventione* I 29. [Cicero, *De inventione*, trans. H. B. Hubbell (Cambridge, MA: Harvard University Press, 2006), 61; translation modified.]

11. *Lucullus* 32: *volunt enim . . . probabile aliquid esse et quasi verisimile.* [For they hold . . . that something is 'probable,' or as it were resembling the truth; *Academica*, trans. Rackham, 509.]

12. τὸ πιθανολογούμενον . . . δεόντως καταλιπεῖν. *Ep. ad Pythoclem.* [Epicurus, *The Philosophy of Epicurus*, trans. George K. Strodach (Evanston, IL: Northwestern University Press, 1963), 158–59.]

13. *De rerum natura* II 1052–57: *nullo . . . pacto veri simile esse putandumst . . ./ hunc unum terrarum orbem caelumque creatum . . .* [It cannot by any means be thought likely that this is the only round earth and sky that has been made; Lucretius, *De rerum natura*, trans. Martin Ferguson Smith (Cambridge, MA: Harvard University Press, 2002), 158–59.]

teleological assumption that makes it all too easy to operate with the 'probable' on this basis.

If we turn now to the *verisimile* in Lactantius, we find that we can both draw on and complete the material we collated earlier on his concept of truth. His understanding of truth as a good placed entirely in divine hands, which God has seen fit to share with us, through revelation, in a dosage conducive to our salvation (note the influence of Ciceronian economy!), already leads us to expect that 'verisimilitude' will here appear predominantly, if not exclusively, in the negative sense of mere semblance. This expectation proves to be fully justified. In "De ira Dei" [On the Anger of God] (IV 7–10), Lactantius refers to a saying of Poseidonius reported by Cicero, according to which Epicurus was really an atheist who kept the gods in his system only for the sake of appearances. Lactantius's treatment of Epicurus at this point is remarkably lenient and sympathetic: he acquits him of the charge of being a double-tongued deceiver (*deceptor bilinguis*) by showing that a contradiction already inheres in the claim that there are gods to whom any function (*officium*) is denied. Epicurus thus fell victim to his own premise about the nature of the divine: ". . . But he erred through ignorance of the truth. For, being led from the beginning by a single opinion's resemblance to truth, he necessarily fell into those things which followed."[14] Concerning the interpretation of the Saturn myth offered by Minucius Felix in the "Octavius," Lactantius remarks critically: "These things, indeed, have some resemblance to the truth, but are not true."[15] The formulation applied to Epicurus crops up again in relation to certain cosmological theses: "The origin of this error must also be set forth by us. For they are always thought deceived in the same manner. For when they have assumed anything false in the commencement of their investigations, led by the resemblance to truth, they necessarily fall into those things which are its consequences."[16] Finally, Lactantius fully demonizes verisimilitude by denouncing it, in his dualistic parlance, as the seductive means for making the path of damnation indistinguishable from the path of salvation: "For how could the forerunner of that way, whose strength and power are altogether in deceit, lead men altogether into fraud, unless he showed them some things which resembled the truth?"[17] When one considers Cicero's immense authority for Lactantius, this transvaluation of the *verisimile,* the new premises

---

14. . . . *ignorantia veritatis erravit. Inductus enim a principio veri similitudine unius sententiae, necessario in ea quae sequebantur incurrit.* [*Ante-Nicene Fathers,* ed. Alexander Roberts and James Donaldson, trans. William Fletcher (Peabody, MA: Hendrikson Publishers, 2004), VII, 261; translation modified.]

15. *sunt haec quidem similia veri, non tamen vera. Div. inst.* I 11, 56. [*Ante-Nicene Fathers,* trans. Fletcher, VII, 23.]

16. *Huius quoque erroris aperienda nobis origo est. Nam semper eodem modo falluntur. Cum enim falsum aliquid in principio sumserint, veri similitudine inducti, necesse est, eos in ea, quae consequuntur, incurrere* (III 24, 2). [*Ante-Nicene Fathers,* trans. Fletcher, VII, 94; translation modified.]

17. *Quomodo enim praecursor eius viae, cuius vis et potestas omnis in fallendo est, universos in fraudem posset inducer, nisi verisimilia hominibus ostentaret?* (VI 7, 3). [*Ante-Nicene Fathers,* trans. Fletcher, VII, 170.]

notwithstanding, is nothing short of astonishing. On closer inspection, we see that Lactantius has eliminated the 'Platonic residue' by deploying a traditional element neglected by Cicero when tackling this question: the Stoic view of probability. The significance of this side branch of the tradition can be found, above all, in the later influence of Descartes, for whom to admit that something seems to be true is to succumb to falsehood. In their logic, the Stoics had elaborated the doctrine of judgmental qualities from the standpoint of a 'position' taken by reason in relation to the pure contents of utterances: the sovereignty of reason is manifested in its freedom to suspend judgment in the ἐποχή, in its refusal to give its assent until the object has been fully ratified. Yet here the probable reveals its power to seduce the judging subject to precipitancy (προπτωσία). This power became especially virulent in rhetoric, which Stoic dialectics, with its goal of avoiding rashness in assent (ἀπροπτωσία), seeks to equip its students to withstand.[18] Stoic dialectics wants to immunize reason against the probable; it inculcates an attitude of wariness as the stronghold from which reason can best hold out against the allurements of probability: "By wariness they mean a strong presumption against what at the moment seems probable, so as not to be taken in by it."[19] In the stark Stoic diathesis of interiority and the exterior world, the πιθανότης becomes the basic characteristic of the effect of things that intrude 'from outside', comparable to the 'rhetorical' effects of those who have an 'interest' in making others agree with what they have to say.[20]

In Augustine, the ambivalence of 'verisimilitude' makes itself felt in both its aspects. The 'Platonic residue' is fully rehabilitated when he takes to the field against Academic Skepticism. In the dialogue "Contra Academicos" [Against the Academicians] (II 7, 16), Augustine asks his interlocutor whether he holds the doctrine peddled by the Academicians to be true. Licentius replies: "I don't know whether it is the truth, but it is probable . . ." Allowing himself to be guided by the thread of metaphor, Augustine now switches to the *verisimile:* "You do know . . . that they also name the probable 'truthlike'?"[21] And this metaphor does indeed offer the point of entry to Platonism. If a man unacquainted with your father, Augustine puts to his interlocutor, were to set eyes on your brother and say that he looks like your father—would not such a man seem to you crazy or simpleminded? Augustine's metaphor permits the 'truthlike' to be set, as a copy, in a derivative relationship to

---

18. See the example of the 'precipitant' definition of 'mother' given in Diogenes Laert. VII 75. ["A probable judgement is one which induces to assent, e.g. 'Whoever gave birth to anything, is that thing's mother.' This, however, is not necessarily true; for the hen is not mother of an egg." Diogenes Laertius, *Lives of Eminent Philosophers,* trans. R. D. Hicks (Cambridge, MA: Harvard University Press, 2005), 2: 183.]

19. τήν τε ἀνεικαιότητα ἰσχυρὸν λόγον πρὸς τὸ εἰκός, ὥστε μὴ ἐνδιδόναι αὐτῷ. Diogenes Laert. VII 46. [*Lives of the Eminent Philosophers,* trans. Hicks, 2: 157.]

20. This equation in Diogenes Laert. VII 89.

21. *Ultrum verum sit, nescio: probabile est tamen . . . Probabile . . . scisne ab ipsis etiam verisimile nominari?* [Augustine, *Against the Academicians, The Teacher,* trans. Peter King (Indianapolis, IN: Hackett, 1995), 41; translation modified.]

the original image of truth. Following a digression in the dialogue, the story arising from the metaphor—that of the man who claims to detect a likeness to the father he has never seen—is scenically and vividly recapitulated before being brought to a conclusion: "The example makes it obvious that your Academicians should likewise be laughed at, since they say that in this life they follow something truthlike, although they do not know what the truth is."[22] A certain Trygetius now enters the conversation to lead Augustine from the *verisimile* back to the *probabile,* hoping thereby to steer clear of the Platonic consequences (II 8, 20); Alypius, too, charges Augustine with clinging to a word that happens to suit his purpose, yet which could just as well be replaced by another. But Augustine refuses to budge: "This isn't a controversy about words! Instead, it's a serious controversy about the issues themselves. I don't think the Academicians were the sort of men who didn't know how to give names to things. On the contrary, these terms (sc. 'probable' and 'truthlike') seem to me to have been chosen to conceal their view from the unintelligent and to reveal it to the more penetrating."[23] Depending on the stance taken by the subject, words conceal and reveal the matter in question; that is one of the basic tenets of Neoplatonism. In the present case, this conditioning of the matter by the stance adopted in relation to it means that the metaphor ought to be heeded and its guidance accepted. Thus, by the next day of the dialogue, Licentius has become fully alert to the metaphor's implications: "Nothing seems more absurd than for someone who doesn't know the truth to say that he's following something truthlike."[24] The positivity of the truthlike lies in its referential function: it is impossible to rest content with verisimilitude alone. Taken for itself, in the self-sufficiency embraced by the Skeptics, it veers to the negative; that emerges from book III of "Contra Academicos" (15, 33–16, 36) and is underscored again in the "Retractiones" (I 1, 4). At the point where the truth has its own unmediated presence and there is no need for referentiality, in the rock-solid certainty of the trinitarian *et sumus et nos esse novimus et id esse ac nosse diligimus* |we exist, we know that we exist, and we are glad of this existence and knowledge|, the verisimilar falls away toward falsehood: "In these three things there is no false resemblance to truth to trouble us."[25]

    The decisive functional transformation of 'verisimilitude' occurs in the late Middle Ages. The process is structurally similar to the genesis of Academic Skepticism:

---

22. *Ipsa res clamat similiter ridendos esse Academicos tuos, qui se in vita veri similitudinem sequi dicunt, cum ipsum verum quid sit, ignorent.* |Augustine, *Against the Academicians,* trans. King, 44.|

23. *Non est ista . . . verborum, sed rerum ipsarum magna controversia: non enim illos viros eos fuisse abritror, qui rebus nescirent nomina imponere; sed mihi haec vocabula videntur elegisse et ad occultandam tardioribus, et ad significandam vigilantioribus sententiam suam* (II 10, 24). |Augustine, *Against the Academicians,* trans. King, 47.|

24. *nihil mihi videtur esse absurdius, quam dicere, se verisimile sequi eum qui verum quid sit ignoret* (II 12, 27). |Augustine, *Against the Academicians,* trans. King, 49.|

25. *in his autem tribus quae dixi nulla nos falsitas verisimilis turbat* (*De civitate Dei* XI 26). |Augustine, *Concerning the City of God against the Pagans,* trans. Henry Bettensen (Harmondsworth: Penguin, 1972), 459; translation modified.|

inflationary pressures on the transcendent character of the true lead to the autarky of the seemingly true. The new skepticism of the fourteenth and fifteenth centuries enlists in the service of *fideism:* in the famous *credo quia absurdum* ['I believe because it is absurd'], the truth that reason is duty-bound to accept 'on faith' itself becomes an unlikelihood; this kind of truth 'does not look' as though it could or should be taken to be true. On the other hand, the verisimilar, having forfeited its commensurability with a truth deemed to be absolute, now achieves full autonomy. Plato's determination of their relationship, in the passage from the "Critias" cited above, has been turned on its head, and the divine and the celestial have been torn asunder: while the divine offers a lonely certitude in faith, the heavens have been integrated into nature, concerning which the theologian considers it not even likely (*ne verisimiles quidem*) that the astronomer can acquire sure knowledge.[26] The new indifference of 'truth' and 'probability' is clearly demonstrated in the question of the relationship between scriptural authority and Copernican cosmology. When Cardinal Bellarmine, in a letter from 12 April 1615, advises the Carmelite Foscarini to declare the Copernican teaching to be probable but not true, there stands behind this advice the idea that no mere probability can challenge the truth of the biblical story about how God brought the sun to a standstill, but also, conversely, that this truth does not automatically rule out the probability of the Copernican teaching. This entire structural complex was deformed by theology in the throes of its late medieval crisis; we cite here a piece of evidence that is of particular interest to us owing to the curiously Latinized occurrence of the ancient Greek word εἰκός, theses 12–15 of Melanchthon's baccalaureate disputation from 1519: "12. The intellect can give assent to no given proposition without reason or experience. 13. Nor can the will by itself force the intellect to give assent to what is probable [*eicotibus*]. 14. The will, drawn away by love to an object of faith, orders the intellect to give assent. 15. This assent is faith or wisdom."[27] What is striking here is the way in which the concept of faith is embedded in a Stoic conceptual schema and contrasted with the *eicota;* the originality with which Melanchthon manipulates old linguistic means to say something new is equally evident in his negative use of the *verisimile* in the

---

26. Andreas Osiander, in the foreword to the "Revolutiones" of Copernicus: *Neque enim necesse est, eas hypotheses esse veras, immo ne verisimiles quidem, sed sufficit hoc unum, si calculum observationibus congruentem exhibeant.* [It is not necessary that these hypotheses should be true, or even likely; but it is enough if they provide a calculus which fits the observations; Copernicus, *On the Revolutions of Heavenly Spheres,* trans. Charles Glen Wallis (Philadelphia: Running Press, 2003), 1; translation modified.]

27. *12. Intellectus nulli propositioni assentiri potest citra rationem aut experientiam.—13. Nec voluntas per sese intellectum eicotibus cogere potest, ut assentiatur.—14. Voluntas per charitatem rapta ad obiectum credibile imperat, intellectui, ut assentiatur.—15. Hic assensus fides est seu sapientia.* [Melanchthon, *Selected Writings,* trans. Charles Leander Hill (Minneapolis: Augsburg Publishing House, 1962), 17–18; translation modified.] In his *Lehrbuch der Dogmengeschichte* (4th ed.) IV, 426 n. 1, R. Seeberg reads *sine eicotibus.* It seems to me that *eicotibus* is here a dative object, contrasting with *ratio* and *experientia* in the preceding thesis. In Stoic terms, it thus designates a deficiency over against the cataleptic presentation. The *obiectum credibile* towers over the *eicota* and has the same effect as the cataleptic presentation, despite not being identical with such a presentation.

reformational paradox of thesis 11: "Therefore, for good deeds to be sins is not dissimilar to the truth"[28]—this is theological prudence made word!

In the battles fought over the new world-picture, the metaphorical ambivalence of 'verisimilitude' once again loomed large, as the names of Osiander and Bellarmine already indicate—nowhere larger, perhaps, than in the trial of Galileo. Galileo had taken the line that something that goes against the biblical source of faith may very well be scientifically probable, since probability leaves room to suppose that it could be otherwise. The final judgment against Galileo from 22 June 1633 pronounced it a grave error to say that an opinion could still be probable even though its opposite had been expressly revealed in the Bible.[29] The *probabile* is here regarded entirely from the act of subjective assent; something like a nuanced agreement is considered out of the question. To be found worthy of our assent, however, the probable must be in possession of a metaphysical right. Galileo, by contrast, had defended himself by pointing out that he had presented the Copernican system in his contentious "Dialogo" with the argumentative skill of a man who could make even falsehood appear probable: "by finding ingenious and apparently probable arguments even in favor of false propositions."[30]

The *logicization* of 'verisimilitude' stems from the importance that must be accorded 'chance' in any explanation of the world that wants, at least in theory, to abstain from theological and teleological premises. The question of whether the recognition of blind chance entails a renunciation of rationality provokes the new urgency and the new formulation given the problem of probability. The task of making probabilities comparable and hence decidable found its model—oriented toward the partiality for the *arte factum* so characteristic of the modern age—in the game of chance, in a 'throw of the dice' that was technically isolated, constant in its determining factors, and quantifiable according to occurrences and possibilities. What Pascal, in his correspondence with Fermat, called the 'art of chance' is the attainment, limited in scope yet lucidly aware of its limitations, of rational mastery over a previously unilluminated, structurally unexplored domain. In 1654, Pascal addressed the Académie Parisienne with a list of his finished, incomplete, or planned mathematical works. They include a study on the laws of chance: "The

---

28. *Ergo et bona opera peccata esse non est absimile vero.* [Melanchthon, *Selected Writings,* trans. Hill, 17; translation modified.]

29. *Il che pure è errore gravissimo, non potendo in modo niuno esser probabile un'opinione dichiarata e definita per contraria alla Scrittura Divina.* [This is still a very serious error, since there is no way an opinion declared and defined contrary to divine Scripture may be probable; trans. Maurice A. Finocchiaro, in *The Galileo Affair: A Documentary History* (Berkeley: University of California Press, 1989), 290.] And in the index of theses concerning which Galileo was *veementemente sospetto d'eresia* [vehemently suspected of heresy], we find listed again, as a formal element in its own right, *che si possa tenere e difendere per probabile una opinione dopo d'essere stata diachiarata e difinita per contraria alla Sacra Scrittura* [that one may hold and defend as probable an opinion after it has been declared and defined contrary to Holy Scripture; *The Galileo Affair,* trans. Finocchiaro, 291.]

30. *in trovar, anco per le proposizione false, ingegnosi et apparenti discorsi di probabilità.* [*The Galileo Affair,* trans. Finocchiaro, 290.]

obscure workings of fate are justly ascribed to chance rather than to natural necessity. This object has thus previously been left in the dark; yet after having proved inaccessible to experience, it has now been brought within reach of the intellect. Through geometry, I have so securely raised it to the level of an art that it now partakes of the reliability of geometry and can progress with confidence. And so it receives its name from both sides, connects mathematical proof with the uncertainty of chance, unites the apparently un-unitable, and rightly claims for itself the astonishing title Geometry of Chance." Leibniz took up the demand for a *logica probabilium* and granted it the right of residence in philosophy.[31] Yet even here, the metaphorical background still shines through. In the "Théodicée," Leibniz dismisses Bayle's claim that there are rational objections to religion that cannot, or cannot yet, be refuted; Leibniz maintains (§27) that Aristotelian logic is more than capable of dealing with any such line of argument, to the extent that it is genuinely purely deductive and rational. Things are quite different when it comes to objections based on probability, however, "for the art of judging from probable reasons is not yet well established, so that our logic in this connexion is still very imperfect, and to this very day we have little beyond the art of judging from demonstrations."[32] But this insuffiency of logic has no bearing on the defense of religion, since it is pointless to contest arguments of probability (*vraisemblance*) when the mysteries of religion already have the semblance of truth against them, and thus cannot be made probable or shielded from the charge of implausibility: "When it is a question of opposing reason to an article of our faith, one is not disturbed by objections that only attain probability. Everyone agrees that appearances are against mysteries, and that they are by no means probable when regarded only from the standpoint of reason."[33] It is possible for truth to have the semblance of truth against it, and even for it to appear quite 'unseeming'. In this passage, uniquely significant for our

---

31. The surest indication of this is the 'scholastic' reception in Christian Wolff, *Logica* §593: *Enimvero ad aestimandam probabilitatem opus est principiis specialibus quae a principiis ontologicis et philosophicis aliis pendent. Sed ea constituunt Logicam probabilium, quam in desideratis esse Leibnitius iam agnovit.* [Indubitably, the estimation of probability is a task for the 'Special Principles', which depend upon ontological and other philosophical principles. But these establish the logic of probability, which Leibniz now acknowledges to be among his desiderata.] In §578, Wolff had already given a definition of probability: *Si praedicatum subiecto tribuitur ob rationem insufficentem, propositio dicitur probabilis. Patet ad eo, in probabili propositione praedicatum subjecto tribui ob quaedam requisita ad veritatem.* [If a predicate is assigned to a subordinate position because of insufficient proof, the proposition is called probable. It is clear from this that I have assigned the predicate in a probable proposition to a subordinate position because of certain requirements pertaining to truth.] Probability is thus an 'incomplete' truth.

32. *car l'art de juger des raisons vraisemblables n'est pas encor bien établi, de sorte que nostre Logique à cet égard est encor très imparfaite, et que nous n'en avons presque jusqu'icy que l'art de juger des demonstrations* (§28). [Gottfried Wilhelm Leibniz, *Theodicy,* trans. E. M. Huggard (London: Routledge & Kegan Paul, 1952), 90–91.]

33. *quand il s'agit d'opposer la raison à un article de nostre foy, on ne se met point en peine des objections qui n'aboutissent qu'à la vraisemblance: puisque tout le monde convient que les mystères sont contre les apparences, et n'ont rien de vraisemblable, quand on ne les regarde que du côté de la raison* (§28). [Leibniz, *Theodicy,* trans. Huggard, 91.]

context, an awareness of the need to logicize the verisimilar goes hand in hand with a blithe exploitation of its metaphorical implications.

It cannot be our task to demonstrate in detail how the Leibnizian demand was addressed through the logicization and calculization of 'verisimilitude'. Several motivating factors behind the 'transition' from the metaphor to the terminological expression will nonetheless be outlined here, since they equally represent essential driving forces in the intellectual history of the modern age. The logical dissolution of *fortuna,* which had ruled imperiously over the age until investigation into the ludic model began to reveal its inner workings, provided the impetus for the true founding work of probability theory, Christian Huygens's treatise "De ratiociniis in ludo aleae" [On Reckoning in Games of Chance] (1657). A very different concern, programmatically formulated for the epoch by Descartes in his *marcher avec assurance dans cette vie,* is evident in Edmund Halley's "An Estimate of the Degrees of the Mortality of Mankind, Drawn from Curious Tables of the Births and Funerals of the City of Breslaw; with an Attempt to Ascertain the Price of Annuities upon Lives" (1693). An interest that was obviously purely statistical, yet guided by a question that, posed now for the first time, was to play a key role in the history of the modern mind, moved the founder of statistics, William Petty, to compose his "Essay concerning the Multiplication of Mankind" (1686).[34] The critical erosion of the teleological principle and its theological correlate, Divine Providence, first made acutely relevant the issue of whether the human race could grow beyond the finite possibilities provided for it by nature, and indeed whether it had not already begun to do so. Abraham de Moivre's "De mensura sortis" [On the Measurement of Lots], a title that directly flags the desire for knowledge, appeared in the "Philosophical Transactions" in 1712. In 1699 there appeared in the same venue a publication that did what Leibniz, in the passage cited above, declares to be impossible: in "A Calculation of the Credibility of Human Testimony," as in John Craig's "Theologiae Christianae principia mathematica" [Mathematical Principles of Christian Theology], the overwhelming historical probability of the biblical documents was to be proven mathematically. Needless to say, these pious computations did nothing to overturn Leibniz's verdict on the use of probability arguments in support of religion. Drawing on Jacob Bernoulli's unfinished, posthumously published "Ars conjectandi" [The Art of Conjecturing] (1713), Niclaus Bernoulli first made juristic use of probability theory in his "Specimina artis conjectandi ad quaestiones juris applicatae" [Examples of the Art of Conjecture Applied to Questions of Law] (1709), a field into which Poisson later introduced the terminological distinction between *probabilité* and *chance.*[35] Andreas Rüdiger, who in "De sensu veri et falsi" [On the Meaning of Truth and Falsehood] (1709) had already enumerated a veritable host

---

34. Petty's "Political Arithmetic" also appeared posthumously in 1691.

35. *Recherches sur la probabilité des jugements en matière criminelle et en matière civile* . . . (Paris, 1837).

of 'probabilities', defines among others a medical variety, as "a probability by means of which we draw conclusions from the consistency of physical experience concerning a future event although contradicted by fear."[36] An application to the study of weather patterns was ventured by Anton Pilgram in his "Untersuchungen über das Wahrscheinliche der Wetterkunde" |Investigations into Meteorological Probability| (Vienna, 1788), a work that can still be read with amusement today. But I will break off here in order to avoid arousing the false semblance (or 'verisimilitude', in the negative sense) of exhaustiveness.

Let us return to the authentically philosophical 'transition' in this metaphorical-conceptual history. In 1756 Moses Mendelssohn published his "Gedanken von der Wahrscheinlichkeit" |Thoughts on Probability|.[37] Here we are again afforded, as from an eminence, an overview of the entire representational complex. "Of all the knowledge that the human mind is impelled to acquire, that of probability can perhaps be deemed the noblest, since it befits our limited insight and must in most cases take the place of certainty. Its influence upon the actions and inactions of men, and through these on their happiness, has always so impressed itself upon the sages of this world, that they have preferred rather to undermine the pillars of truth itself, than the pillars of probability."[38] The 'great discoveries' made by mathematicians in the preceding century had all been made in the field of probability: "In all kinds of games of chance, wagers, insurance schemes, lotteries, in a number of legal disputes, and even with regard to historical credibility, they have weighed the probable cases against each other, and determined the magnitude of expectation, or degree of probability, in accordance with these calculations . . . A sage who, in order to fulfill the wish of Herr Leibnitz, wanted to invent a rational art of the probable, would have to be skillfull enough to abstract the general from the particular rules given us by these great mathematicians, and then to extrapolate *a priori*, as it were, a greater number of particular rules."[39] Mendelssohn arrives at this general rule

---

36. *probabilitas qua a constantia experientiae physicae ad futurum eventum physicum cum metu oppositi concludimus . . .*

37. *Gesammelte Schriften*, ed. Elbogen, Guttmann and Mittwoch (Berlin, 1929), 1: 147 ff.

38. *Unter allen Erkenntnissen, zu welchen der menschliche Verstand aufgelegt ist; kann die Erkenntniß der Wahrscheinlichkeit vielleicht für die vornehmste gehalten werden, weil sie unsrer eingeschränkten Einsicht angemessen ist, und in den meisten Fällen die Stelle der Gewißheit nehmen muß. Ihr Einfluß in das Tun und Lassen der Menschen, und vermittelst dieser in ihre Glückseligkeit, hat den Weltweisen von jeher so in die Augen geleuchtet, daß sie sich eher haben einkommen lassen, die Stützen der Wahrheit selbst, als die Stützen der Wahrscheinlichkeit wanken zu machen.* Ibid., 149. A slightly but tellingly amended version of the same passage is found in the 'improved edition' of the "Philosophical Writings" (Berlin, 1771; cited in ibid., 497): *Unter den Erkenntnissen, die wir zu erlangen haben, kann die Wahrscheinlichkeit vielleicht für die nothwendigste gehalten werden; weil sie unsrer eingeschränkten Sphäre angemessen ist, und in den meisten Fällen die Stelle der Gewißheit vertreten muß.* |Of all the knowledge we should acquire, that of probability can perhaps be deemed the most necessary, since it befits our limited sphere and must in most cases take the place of certainty.|

39. *In allen Arten von Glücksspielen, Wetten, Assekuranzen, Lotterien, in einigen Rechtshändeln, ja sogar in Ansehung der historischen Glaubwürdigkeit, haben sie die wahrscheinlichen Fälle gegeneinander berechnet, und die Größe der Erwartung, oder den Grad der Wahrscheinlichkeit nach dieser Ausrechnung*

aided by Wolffian logic, which makes a sentence's degree of certainty depend on the degree to which the grounds permitting the predicate to follow from the subject are known: "The degree of probability is determined by the relationship of the given grounds for truth to those that pertain to complete certainty."[40] Against the definition of probability by the *genus proximum* of 'expectation', Mendelssohn holds that past as well as future events have their probability: "Just as it is probable that whatever is lacking the fewest grounds for truth will occur; so it is equally probable that whatever provided us with the most grounds for truth has occurred."[41] The Wolffian interpretation of probability as an incomplete truth recurs in Mendelssohn in the idea of assimilating the probable to the true: "Probability is often the path by which one arrives at indubitable certainty. Whenever we cannot immediately survey all the grounds for truth lying in a subject, we provisionally accept several of these grounds, in order to see what would follow from them if they alone exhausted the essence of the subject. We call the success brought about in this way a *hypothesis*."[42] The theological element that crops up time and again throughout the entire history of the idea of probability plays a role in Mendelssohn as well: "S'Gravesand proves, in his introduction to worldly wisdom, the reliability of these (sc. inductive) conclusions from God's will, since the most perfect being must always act in accordance with universal laws. Yet I have my doubts about basing our experimental conclusions on God's will."[43] Noteworthy in this context

---

bestimmt . . . Ein Weltweiser, der den Wunsch des Herrn von Leibnitz zu erfüllen, eine Vernunftkunst des Wahrscheinlichen erfinden wollte, müßte die Geschicklichkeit besitzen, von den besondern Regeln, die uns diese großen Mathematiker gegeben, das Allgemeine zu abstrahieren und hernach eine größere Anzahl von besonderen Regeln gleichsam a priori heraus zu bringen. Ibid., 498.

40. *Aus dem Verhältnisse der gegebenen Wahrheitsgründe zu denjenigen, die zur völligen Gewißheit gehören, wird der Grad der Wahrscheinlichkeit bestimmt.* Ibid., 499.

41. *So wie es wahrscheinlich ist, daß sich dasjenige zutragen wird, wozu die wenigstens Wahrheitsgründe fehlen; ebenso wahrscheinlich ist es, daß sich dasjenige zugetragen hat, wozu uns die meisten Wahrheitsgründe gegeben sind.* Ibid., 502. This view of probability as a real predicate is not to be confused with Jacob Bernoulli's distinction between a priori and a posteriori probability (*Ars conjectandi* IV); an event's probability can be determined a priori if the circumstances speaking for and against the event's occurrence are weighed against each other; it can be determined a posteriori (inductively) from frequent success under similar or identical conditions, which, however, need not be more closely determined and adjudged as favorable or unfavorable to the outcome: *quod apriori elicere non datur, saltem a posteriori hoc est ex eventu in similibus exemplis multoties observato eruere licebit* [What cannot be ascertained a priori, may at least be found out a posteriori from the results many times observed in similar situations; Jakob Bernoulli, *The Art of Conjecturing*, trans. Edith Dudley Sylla (Baltimore: Johns Hopkins University Press, 2006), 327].

42. *Öfters ist die Wahrscheinlichkeit auch der Weg, dadurch man zur untrüglichen Gewißheit gelangt. Wenn wir alle Wahrheitsgründe, die in einem Subjekte liegen, nicht auf einmal übersehen können, so nimmt man vorerst einige von diesen Wahrheitsgründen an, um zu sehen, was aus ihnen erfolgen würde, wenn sie allein das Wesen des Subjekts wirklich erschöpfeten. Den Erfolg, den man solchergestalt herausgebracht, nennet man eine Hypothese.* Ibid., 504.

43. *S'Gravesand beweiset, in seiner Einleitung in die Weltweisheit, die Zuverlässigkeit dieser (sc. induktiven) Schlüsse aus dem Willen Gottes, weil das allervollkommenste Wesen beständig nach allgemeinen Gesetzen handeln müsse. Allein ich trage Bedenken, den Grund unserer Experimentalschlüsse auf den Willen Gottes zu legen.* Ibid., 506. Wilhelm Jacob s'Gravesand's "Einleitung in die Weltweisheit," the German translation of his "Introductio ad philosophiam, logicam et metaphysicam" (1736), distinguishes

is Mendelssohn's discussion of the thesis, advanced by 'several sages', that if moral subjects are to be able to perform free acts, there must be a probability that is essentially unsurpassable even for an infinite intellect. That would necessarily affect both the definition of probability as an 'incomplete truth' and the traditional notion of omniscience. Yet freedom as conceived by Mendelssohn, namely as *indifferentia aequilibrii,* does not even allow for probable knowledge and would thus deny such knowledge even to God. This conclusion makes Mendelssohn resolve to set his own, deterministic conception against the idea of an essential probability: "I therefore believe that I have demonstrated, as much from the qualities of the divine as from common experience, that all arbitrary decisions must be preceded by their own particular certainty . . ."[44]

We indicated earlier the role played by 'verisimilitude' in the battles fought over the Copernican worldview. Here Mendelssohn gives us an opportunity to provide authenticating evidence for the transition from metaphorical to terminological discourse specifically in this regard: "The Copernican model of the universe is now widely acknowledged to be more probable than the old Ptolemaic model, even if, like its predecessor, it is not lacking in eccentricities and epicycles to explain all observed phenomena. In the more recent construction of the universe, however, everything is explained by simple postulates, and consequently traced back to a few causes; for the ancients had to think up a new hypothesis for each irregular phenomenon. One can thus to a certain extent gauge the degree to which the new construction of the world is more probable than the old one."[45] Assuming the number of observed phenomena to be identical, fewer factors are needed to explain these phenomena in the Copernican system than in the Ptolemaic. The smaller the number of factors needing to be admitted into the system, the more unlikely it is that each phenomenon could have a different cause. If I can adequately explain phenomena a, b, and c by cause d, then a theory that draws on causes A, B, and C to the same end will be the less probable. In Mendelssohn's words: "For since these phenomena a, b, c, etc., agree inasmuch as they can all be explained from a single cause d, this agreement would have to be regarded as a mere coincidence if each of these phenomena had its own separate cause. The probability of such a coincidence

---

between mathematical and moral evidence: "The former is in itself a characteristic of truth; the latter, however, exists because God wants it to exist, and pertains merely to a certain arrangement of things." (§582) Probability relates only to matters of moral evidence: "Probability stands in the middle between ignorance (!) and an insight that wants for nothing and gives rise to complete conviction" (§584).

44. *Ich glaube also aus den göttlichen Eigenschaften sowohl, als aus der gemeinen Erfahrung dargethan zu haben, daß alle willkürlichen Entschließungen zum voraus ihre bestimmte Gewißheit haben müssen* . . . (515).

45. *Das kopernikanische Weltgebäude wird jetzt durchgehends als wahrscheinlicher erkannt, als das alte ptolemäische, ob es gleich den Alten nicht an Excentricitäten und Epicyklen gefehlt haben dürfte, all nachher beobachtete Erscheinungen zu erklären. Allen nach dem neuern Weltgebäude erkläret man alles durch einfache Voraussetzungen, und folglich aus wenigen Ursachen; da die Alten für eine jede besondere Erscheinung auf eine neue Hypothese bedacht seyn mußten. Man kann also gewissermaßen den Grad der Wahrscheinlichkeit bestimmen, den das neue Weltgebäude vor dem alten voraus hat.*

= $1/n+1$; therefore the probability of the opposite case = $n/n+1$."[46] The logicization of probability implies the commensurability of hypothetical statements and thus requires a statement to be made about these statements. Metaphorical 'verisimilitude', which figured so prominently in the texts of the Copernican dispute, tended to neutralize the cosmological claim to truth that had been raised by Copernicus himself and, with incomparably greater pathos, by his successors.

Logicized probability becomes an instrument of the critical spirit, as another eighteenth-century document from the history of cosmology attests. In his "Essai de cosmologie,"[47] Maupertuis objects to the manner in which Newton used the uniformity of the planetary orbits to prove God's existence. Maupertuis shores up his argument by adjudging the chance occurrence of the fact that the planetary orbits all lie on a plane taking up only one-seventeenth of the imaginary sphere surrounding the solar system to be highly improbable. What he rejects, however, is precisely the idea that probability is an 'incomplete truth' that could somehow be converted into truth; no path leads from the improbability that the universe arose by chance to the necessity that it was brought into being by an act of will;[48] theories cannot even be compared here in probabilistic terms: "If one takes the earth's orbit as the blueprint for the other planetary orbits, and if one regards their position as the effect of chance, then the probability that the five other orbits should fall outside this zone is 17^5—1 to 1; that is to say, 1,419,856 to 1 . . . Some probability nevertheless remains, and one therefore cannot say that such uniformity is the necessary result of a choice."[49] Moreover, Newton found the alternative of conscious creation and chance occurrence compelling only because he was unable to identify a physical

---

46. *Denn da diese Erscheinungen a, b, c usw. dergestalt übereinstimmen, daß sie alle aus einer einzigen Ursache d erkläret werden können; so wäre diese Übereinstimmung als ein bloßer Zufall anzusehen, wenn eine jede Erscheinung ihre besondere Ursache haben sollte. Die Wahrscheinlichkeit eines solchen Zufalls* = $1/n+1$; *daher die Wahrscheinlichkeit des entgegengesetzten Falles* = $n/n+1$.

47. "Première partie, où l'on examine les preuves de l'existence de Dieu tirées des merveilles de la Nature," in *Oeuvres* (Lyon, 1768) 1, 8.

48. The hiatus between probability and truth is here no less unbridgeable than that claimed by Lessing for the relationship between *historical* probability and *religious* truth: *Die wunderbare Religion muß die Wunder wahrscheinlich machen, die bei ihrer ersten Gründung sollen geschehen sein. Aber auf die historische Wahrscheinlichkeit dieser Wunder die Wahrheit der Religion gründen; wenn das richtig, wenn das auch nur klug gedacht ist!—Es sei herausgesagt! Wenn ich jemals so richtig, so klug zu denken fähig bin, so ist es um meinen Verstand geschehen. Das sagt mir meinen Verstand itzt. Und habe ich jemals einen andern Verstand: so hatte ich nie einen.* [The miracle of this religion must render probable the miracles which are said to have occurred when it was first founded. But to base the truth of the religion on the historical probability of these miracles—is this right, or even well advised?—Let it be clearly stated: if I am ever capable of such right and well-advised thinking as this, my understanding has deserted me. My understanding tells me so now. And if ever I have an understanding other than this, I can never have had one in the first place.] *Eine Duplik,* 1778 (*Ges. Werke,* ed. Rilla, VIII, 36). ["A Rejoinder," in Gotthold Ephraim Lessing, *Philosophical and Theological Writings,* trans. H. B. Nisbet (Cambridge: Cambridge University Press, 2005), 105.]

49. *Si l'on prend donc l'orbe de la Terre pour le plan auquel on rapporte les autres, et qu'on regarde leur position comme l'effet du hasard, la probabilité, que les cinq autres orbes ne doivent pas être renfermés dans*

cause for the uniformity of the planetary motions; indeed, he did not even believe that such a cause was possible. Maupertuis cites a prize-winning essay by Daniel Bernoulli, "Sur l'inclinaison des plans des orbites des planètes" [On the Inclination of the Planetary Orbits], published in 1734 by the Paris Academy of Sciences, in which the problem was tackled by hypothesizing a fluid medium filling up cosmic space—not in order to throw his weight behind this hypothesis, but to underscore the vagueness of any approach based on considerations of probability. Here the critical function of the probability concept is maintained; but it would be exceeded before the century was out, as it was brought into connection with new metaphysical background representations: the infinity of time, permitting innumerable 'throws of the dice', makes it likely that *every* conceivable event, including the genesis of our world, occurred at random. The classic formulation of this idea was given by Diderot in the twenty-first of his "Pensées philosophiques," initially in relation to the chance emergence of the "Iliad": "According to the laws of probability . . . the occurrence of a possible event should cause me no surprise; and the improbability of the event can be compensated for by the number of throws . . . my advantage would even be infinite if the number of throws allowed were infinite too."[50] Once the premise has been established that matter is eternal and inherently motile, there result "an infinite number of marvelous arrangements proceeding from the infinite number of possible combinations," among which even so complicated an event as 'this world' assumes, in the eyes of the thinker, a degree of probability that leads him to exclaim: "It follows, then, that the mind ought to be astonished less by the actual birth of the universe than by a hypothetical continuation of the original chaos."[51] Newly wedded to the postulate of infinity, probability becomes capable of explaining everything. It is obvious that here a deity whose essential function had been to 'explain' the world has been usurped by infinite chance, eternal truth usurped by eternal probability; only the names have changed. For it is no less obvious that only a God who had himself been conceived as unfathomably arbitrary, as *deus mutabilissimus, could* be replaced by infinite chance, indeed that this substitution responded to a deeply felt need, as Diderot again makes clear: "The thought that a God does not exist has never terrified humanity, but the thought that there is such a God as the one represented to me is indeed terrifying."[52] It only appears

---

cette zone, est de 17⁵ – 1 à 1; c'est-à-dire, de 1 419 856 à 1 . . . Il y restoit cependant quelque probabilité, et dèslors on ne peut pas dire que cette uniformité soit l'effet nécessaire d'un choix.

50. *Selon les lois de l'analyse des sorts . . . je ne dois point être surpris qu'une chose arrive lorsqu'elle est possible, et que la difficulté de l'événement est compensée par la quantité des jets . . . mon avantage serait même infini si la quantité des jets accordée était infinie.* [Denis Diderot, *Diderot's Selected Writings,* trans. Derek Coltman (New York: Macmillan, 1966), 6.]

51. *dans la somme infinie des combinaisons possibles un nombre infini d'arrangements admirables . . . Donc, l'esprit doit être plus étonée de la durée hypothétique du chaos que de la naissance réelle de l'univers.* [Diderot, *Diderot's Selected Writings,* trans. Coltman, 6.]

52. *la pensée qu'il n'a point de Dieu n'a jamais effrayé personne, mais bien celle qu'il y en a un tel que celui qu'on me peint. Pensées philosophiques* (1746) IX. [Denis Diderot, *Diderot's Early Philosophical Works,* trans. Margaret Jourdain (New York: Burt Franklin, 1972), 30; translation modified.]

as though man is now at the mercy of physical chance in the same way that he had once been at the mercy of theological capriciousness. In fact, the emotional correlates are radically different, not least because chance conforms to laws that allow man to pit his existence *against* its blind decrees.

It is easy for us today to overlook a further field of importance in the history of the expression 'verisimilitude' (or 'probability'), the field of *aesthetics*. Our metaphysical elevation of the work of art has made us so accustomed to according art its own 'truth', or even 'truth' in special measure, that 'verisimilitude' strikes us as being too common and shabby a term to merit a place in discussions of art-theoretical questions. In classical aesthetics, by contrast, the opinion that 'verisimilitude' in works of art was preferable to 'truth' was frequently expressed. This was still conceived entirely within the bounds of Aristotelian poetics: mimesis concerns not the 'truth' of the 'real' in its concrete singularity and materiality, but the 'verisimilitude' of a universal devoid of real existence. Aesthetic verisimilitude sticks closely to the metaphorical meaning of the word, since what is considered essential to the work of art is not its *being* true, a quality that could be checked with reference to the facts 'out there', but its self-evidently *seeming* true. Lessing criticizes Caylus's thesis of the equivalence of poetry and painting in Homer by pointing out that the image of a goddess hurling a massive boulder, while possible in the epic, becomes a "manifest improbability" (*anschauliche Unwahrscheinlichkeit*) when imagined in a painting.[53] In another passage of "Laokoon" (XXIX), Lessing summarizes Winckelmann's argument that, "by merely imitating nature, art can no more attain perfection than poetry, and that both poet and painter must choose the impossible that is probable, rather than the merely possible."[54] Here, the two metaphorical meanings are conjoined in such a way that verisimilitude is seen to be 'mere semblance'—it simply cannot be true—while, on the other hand, this semblance is nonetheless the appearing of a truth that has nothing to do with the 'impossibly' unreal object depicted in the work of art. Kant would have been the most likely candidate to have drawn the conclusion overlooked by both Winckelmann and Lessing: that all reference to an object, as a contributing factor to the work's truth value, would have to be

---

53. *Laokoon* XII (*Werke*, ed. Rilla, V, 102). A striking explication of the 'probable' in Lessing can be found in the thirty-ninth of his "Briefe antiquarischen Inhalts" [Letters of Antiquarian Content] (V, 521). Lessing had revoked his interpretation of the Borgesian fencer in letter 38 and now seeks to defend the aesthetic value of the thesis as such: *In dem antiquarischen Studio ist es öfters mehr Ehre, das Wahrscheinliche gefunden zu haben, als das Wahre* [In the antiquarian studio, it is often more honorable to have found what is probable than what is true]. The justification given for this is important, since it views 'truth' as a purely receptive quality, whereas 'probability' is regarded as a productive quality: *Bei Ausbildung des erstern (sc. des Wahrscheinlichen der Chabrias-These) war unsere ganze Seele geschäftig: bei Erkennung des andern (sc. des faktischen Sachverhalts) kam uns vielleicht nur ein glücklicher Zufall zustatten* [In establishing the former (sc. the probability of the Chabrias theory), our entire soul was active; in recognizing the latter (sc. the factual state of affairs), it may be that only a happy coincidence came to our aid].

54. *sich durch die bloße Nachahmung der Natur das Höchste in der Kunst eben so wenig wie in der Poesie erreichen lasse, daß sowohl Dichter als Maler lieber das Unmögliche, welches wahrscheinlich ist, als das bloß Mögliche wählen müsse.* [Gotthold Ephraim Lessing, *The Laocoon, and Other Prose Writings of Lessing*, trans. W. B. Rönnfeldt (London: Walter Scott, n.d.), 77.]

dropped if the work of art were no longer to be regarded under the aspect of its 'verisimilitude', but solely under that of its 'truth'. As far as Lessing is concerned (to whom we shall confine ourselves so as not to cause this section to swell into a study in its own right), a more detailed investigation could show that his concept of aesthetic 'verisimilitude' corresponds very precisely to that of 'inner truth' in his philosophy of religion. 'Inner truth' signifies, above all, the independence of religious propositions from historical facts and their degree of verifiability.[55] The work of art's 'verisimilitude' is likewise an immanent quality manifested solely in its persuasive force, consigning to irrelevance the question of whether what is presented as a real occurrence in a fable, for example, bears any resemblance to what actually happened: "For we are only convinced of the truth of that which we have not beheld by its probability, or when, from the reasons given, it is more probable than otherwise. Now, as it is solely our internal sense of probability which produces our belief in the reality of an event, and as this inward sense of probability will apply equally to an invented case, what greater effect on my conviction is produced by the historical passage than by the invented fable?" Moreover, because "much may be historically true which is very improbable," whereas the poet "has full power" to "make everything appear probably which he offers as true," the fable is even to be preferred to the "historical example."[56] Lessing's reflections can be seen as contributing to the aesthetic extension of the doctrine of probability called for by Leibniz, and already transferred to the artistic domain by Johann Jakob Bodmer in his "Critischen Betrachtungen über die poetischen Gemählde der Dichter" [Critical Remarks on the Poetic Paintings of the Poets] (1741): "It is therefore to be deplored that so little progress has been made in the art of things probable, which not only has need of a deep thinker to expound it in dogmatic fashion, as frequently urged by Herr von Leibnitz, but which cuts a sorry figure indeed even in those places where it has been tried and tested in public."[57] Needless to say, Lessing was to play a decisive role in leading the problem away from the 'poetic paintings of the poets' and giving it a new, still unexhausted potentiality.

---

55. Compare the passages in the edition cited above, VIII, 171, 179, 189, 190, 193.

56. *Ich glaube bloß deswegen, daß ein Ding geschehen, und daß es so und so geschehen ist, weil es höchst wahrscheinlich ist, und höchst unwahrscheinlich sein würde, wenn es nicht, oder wenn es anders geschehen wäre. Da also einzig und allein die innere Wahrscheinlichkeit mich die ehemalige Wirklichkeit eines Falles glauben macht, und diese innere Wahrscheinlichkeit sich ebensowohl in einem erdichteten Falle finden kann: was kann die Wirklichkeit des erstern für eine größere Kraft auf meine Überzeugung haben, als die Wirklichkeit des andern? . . . das historisch Wahre nicht immer auch wahrscheinlich ist . . . freie Gewalt . . . alles, was er für wahr ausgibt, auch wahrscheinlich zu machen. Abhandlungen über die Fabel* I (IV, 45). [*Fables and Epigrams, with Essays on Fable and Epigram,* trans. anon. (London: John and H. L. Hunt, 1825), 100–101.]

57. *Darum kann ich nicht gutheißen, daß man so wenig Fleiß auf die Kunst der wahrscheinlichen Dinge wendet, welcher es nicht nur an einem tiefsinnigen Mann fehlet, der sie in einer dogmatischen Lehrart abhandle, wie schon Herr von Leibnitz vielfältig darauf gedrungen hat, sondern welche auch an denen Orten, wo sie sich in der Ausübung und Ausführung zeigen sollte, ziemlich mangelhaft erscheinet.*

IX

METAPHORIZED COSMOLOGY

The impression might arise that our lengthy exemplification of the 'transition' from metaphors to concepts (and thus our entire attempt at a typology of metaphor histories) remains beholden to a primitive evolutionary schema. We shall seek to dispel this impression by surveying a type of metaphor history that proceeds in the opposite direction, *from concepts to metaphors*. With respect to the evidence presented, we must fear having to hear the same reproach once leveled by Lessing against Privy Counselor Klotz: "And how many of them do you suppose that he cites? In all, *summa summarum,* rightly counted—one."[1] But we think this piece of historical evidence weighty enough to withstand the objection.

In 1543 there appeared in Nuremberg a work in six books by the Frauenburg canon Nicolas Copernicus, who died in the same year, entitled "De revolutionibus orbium caelestium" [On the Revolutions of Heavenly Spheres]. This work is a sober theoretical treatise that, where it does not define the terms with which it operates, borrows terms long since defined by others. It seeks to overcome the difficulties arising from the traditional Ptolemaic system for the phoronomic explanation of observational data by constructing a new model of the universe, bolstering its claim to legitimacy by pointing in good humanist fashion to a row of ancient

---

1. *und wie viele meinen Sie, daß er deren anführt? In allen, summa summarum, richtig gerechnet,—einen.*

precursors. There is not the slightest hint that this new astronomical conception—for all that its author wanted it to be taken as a true account of the divinely created cosmos, rather than as a theoretical model for calculations—was destined, more than anything else, to provide a new formula for how humans perceived themselves and their place in the universe.[2] The virulence with which a purely theoretical process could seize hold of people's imaginations was made explicit, at the very latest, when Goethe famously asserted in his "Materialien zur Geschichte der Farbenlehre" [Materials on the History of the Theory of Color] that "of all discoveries and opinions, none may have exerted a greater effect on the human spirit" than this astronomical restructuring of the universe. Goethe, to be sure, saw in this a "demand made on mankind," disclosing a "freedom of view and greatness of thought so far unknown, indeed not even dreamed of," after mankind's supposed securities and certainties had gone up in mist and smoke.[3] Yet Nietzsche took a diametrically opposed view of the same shift in self-awareness. For him, "the self-diminution of man" begins with Copernicus: "his faith in his dignity, uniqueness, irreplaceableness in the rank-ordering of beings" has gone; through the "defeat of theological astronomy," human existence has become "still more arbitrary, peripheral, and dispensable in the visible order of things."[4] That has been the prevailing tone of Copernican self-understanding ever since.[5] Even and especially where its scientific and theoretical consequences are embraced, the significance of the cosmological revolution for mankind is seen to lie in the fact "that the earth, humanity, the individual self, are all dethroned," that "man is no longer important for astronomy, at most for himself."[6] By a not entirely fortuitous historical irony, another work of seminal importance for the modern spirit was published in Basel in the same year, 1543, Vesalius's "Humani corporis fabrica" [On the Fabric of the Human Body], so that it was now easy to say that one had diminished and demeaned man (under

---

2. See Hans Blumenberg, "Der kopernikanische Umsturz und die Weltstellung des Menschen: Eine Studie zum Zusammenhang von Naturwissenschaft und Geistesgeschichte," *Studium Generale* VIII (1955): 637–48. [See also, and above all, Hans Blumenberg, *The Genesis of the Copernican World*, trans. Robert M. Wallace (Cambridge, MA: MIT Press, 1987).]

3. *unter allen Entdeckungen und Überzeugungen . . . nichts eine größere Wirkung auf den menschlichen Geist hervorgebracht . . . Forderung an die Menschheit . . . bisher unbekannten, ja ungeahnten Denkfreiheit und Großheit der Gesinnungen.* [Trans. cited in Stephen Hawking, introduction to *On the Revolutions of Heavenly Spheres*, by Copernicus (Philadelphia: Running Press, 2003), xvi.]

4. *Selbstverkleinerung des Menschen . . . der Glaube an seine Würde, Einzigkeit, Unersetzlichkeit in der Rangabfolge der Wesen . . . Niederlage der theologischen Astronomie . . . noch beliebiger, eckensteherischer, entbehrlicher in der sichtbaren Ordnung der Dinge. Zur Genealogie der Moral (Ges. Werke,* Musarion ed., XV, 438, 440). [Friedrich Wilhelm Nietzsche, *On the Genealogy of Morality,* trans. Keith Ansell-Pearson (Cambridge: Cambridge University Press, 2007), 115; translation modified.]

5. Dilthey is an important exception (*Weltanschauung und Analyse des Menschen seit Renaissance und Reformation* [Leipzig, 1921], 260): "Thus, the sovereign consciousness of the autonomy of the human intellect and its power over things was established through the great discoveries of Copernicus, Kepler, and Galileo, and through the attendant theory of nature's construction by logical-mathematical elements of consciousness given a priori."

6. Max Born, *Die Relativitätstheorie Einsteins,* 3rd ed. (Berlin, 1922), 10.

the dissecting knife) in the same way that the other had diminished and demeaned the earth, and that the church's resistance to them both bore a 'theological and humanistic' stamp.[7] Arthur Koestler has even spoken of a 'fateful shift': "We do not know how many thousands of years ago man first enquired about the meaning of life, but we do know at what point in time—terrifyingly close to our own—he lost the answer to that question."[8]

Such quotations could be multiplied more or less at will. These few will suffice to bring out the decisive point: they all have nothing to do with the process of the Copernican reform taken as a *theoretical, terminological* work of astronomy. They take what happened and was discovered there not as an item of knowledge, nor as an hypothesis, but *as a metaphor!* And an *absolute* metaphor at that, inasmuch as the Copernican reorganization of the cosmos was seen to provide an orienting model for the answer to a question that has never yet been answered by purely theoretical and conceptual means: the question of man's place in the universe, in the sense of his planned and purposeful centrality or his marginality to the cosmic motions and commotions in which he finds himself swept up—the question, that is, of how he stands in relation to everything else that exists and how it stands in relation to him. Geocentrism, heliocentrism, and acentrism were transformed into diagrams from which man's standing in the world was to be 'read off'. This bridling of our self-understanding by the cosmological metaphor has become a commonplace in contemporary critiques of our situation. In the process, the difference between the metaphorical interpretability of a theoretical event and the assumption of its causality for the interpretations to which it gives rise has long since been effaced. Not to mention that theoretical work's underlying intent: although Copernicus felt obliged to make drastic changes to the established construction of the cosmos, his intention was 'conservative' to the extent that he believed he would thereby be better able to preserve the principle of the universe's uniform rationality. In doing so, he endeavored to show that man, by virtue of the theoretical faculty with which he has been endowed, occupies the relational midpoint from which all of creation becomes intelligible.[9] This validation and demonstration upon an object still determined by its ancient divine status, and not yet relegated to the status of a 'natural object', was meant to signify a real self-confirmation for the human mind, not its metaphorical self-localization. Yet even where the positive implications of Copernicus's achievement are grasped, this occurs via the 'detour' of its metaphorization: man, no longer ensconced at the center of creation, is celebrated as a being that, even after it has forfeited its presumed teleological preeminence, still proves capable of contesting its existence and securing for itself its own, 'self-centered' universe. In other words,

---

7. G. Toffanin, *Geschichte des Humanismus* (1941), 268–69.

8. Cited by Margret Boveri in *Merkur* XI (1957): 1183.

9. See my study "Kosmos und System: Aus der Genesis der kopernikanischen Welt," *Studium Generale* X (1957): 61–80.

the Copernican world became a metaphor for the critical disfranchisement of the teleology principle, the removal of the *causa finalis* from the Aristotelian bundle of *causae*; and there can be no doubt that the Copernican metaphor formed the basis of a new self-consciousness, tied to man's cosmic eccentricity, which first allowed the process of deteleologization to make itself felt in all its pathos. Yet the geocentric and teleological 'reaction' that now set in, belatedly discovering all that the old worldview had 'meant' and how precious an asset it had been, also rested on such metaphoric realism. "Behind all the criticism of Copernicus there lurks the fear of cultural revolution; there is a reluctance to recognize life, seen for millennia from the viewpoint of stasis, as a dynamic force. That emerges clearly from Sir Christopher Heydon's 'Defence of Judiciall Astrologie' (1603): 'Copernicus altered the whole order of nature to rectifie his Hypothesis' (p. 386). Ptolemy, on the other hand, is an honest fellow with no intent to deceive (p. 161)."[10] The fact that geocentrism only came to be established as a theologumenon through Copernicus and the ensuing metaphorization of his reform also belongs in this context, comparable to those impulses in the history of Christian dogma that, stung into action by 'heresy', resulted in definitions that retrospectively sanctioned as 'orthodox' the beliefs and opinions from which the 'heterodox' had strayed. We find the argument that geocentrism constituted a theological *opinio communis* strikingly expressed in Bellarmine's letter to Foscarini from 12 April 1615.[11] Now there are doubtless any number of patristic and postpatristic texts one could quote in which the geocentric worldview is taken for granted and used to interpret the relevant biblical passages; but here it appears as a self-evident presupposition, not as an "opinion" (*doxa*) supported by scriptural authority. On the contrary, those patristic authors who were influenced by the Stoic tradition could adopt the Stoic foundation of teleological anthropocentrism upon geocentrism only with grave misgivings and difficulties, since for them the earth

---

10. P. Meissner, *Die geistesgeschichtlichen Grundlagen des englischen Literaturbarocks* (Munich, 1934), 62–63. The entire chapter "Makrokosmos und Mikrokosmos" (44–97) brings together a great deal of useful material about the metaphorical congruence of geocentrism and teleology within the Copernican 'reaction'.

11. First published in D. Berti, *Copernico e le vicende del sistema Copernicano* (Rome, 1876), 121–22. The decisive passage reads: *Dico che, come lei sa, il Concilio proibisce esporre le scitture contra il commune consenso de' Santi Padri, e se la P. V. vorrà leggere non dico solo il Santi Padri, ma il commentarii moderni sopra Giosuè, trovarà, che tutti convengono in esporre ad literam ch'il sole è nel cielo e gira intorno alla terra con somma veolcità e che la terra è lontanissima dal cielo e sta nel centro del mondo immobile. Consideri hora lei con la sua prudenza, se la chiesa possa supportare, che si dia alle scritture un senso contrario alli Santi Padri, et a tutti li espositori greci e latini.* [I say that, as you know, the Council prohibits interpreting Scripture against the common consensus of the Holy Fathers; and if Your Paternity wants to read not only the Holy Fathers, but also the modern commentaries on Genesis, the Psalms, Ecclesiastes, and Joshua, you will find all agreeing in the literal interpretation that the sun is in heaven and turns around the earth with great speed, and that the earth is very far from heaven and sits motionless at the center of the world. Consider now, with your sense of prudence, whether the Church can tolerate giving Scripture a meaning contrary to the Holy Fathers and to all the Greek and Latin commentators; trans. Maurice A. Finocchiaro, in *The Galileo Affair: A Documentary History* (Berkeley: University of California Press, 1989), 67–68.]

not only had to be the site of paradise as the ultimate teleological "place adapted to man" (*locus congruens homini*),[12] but equally the site of the ateleological, arduous existence eked out by man following his banishment from that blissful seat. No, the geocentric *opinio* is a theologumenon after the event, one that could first explicate itself by means of the Copernican metaphor. But on this late and violent explication rests the modern age's widely held conviction—truly an *opinio communis* on an *opinio communis!*—that geocentrism had been defended and debunked as a specifically Christian proposition. In reality, Christianity had no need of a cosmic metaphor for identifying man's place in the world. Christian theology 'knows' far too much about man, his position and purpose in the universe, for it to be conscious of a chink in its dogmatic defenses into which a metaphorically acquired answer would have to be projected. Such a projection had been undertaken by the Stoics, however, and neo-Stoicism, whose finely branched reception has received nothing like the attention it deserves, surely made a decisive contribution to the 'discovery' of the metaphorical potential contained in Copernicus's work.

One therefore cannot understand the metaphorization of the Copernican world, and with it the assumption of its formative influence on the modern mind, without analyzing the structurally analogous process by which the ancient geocentric cosmos, described above all by Aristotle, was transformed into a metaphor by the Stoics. To claim that one can "speak of a geocentric religiosity among the Greeks from Aristotle on," and that the "ideals of Aristotle" were at stake in this matter, is simply incorrect.[13] Geocentric cosmology had not the slightest metaphorical significance within the philosophical system that was to serve as its vehicle for two thousand years, and from which it drew its sanction: for Aristotle, the fact that the earth occupies the midpoint of the cosmos is utterly irrelevant to the question of man's place in the cosmos. There is a cosmological metaphorics in Aristotle, too, but it is constructed according to a different schema, proceeding from top to bottom rather than from the center to the periphery. In other words, it does not begin by bisecting the spherical cosmos but refers to any radius that can be drawn through it. The *center* of the whole is simultaneously the absolute *bottom* of the radially oriented hierarchy of cosmic elements. In "De caelo" (II, 13), Aristotle discusses a metaphorical view of cosmic 'positions' that has much in common with the later metaphorization of his own cosmology: the cosmology of the Pythagoreans. Precisely because they regarded the center of the universe as the most honorable place (τιμιωτάτη χώρα), the Pythagoreans could not, starting out from these premises (ἐκ τούτων ἀναλογιζόμενοι), assign the earth this position, reserving it instead for the most honorable element, fire (293a30–34). Aristotle himself believes "that which encompasses and sets bounds" to be worthier than "that which is bounded,"

12. [The definition is taken from Aquinas, *Summa theol.* 1 q. 102 a. 2 ad 2.]

13. E. Goldbeck, *Der Mensch und sein Weltbild im Wandel vom Altertum zur Neuzeit: Gesammelte kosmologische Abhandlungen* (Leipzig, 1925), 22, 60.

and if the starting point (ἀρχήν) possesses the highest dignity, then the center of the universe is what is lowest and last (293b11–14). Yet this value hierarchy is not the principle underlying the real cosmic structure, since the congruence of the center of the earth and the center of the universe is only accidental (κατὰ συμβεβηκός), best being understood as the result of a physical process (297a12–14; b14–17).[14] Aristotle here clearly delimits his own theory from a view that wants not only to find confirmation for the correspondence of the value hierarchy with the real order of things in space, but also to derive the latter from the former. As far as man and his self-understanding are concerned, there is nothing to be inferred from this whole structure. While man is teleologically privileged, this privilege is conceived solely within the parameters of the axiom that nature does nothing in vain; accordingly, the anthropocentric teleology pertains only to the region in which and from which he contests his existence. The relation to mankind is confined to the sublunary sphere, and one cannot regard the entire cosmos in the aspect of how man, by no means the highest thing in the cosmos (τὸ ἄριστον τῶν ἐν τῷ κοσμῷ),[15] is positioned within it. Man's faculties have been laid out with the utmost economy, fitting him for the preservation of life rather than its fulfillment; such economy permits one to say that everything he needs is to be found in sublunary nature, not that it has been placed there solely for his benefit. From Aristotle's statements on teleology, one could equally conclude that man is there so that all the other beings that serve his needs will not have existed in vain. We should avoid viewing the Aristotelian doctrine of teleology through the distorting lens of its Stoic and Christian reception. This cosmos is not a construct centered around a midpoint; still less *is* man this midpoint or its pampered beneficiary. Entirely missing from Aristotle, too, is the aesthetic dimension that comes to the fore in Stoicism, giving man the partner role, indispensable for the beautiful, of spectator and admirer—a metaphorical consideration that finally concedes him a central function in the cosmos.

The Stoics used the geocentric cosmos as a metaphor for their anthropocentric teleology. They took up the teleological connection to gods and mortals in one of their numerous definitions of the cosmos, which go back at least to Chrysippus.[16] The center of the cosmos derives its physical preeminence above all from a new view of the *unity* of the universe, now understood as dynamic rather than eidetically static in its structure: the *subsistence* of the universe as such is no longer self-evidently eternal, as it had been for Aristotle, but an immanent and self-consuming 'achievement' of this whole, especially of its dominant element, fire, which constitutes the shape of the universe (as creative fire, πῦρ τεχνικόν) before devouring it

---

14. [Aristotle, *On the Heavens,* trans. W. K. C. Guthrie (Cambridge, MA: Harvard University Press, 2000), 217–19, 245.]

15. *Nicomachean Ethics* VI 7; 1141a 20–b3. [Aristotle, *Nicomachean Ethics,* trans. H. Rackham (Cambridge, MA: Harvard University Press, 2003), 343.]

16. *Stoicorum Veterum Fragmenta,* coll. Arnim (= *SVF*) II, 527.

again in its degenerate form (as destructive fire, πῦρ ἄτεχνον). As soul (πνεῦμα), fire gives the whole its tone (τόνος) in an eternally recurring, self-consuming cycle, guaranteeing the unity (ἕνωσις) of the universe and everything in it (*SVF* II 458; I 497). To be able to imagine this dynamic unity, the Stoics had to abandon the statically stratified Aristotelian doctrine of a proper place (τόπος οἰκεῖος) specific to each element. That, in turn, meant detaching the theory of 'natural movements' from this topography. The basic, elemental movement is now *centripetal,* abstracted from downward flight and interpreted as the continuous, self-impelled rotation of the cosmos. This idea, which can be gleaned from a Chrysippus quotation in Plutarch (*SVF* II 550), is already dogmatically ascribed to Zeno: "All the parts of the cosmos have a compulsion to travel toward its center."[17] The whole cosmos is subject to a single law of motion, capable of explaining both the subsistence of the cosmos in the infinite void and the localization of the earth at its center. How this law of motion is itself to be explained can only be surmised from the fragments that have come down to us: the turning of all parts of the cosmos toward the middle appears to correspond to the all-governing principle of οἰκείωσις—self-constitution, self-finding, self-preservation—inasmuch as this middle, representing the point in the cosmos at the furthest remove from κενόν = μὴ ὄν |emptiness = nonbeing|, simultaneously offers the greatest security against the onslaught of nothingness. Everything strives to push its way back to the sheltering womb of Being, so to speak; that is an authentically Stoic idea: "It is said that the cosmos endures in infinite emptiness due to its impetus toward the center."[18] The attraction exerted by the center as the highest concentration of Being is accordingly determined by the metaphysical presupposition that Being, squeezed into a cosmic ball, must struggle to subsist while under constant threat from the surrounding void (*SVF* II 549). This dualistic premise inverted the Aristotelian cosmos, especially when one considers that the higher and highest ontological dignity had been transferred from the periphery of the cosmos, indeed from beyond its outermost sphere (where the Aristotelian unmoved mover dwells), to its center. Despite this inversion, however, the solution to the problem of kinetic causality in the cosmos remained *formally* the same as in the Aristotelian schema: the Supreme Being, now the midpoint of the universe, is unmoved as a point, yet moved through the attractive force it exerts on everything else that exists. Striving to secure its own existence, and so come 'to itself', each of these other 'eccentric' beings presses toward the center. In doing so, it necessarily displaces something else *from* the center, giving rise to an incessant circulation of elements. For each physical element, the center itself remains an essentially unattainable and ideal goal, like the unmoved mover for the eros of the first sphere. At bottom, what is sought here in metaphorical terms—the Stoic cosmos is an organism (ζῷον) no less than the Platonic—is the mystery of a subject's

---

17. πάντα τὰ μέρη τοῦ κόσμου ἐπὶ τὸ μέσον τοῦ κοσμου τὴν φορὰν ἔχειν. *SVF* I 99.
18. φασὶ δὲ μένειν τὸν κόσμον ἐν ἀπείρῳ κενῷ διὰ τὴν ἐπὶ τὸ μέσον φοράν. *SVF* II 554.

self-identity under the presuppositions of a materialistic metaphysics, and this is conceived as the constant availability of a totality of elements for a center. The cosmos literally 'comes' to itself at its center, grasping itself in the totality of its parts. It is easy to see how, through a curious 'translation', the inversion of the Aristotelian cosmos has retained not only the functions but also the immanent essence of the 'unmoved mover': centripetal movement is nothing other than thought thinking itself (νόησις νοήσεως) in materialized form.

For the Stoics, man thus exists at a metaphysically distinguished cosmic location, and he may justifiably refer this whole cosmic arrangement to himself and his needs. Developing elements of the Platonic "Timaeus" in particular, the Stoics bestowed upon man his loftiest definition as 'contemplator of the heavens' (*contemplator coeli*), lending this concept an aesthetic as well as theoretical significance. The church fathers sought to tack on the theological dimension by 'lengthening' the perspective of the *contemplator coeli,* so to speak,[19] but they thereby abandoned the inverted Aristotelianism of the ancient Stoics and paved the way for the medieval 'mixed form', in which the Aristotelian construction was inflected by Stoic emotional accents. For the Stoics, the congruence of geocentrism and anthropocentrism provided a securely confirmed principle for making sense of the world. If a Stoic astronomer wanted to prove that the cosmos was homogeneous and without void, he could always argue that if the cosmos were indeed heterogeneously composed, the human senses could not be reached by everything contained within it. The universe would thus not be fully accessible to our perception, and this possibility is ruled out by the anthropocentric premise (Cleomedes, *SVF* II 546). The popular *consensus* argument had a similar metaphysical foundation: we can be quite sure that the gods exist, since otherwise religion would be a monstrously wasteful investment, a possibility excluded on teleological grounds: as the midpoint and reference point of the entire cosmos, man can do nothing in vain in terms of how he allocates his existential resources.[20] Explicitly or implicitly, 'everything for the sake of man' (*omnia hominum causa*) was the principle applied without question and without fail to problems of a metaphysical and physical nature, a general presupposition underpinning the Stoic understanding of the world. Two doctrinal elements of independent origin thus flow together in medieval cosmology, amalgamating into the durable compound that would determine the divergence of opinions after Co-

---

19. This still occurs without the interposition of a deductive procedure (such as that found in the cosmological proof of God) through an act of direct and almost physiognomic perception: *homo autem recto statu, ore sublimi ad contemplationem mundi excitatus confert cum deo vultum et rationem ratio cogniscit* (Lactantius, *De ira Dei* 7, 5). [But man, with his erect position, with his elevated countenance raised to the contemplation of the universe, compares his features with God, and reason recognises reason; *Ante-Nicene Fathers,* ed. Alexander Roberts and James Donaldson, trans. William Fletcher (Peabody, MA: Hendrikson Publishers, 2004), VII, 263.] Under Stoic premises there can be no transcendence, which would entail a leap into the void (or nonexistence). At the same time, however, we see here that the Stoics' attempt to dissolve the connection between the celestial and the divine failed to 'catch on'.

20. Sextus Empiricus, *Adv. math.* IX 61, 123 sq.

pernicus: on the one hand, the dreaded dethronement of man through the demise of geocentrism; on the other, the welcomed liberation from anthropocentric teleology through the same process. What was overlooked, however, is that Copernicus sacrificed the ballast of a cosmology whose effectiveness was purely metaphorical precisely in order to salvage for man his theoretical determination as *contemplator coeli,* a being fit for the truth and rationally equal to the cosmos. He thereby set out to redeem at a higher level the principle of *omnia hominum causa* as well, reprised in the 'world made for us' (*mundus propter nos conditus*) of the dedicatory preface to the "Revolutiones."[21] Copernicus preferred to discard the image for the sake of the matter to which it referred; yet as we have seen, what prevailed in the reception history of Copernicanism was the eye-catching superficiality of the metaphor instead.

Metaphorical realism is a factor of the first importance in the formation of historical life. No paradigm is better suited to demonstrating this than the one discussed here. Subtle idealizations, such as those undertaken by Copernicus on the model of teleological anthropocentrism, fail to take hold and revert to their metaphorical quality. The replacement of the central *position* by a central *function* proved unable to establish itself as a legitimate 'transition', even if it was wrested as an 'achievement' from man's metaphorical eccentricity; this much has already emerged from our discussion of truth metaphorics. Indeed, the direction in which the metaphorization of the Copernican cosmology unfolded was by no means so rigidly predetermined as Nietzsche, for one, would have us believe. An important role—albeit one we can no longer adequately comprehend today, although its effects continue to be felt in the axiomatic foundation of astromomy—was played by the 'stellarization' of the earth, its classification among the other heavenly bodies. Theoretically, this had the sobering consequence (first put into practice by Galileo) that the earth could now be taken as the starting point for physical extrapolations, and thus utilized as a cosmological paradigm. But Copernican pathos sought and found food for metaphor in this: Galileo prides himself on having *raised* the earth to the rank of a star, and he lets the foolish Simplicio (in the "Dialogo") give vent to his violent antipathy on just this point. Many specific interests of Galilean research and speculation can only be understood against the metaphorical background of the earth's stellar 'elevation'. Aristotle had been able to defend himself against the worldview of the Pythagoreans by drawing attention to the logical consequence that would arise from their construction, namely, that the earth would be one of the stars (ἓν τῶν ἄστρων)[22]—a consequence whose absurdity he took entirely for granted, probably due to the unquestioned and unattainable divinity in which the stars still stood for him. Notwithstanding the altered theological premises, the Middle Ages proved reluctant to challenge Aristotle's authority on this point, in-

---

21. [Copernicus, *On the Revolutions,* trans. Edward Rosen (Cracow: Polish Scientific Publishers, 1978), 4.]

22. *De caelo* II 13; 293a21–23; 296a25. [Aristotle, *On the Heavens,* trans. Guthrie, 217.]

sisting on the stars' quasi-divine special nature; this was still causing headaches for Tycho Brahe when he came to interpret the 'new star' (*Stella Nova*) that appeared in Cassiopeia in 1572. This mythic status plays into the metaphor of the earth's stellarization, which a more sober appraisal of the methodological situation would have greater cause to describe as a tellurization of the stars. After all, the assumption that the laws governing the universe are homogeneous with the stuff from which the universe is made meant that terrestrial findings could now be projected onto extraterrestrial phenomena. But the metaphor is unconcerned with theoretically verifiable problems, such as those that could be settled by sending astronauts on fact-finding missions into outer space; it wants to know 'more' than any space probe will ever be able to ascertain. The earth as a 'star among stars' is primarily a metaphysical index. Nicolaus of Cusa first made it as much in the twelfth chapter of book II of his "Docta ignorantia" [Of Learned Ignorance], where he lists the two characteristics that, for Galileo, would guarantee the earth's stellar essence: motion and brightness (or receptivity to light). For Cusanus, it is no longer true "that this earth is the basest and lowest planet."[23] To an observer from some other planet, the earth would appear no less luminous a body than the sun, since the fiery mantle that, for us, is hidden from view can only be seen from outside. "The earth, then, is a brilliant star having a light, heat and influence distinctively its own"—even the earth's astrological equality, its power to shape the destiny of beings on other stars, is taken into account, as the technical term *influentia* suggests.[24] Precisely the illusion that we stand at the center of the universe is what first gave rise to the impression that the earth is only passively influenced by these other stars and does not exert an influence of its own: "We have no knowledge from experience of that influence, since we have no experience beyond that of our existence in the center where the influences merge."[25] Having become one star among others, the earth forfeits any special qualities that man could refer to himself and his standing in the universe. Cusanus puts an end to the earth's relegation within the Aristotelian system of elements, but no new trait has been won in the process. For Cusanus, however, that is the decisive advance: the earth's cosmological neutrality as a star among stars now allows man to grace this one star with the metaphysical distinction of his presence: "Rather than think that so many stars and parts of the heavens are uninhabited and that this earth of ours alone is peopled—and that with beings, perhaps, of an inferior type—we will suppose that in every region there are inhabitants, differing in nature by rank and all owing their origin to God, who is the center and circumference of all stellar regions. Now, even if inhabitants of another kind should exist

---

23. *quod terra ista sit vilissima et infima.* [Nicholas of Cusa, *Of Learned Ignorance,* trans. Germain Heron (London: Routledge & Kegan Paul, 1954), 112.]

24. *Est igitur terra stella nobilis, quae lumen et calorem et influentiam habet.* [Nicholas of Cusa, *Of Learned Ignorance,* trans. Heron, 113.]

25. *et cum non experiamur nos aliter quam in centro esse, in quo confluunt influentiae, de ista refluentia nihil experimur.* [Nicholas of Cusa, *Of Learned Ignorance,* trans. Heron, 114.]

on the other stars, it seems inconceivable that, in the line of nature, anything more noble and perfect could be found than the intellectual nature that exists here on this earth and its region. The fact is that man has no longing for any other nature but desires only to be perfect in his own."[26] This remarkable text marks a caesura in the history of human self-understanding. For the first time, the attempt is made to break the power of cosmological metaphorics over human self-awareness. The hierarchical gradations of the Aristotelian cosmos are literally razed to the ground; the earth is no longer the universe's dark and heavy sediment, nor a privileged center of attraction for cosmic strivings in the Stoic sense, but merely one astral body among others without any distinguishing features. All that relieves the ordinariness of this natural object we call the 'earth' is the quite accessory fact that it happens to be populated by human beings. Solely the metaphysics of man—the "second god" (alter deus), the creative intellect, the "internal founder of the world" (conditor mundi internus)—distinguishes this cosmic point that, in physical terms, scarcely differs from any other. One sees that this conception, which was to exert such a lasting influence on Renaissance anthropology, has no use for a geocentric cosmology, indeed that it must emphatically reject the all too generous 'allowances' such a cosmology makes for man—cause enough for Cusanus, aided by his axiom of imprecision, to dislodge the earth from the center of the universe without having any new constructive solution in mind. Unlike most of his commentators, who purport to see in him a forerunner of modern astronomy and natural science, Cusanus shows not the slightest interest in this question. He is more concerned with pursuing what might be called a *negative metaphorics:* a being of man's metaphysical dignity must learn to do without the geocentric metaphorics that has steered his self-conception hitherto.

Galileo undoubtedly never arrived at this point. When he sings his own praises for having raised the earth from the sediment of the universe[27] to a star, the Cusan

---

26. *nam et si deus sit centrum et circumferentia omnium regionum stellarum et ab ipso diversae nobilitatis naturae procedant in qualibet regione habitantes, ne tot loca coelorum et stellarum sint vacua et non solum ista terra fortassis de minoribus habitat, tamen intellectuali natura, quae hic in hac terra habitat et in sua regione, non videtur nobilior atque perfectior dari posse secundum hanc naturam, etiam si alterius generis inhabitatores sint in aliis stellis. Non enim appetit homo aliam naturam, sed solum in sua perfectus esse.* [Nicholas of Cusa, *Of Learned Ignorance,* trans. Heron, 114–15.]

27. The formula of the sediment and excrement of the universe, so handy as a foil to the earth's stellarization—*non autem sordium mundanarumque fecum sentinam esse demonstrabimus,* Galileo writes in his "Siderius nuncius" of 1610 [I will prove that the Earth ... is not the place where the dull refuse of the universe has settled down]—appears to have originally illustrated the process by which the earth came to be deposited in the middle of the universe. [Galileo Galilei, *The Sidereal Messenger,* trans. Edward Stafford Carter (London: Dawsons, n.d.), 38.] Otherwise, it would hardly be likely to have been connected in ancient Stoic texts with the emphasis placed on the earth's central position: ὑποσταθμὴν δὲ πάντων τὴν γῆν, μέσην ἁπάντων οὖσαν [The earth is the foundation of everything, being at the center of all] (*SVF* I, 105). The anti-Stoic polemics of the Epicureans may have exploited this metaphorically, as Lucretius V 496 sq. leads us to suppose: *Sic igitur terrae concreto corpore pondus / constitit atque omnis mundi quasi limus in imum / confluxit gravis et subsedit funditus ut faex . . .* [In this way, therefore, the heavy earth became solid with compact body, and all the mud of creation, so to speak, flowed to-

view that the earth owes its preeminence solely to the general nature of mankind has been forgotten, replaced by the feat of an intellect that, in 'single-mindedly' bringing about a shift in worldview, credits itself with having converted a metaphor derogatory to mankind into its opposite. This metaphorical understanding of the theoretical act, as a deed that impinges upon the matter itself, recurs time and again as a stylistic trait of Copernican pathos. We still find it concisely reflected in Friedrich Tieck's inscription on the Copernicus monument in Torun: "Mover of the Earth, Holder of the Sun and the Heavens" (*Terrae Motor, Solis Caelique Stator*). It may be that such heroic phraseology had been coined in advance by the enemy camp; an unpublished manuscript of the Jesuit Inchofer, who acted as a consultant in the trial of Galileo, bears the title "Vindiciae sedis apostolicae . . . adversus Neo-Pythagoreos terrae motores et solis statores" [Opinions of the Apostolic Seat . . . against the Neo-Pythagoreans, the Movers of the Earth and Holders of the Sun].[28] In this context, it is important to note that in the texts documenting the Galileo affair, the question of the central body recedes in significance behind the alternative 'stationary earth/mobile earth'. Several factors go hand in hand here: the well-known passage in Joshua, which presupposes solar motion, at the very least; then also the metaphysical dignity accorded the unmoved in the Aristotelian system; most of all, perhaps, the interest shown by Galileo in the movement of the earth, since if this could be proved, its stellar rank would count for him as assured. Today, we see the right and merit of this interest in the fact that it created, in the axiom of the homogeneous universe, one of the essential prerequisites for an astronomy that operated with physical laws and concepts; a historical inquiry, however, must bear in mind that this interest was sustained by Galileo's Copernican pathos, emblematized in the stellarization of the earth. One could say that Galileo resolves 'upward' the Aristotelian (and Ptolemaic) dualism of sublunary and supralunary worlds; thus the discovery of the moon's similarity with the earth, far from leading him to conclude that the moon is something like a smaller 'earth', prompts him to approximate the earth to a kind of cosmic being that, since Aristotle, had been deemed incomparably superior to all things terrestrial. It says a great deal about the immanent 'interest' of Galileo's cosmology that he seeks to uphold the stellar world's Aristotelian primacy in order that the earth, too, may now partake of it, rather than 'tellurizing' the stars, which is what *methodologically* in fact occurs. That is why the earth must move—and in a perfect circle at that!—and shine like the other stars.

---

gether by its weight and settled to the bottom like dregs; Lucretius, *De rerum natura,* trans. W. H. D. Rouse, rev. Martin Ferguson Smith (Cambridge, MA: Harvard University Press, 2002), 417.] Yet even in the School itself, Poseidonius deviated from the geocentric line by glorifying the sun; Plutarch, in his text "De facie in orbe lunae" (a major source for both Galileo and Kepler), ascribes to him the formula of the earth as ὑποσταθμὴ καὶ ἰλὺς τοῦ παντός [the sediment and dregs of the universe] (940e). [Plutarch, *Moralia, Volume XII,* trans. Harold Cherniss and William C. Helmbore (Cambridge, MA: Harvard University Press, 2001), 179.]

   28. Cf. H. Grisar, *Galileistudien* (Regensburg, 1882), 168.

Galileo's lively interest in the phenomenon of tidal flows is aimed at gathering evidence for the earth's absolute motion.[29] Much time is spent discussing this point on the fourth day of the "Dialogo." Galileo wants to do more than just shore up the Copernican system.[30] His strict adherence to the exact circularity of the planetary orbits, and hence now to the circularity of the earth's orbit as well, likewise belongs in the context of this tendency to have the earth partake of the characteristics of the utmost cosmic perfection. Not Simplicio, but the 'authorized' Salviati is the speaker who deduces circular motion as the stigma of perfection,[31] a position that even Kepler, so much more convinced of the sacredness of the basic geometric figures, could abandon. For Galileo, however, the 'sign' of the circle further indicates both the earth's 'equality' with the stars and the dignity of the standing it has thereby acquired—for what would the earth's elevation to stellar rank matter if the metaphysical privileges enjoyed by this cosmic aristocracy were to be secularized at the same time! Galileo's oft-criticized Aristotelianisms and teleological deductions are anchored in this metaphorical background; they formally conserve the 'position' to which the earth can now be raised. The characteristic of the earth's luminosity also bears on this interest: the well-known phenomenon of ash-gray moonlight following a new moon, correctly interpreted by Galileo as sunlight reflected by the earth, counts for him as proof that the earth could not be what the ancients had proclaimed it to be: the darkest, most light-sensitive of bodies. In the "Sidereus nuncius" (1610), Galileo gives advance notice of his "System of the World" where, he announces, "by very many arguments and experimental proofs, there is shown to be a very strong reflexion of the Sun's light from the Earth, for the benefit of those who urge that the Earth must be separated from the starry host, chiefly for the reason that it has neither motion nor light."[32] The motivation of a great theoretical complex in the form of a metaphor could be no more beautifully presented: what the historian of science, retrospectively searching for the basis on which a discipline established a sequence of results, takes for a rational and methodical foundation (in this case, the universal principle of homogeneity) shoots up from an underground of impulses formed on images, impulses that draw both their force and their direction from representations of a metaphorical kind. The critical and receptive relationship to tradition takes second place to the regulation of overriding metaphorical 'needs'; where Galileo has need of Aristotelianism in order to bring out the required difference in status for the earth's Copernican triumph, he is prepared to recognize its authority; where it stands in his way, he dismisses it without further ado. Thus he vehemently polemicizes against the metaphysical evaluation of the

---

29. A point already made by E. Goldbeck, 129 ff.

30. "We see from this just how important it was for him to be able to prove the earth's movement, and thereby secure it a place among the heavenly bodies" (Goldbeck, 131).

31. *Giornata prima,* ed. Albèri, I, 24. [Galileo Galilei, *Dialogue on the Great World Systems,* trans. Thomas Salusbury (Chicago: University of Chicago Press, 1953), 22.]

32. *Opere,* ed. nazionale, II, 75. [Galileo, *The Sidereal Messenger,* trans. Carter, 37–38.]

difference between rest and motion prescribed for the tradition by Aristotle's unmoved mover; here, too, what is at stake is the earth's rehabilitation as the site of
incessant change, growth, and decay: "It is my opinion that the Earth is very noble
and admirable by reason of the many and different alterations, mutations, genera-
tions, etc., which incessantly occur in it."[33] Had the earth frozen into an "immense
globe of crystal" void of all growth, decay, and transformation, comparable to the
spherical shells of antiquity, "I should have esteemed it a wretched lump of no benefit to the Universe, a mass of idleness, and in a word superfluous, exactly as if it
had never been in Nature."[34] This radical, truly 'Copernican' turn, which takes the
astronomically necessitated mobilization of the earth in Copernicus only as the
metaphorical occasion for a transvaluation of the ultimate metaphysical standards,
was passed over in silence by the Congregation of the Index and the inquisitorial
tribunals. It is nonetheless striking that the censorship decree of 1616 characterizes
each of the condemned propositions as "foolish and absurd in philosophy,"[35] particularly when one considers that philosophical censorship was so rare (because so
difficult to justify) in curial practice.[36] For Galileo, the philosophical tradition defended in this way stands under the entry "the vanity of popular discourse," since
any talk of the earth's baseness, or that of the element of which it consists, is arrant
folly; the worth of a matter (or its lack thereof) is for him merely relative, depending on its scarcity and plenty—and so it is with the precedence enjoyed by the unmoved and eternal over the moved and temporal: fear of death, and the great desire
to tarry in this world, made men extol incorruptibility and inalterability, without
considering that "if men had been immortal, they would not have had to come into
the world."[37] Only as a moved star does the earth represent the form of being ap-

---

33. *Io per me reputo la Terra nobilissima ed ammirabile per le tante e si diverse alterazioni, mutanzioni,*
generazioni, etc., che in lei incessabilmente si fanno. Giornata prima (Sagredo), ed. Albèri, I, 67. [Galileo,
Dialogue on the Great World Systems, trans. Salusbury, 68.]

34. *globo immense di cristallo . . . io la stimerei un corpaccio inutile al mondo, pieno di ozio e, per dirla*
in breve, superfluo e come se non fusse in natura. [Galileo, *Dialogue on the Great World Systems,* trans. Salusbury, 68.]

35. *stultam et absurdam in Philosophia.* Cited in Grisar, 38. [*The Galileo Affair,* trans. Finocchiaro,
146.]

36. See Grisar, 224. The 1633 sentence against Galileo also repeats the *proposizione assurda e falsa in*
filosofia [proposition that is philosophically absurd and false], followed by the *formamente eretica* [for-
mally heretical]. Of interest here is the nuance that the *philosophical* censorship for both of the condemned Galilean theses—the heliostatic and the geokinetic—has the same wording, whereas the
theological censorship condemns the first in much stronger terms—namely, as formally heretical—than
the second (*ad minus erronea in fide* [at least erroneous in the Faith]). The church does not defend Aris-
totelian-Stoic geocentrism with the same zeal as the miracle of the solar standstill in Joshua. [*The Gal-*
ilei Affair, trans. Finocchiaro, 288.] The 1664 decree placing all Copernican writings on the Index has
nothing to say about the problem of which body occupies the center of the universe, condemning only
libri omnes docentes mobilitatem terrae et immobilitatem solis [all books that teach that the earth moves
and the sun does not].—So 'valiant' an anti-Copernican as the mathematics professor in Bologna, G. A.
Magini, had denounced the Copernican worldview in his "Confutatio diatribae Scaligeri" (1617) as an
affront to philosophy.

37. *vanità de i discorsi populari . . . e non considerano che quando gli uomini fussero immortali, a loro non*
toccava a venire al mondo. [Galileo, *Dialogue on the Great World Systems,* trans. Salusbury, 69.]

propriate to man, not the form of being assumed by his illusions and fears. Metaphorized Copernicanism explicates itself as the ontological model of the modern age.

The road leading from the ennoblement of the earth in Galileo to Nietzsche's lament about "man's diminution since Copernicus"[38] appears long indeed. Following its twists and turns would mean laying bare an essential vein in the 'inner history' of the modern age; that cannot be our task here. Leaping forward half a century, I want to show only how the Copernican metaphor begins to acquire a certain ambivalence through the spirit of the early Enlightenment, as mirrored in Fontenelle's famous "Entretiens sur la pluralité des mondes" |Conversations on the Plurality of Worlds| (1686). In the conversation with the marchioness on the first evening, the discussion turns to the relationship between geocentrism and anthropocentric teleology. It is remarkable that Fontenelle, far from deriving the teleological principle from the geocentric illusion, declares the teleological presumption to be so ingrained in human nature that it created the geocentric system for purposes of illustration and confirmation. Fontenelle apostrophizes the aesthetic component of Stoic geocentrism in particular: "When we enquire of some philosophers the use of such a prodigious number of fixed stars, of which a smaller proportion would have been sufficient for all the offices they appear to perform; they coolly answer, they were made to gratify our sight. On this selfish principle it was for a long time supposed that the earth was motionless in the midst of the universe, whilst all the heavenly bodies were created for the sole purpose of journeying round, and distributing their light to her."[39] A very modern irony appears here in Copernican guise.

---

38. No. 18 in Nietzsche's first index to the "Will to Power" plan of 1887 (Musarion ed., XIX, 386).

39. *quand on demande à nos philosophes à quoi sert ce nombre prodigieux d'étoiles fixes, dont une partie suffirait pour faire ce qu'elles font toutes, ils vous répondent froidement qu'elles servent à leur réjouir la vue. Sur ce principe on ne manqua pas d'abord de s'imaginer qu'il fallait que la terre fût un repos au centre de l'univers, tandis que tous les corps célestes qui étaient faits pour elle, prendraient la peine de tourner à l'entour pour l'éclairer.* |Bernard le Bovier de Fontenelle, *Conversations on the Plurality of Worlds*, trans. Elizabeth Gunning (London: J. Cundee, 1803), 13–14.| In order to understand which position Fontenelle may have had in mind here, consider—together with the material cited earlier—the following passage from Seneca's "De otio" (c. 5, 3 sq.): *Curiosum nobis ingenium natura dedit et artis sibi ac pulchritudinis suae conscia spectatores nos tantis rerum spectaculis genuit, perditura fructum sui* (i.e., by depriving herself of the fulfillment of her self-enjoyment), *si tam magna, tam clara, tam subtiliter ducta, tam nitida et non uno genere formosa solitudini ostenderet.* |Nature has bestowed upon us an inquisitive disposition, and being well aware of her own skill and beauty, has begotten us to be spectators of her mighty array, since she would lose the fruit of her labour if her works, so vast, so glorious, so artfully contrived, so bright and so beautiful in more ways than one, were displayed to a lonely solitude.| (The appearing manifold is here presupposed as self-presentation in which a formative principle makes itself perceptible; that is an important intermediate link between the Platonic demiurge, who is only bound to his constructive program by the exemplary world of ideas, and the Christian concept of creation, reflected in the idea of revelation.) *Ut scias illam spectari voluisse, non tantum aspici, vide quem nobis locum dederit: in media nos sui parte constituit et circumspectum omnium nobis dedit; nec erexit tantummodo hominem, sed etiam habilem contemplationi factura, ut ab ortu sidera in occasum labentia prosequi posset et vultum suum circumferre cum toto, sublime fecit illi caput et collo flexibili imposuit . . .* |That you may understand how she wished us, not merely to behold her, but to gaze upon her, see the position in which she has placed us. She has set us in the centre of her creation, and has granted us a view that sweeps the universe; and she not only created man erect,

The enlightener mocks a premise of inequality that is projected out into the cosmos only to retrieve its legitimation from that cosmos. This premise not only enabled the human race to make itself the privileged center of all things, it could also be used to advertise the supposed 'naturalness' of all claims to superiority raised by some human beings over others; Fontenelle cites several forms such pretentions can take. This pre-Rousseauian trait, standing in close proximity to the moralist tradition, emerges even more clearly over the subsequent course of the first evening. The marchioness remarks resentfully of the 'German' (Copernicus) that he would have alienated the earth of the last of its satellites, the moon, had it been in his power to do so, "for one may see, in every part of his hypothesis, that he was but little inclined to favor the earth." The enlightener replies with almost democratic pathos that he, for his part, is grateful to Copernicus for having humbled the vanity of those men who would arrogate to themselves the best situation in the universe: "'Tis with pleasure I consider the world mixing in the croud of planets." The earth as equal among equals! This view reflects critically on the social state of mankind, for geocentrism was only ever the cosmically broadcast manifestation of the egocentricity of a being for whom the place assigned it in a salon, or the rank accorded it in a seating arrangement, is essentially more important than its place and rank in the universe: "The same disposition which induces a man of the world to aspire after the most honorable place in a room, will make a philosopher desirous of placing the globe on which he lives in the most distinguished situation in the universe." The marchioness, otherwise not averse to a little postprandial enlightenment, does not take kindly to this cosmological moral. And so she is piqued into preempting Nietzsche by some two hundred years: "Upon my word . . . you are calumniating human nature—how happened it that the opinions of Copernicus were received, since they are so very humiliating?"[40]

---

but in order to fit him for contemplation of herself, she has given him a head to top the body, and set it upon a pliant neck, in order that he might follow the stars as they glide from their rising to their setting and turn his face about with the whole revolving heaven; Seneca, "On Leisure," in *Moral Essays,* trans. John W. Basore (Cambridge, MA: Harvard University Press, 2001), 2: 191.]

40. *car je vois dans tout son procédé qu'il était bien mal intentionné pout la terre . . . et j'ai du plaisir à voir présentement la terre dans la foule des planètes . . . la même inclination qui fait qu'on veut avoir la place la plus honorable dans une cérémonie, fait qu'un philosophe, dans un système, se met au centre du monde, s'il peut. Il est bien aise que tout soit fait pour lui . . . Franchement . . . c'est là une calomnie que vous avez inventée contre le genre humain. On n'aurait donc jamais dû recevoir le système de Copernic, puisqu'il est si humiliant.* [Fontenelle, *Conversations,* trans. Gunning, 19–20.]

X

GEOMETRIC SYMBOLISM AND METAPHORICS

The Fontenelle text from which I have just quoted implies a distinction, germane to our typology of metaphor histories, which confronts us with a final 'transitional' phenomenon, that of *metaphorics* and *symbolism*. Here we must be wary of formulating all too subtle definitions, tailored to the specifications of some system or other, that risk narrowing the basis of fulfilling intuitions in advance. The concept of symbol, richly shaded by its application to everything from aesthetics to formal logic (at the very least!), has already done much to obscure the expressive phenomena it was called on to illuminate. With its help, we will attempt here solely to elaborate an elementary distinction that we find very nicely exemplified in Fontenelle's text.

The expressive function ascribed by Fontenelle to the image of the geocentric cosmos is not that of 'absolute metaphor'. For Fontenelle, that is to say, the image does not provide the theoretically unanswerable question of man's place in the universe, and his relationship to everything else that exists, with a point of orientation. The critical mind of this early Enlightenment thinker aims instead to show that this metaphysical question no longer needs, and indeed has never needed, a cosmological metaphor to help it *find* an answer, since it has always already *given* itself such an answer through the will to preeminence that prevails in man. This preliminary decision cuts off the question before it can even be asked; it seeks only a fitting image, a manifestation attesting to the self-evidence vouchsafed it by Being, a sign unsullied by any suspicion of egocentric manipulation and given for all to see. At issue here is not the idle question of whether there is any substance to Fontenelle's account of the origin of the geocentric worldview. But the interpretation he gives geocentrism turns the long-antiquated image of the cosmos into a *symbol,* the projection into a cosmic dimension of man's overweening sense of his own importance. At most, this projection can heighten the emotional impact of a preexisting belief; it cannot, considered objectively, confirm and legitimate that belief. Seen in this light, Copernicus's theoretical reform takes on features of a political, indeed revolutionary kind: it destroyed a symbol invented for the purpose of sanctioning and perpetuating a universal inequality. And the destruction of that symbol implies the will to demolish its real basis.

The process we have described as a *metaphorization* of geocentrism among the Stoics is quite different: here a preexisting, theoretically validated image of the cosmos is 'given voice', as it were, through a supplementary hypothesis, namely through the teleological interpretation of man as a being created to contemplate and take pleasure in the universe that offers itself to his gaze. The Stoics not only read off a 'code' from their cosmology; they gleaned from it a comprehensive, internally consistent metaphysical framework in which existence and task, rank and duty, were correlates. Fontenelle presupposes that the cosmocentric position had from the outset been viewed and evaluated, even 'invented', in the sense of courtly ceremonial or social convention, and he assumes these to be purely factual assignations without any relation to Being. Just as the drive for status within society first had to create a scaffold of forms by means of which different status positions could be marked and 'expressed', in order then to comply with this factual 'code' without having to answer to any substantive criteria, so man initially concocted the fiction that nature was ready to instruct him through the architecture of the cosmos about his place in the totality of beings, in order then to posit in geocentrism the symbol of his presumed ontological preeminence. The symbol need only capture the identity of a relationship: what matters is not *where* in a seating arrangement the top-ranking dignitary has been placed, but that he is sitting in the spot to which the prevailing code stipulates that he ought *always* to be assigned. The symbol operates by subserving an identification, but it is meaningless to inquire about its *content.* Where that nonetheless proves possible, symbolic and metaphorical functional elements have come together. Such cases will be examined more closely in what follows.

A case in point is the employment of *mathematical* signs and figures in philosophical contexts. We are fortunate enough to possess, in Dietrich Mahnke's exemplary monograph "Unendliche Sphäre und Allmittelpunkt: Beiträge zur Genealogie der mathematischen Mystik" [Infinite Sphere and Cosmic Center: Contributions to the Genealogy of Mathematical Mysticism] (Halle, 1937), one of the few truly rigorous and thorough studies of the material in this field, or more precisely of a particular selection from that material. Mahnke consistently refers to *circle and sphere* as

'geometric symbols' that become expressive means of *mysticism* through the supplementary element of their infinitization. Although we cannot hope to compete with
Mahnke's monograph in its wealth of detail, we will draw on some of the material
assembled there to explore, in as productive a manner as possible, the question
that has arisen in our context concerning the relationship between symbolism and
metaphorics. The interest in a *cosmological metaphorics* that guided our last section
will be maintained in this section, too, insofar as circle and sphere will primarily
be encountered as forms of cosmic orbits and bodies. We will also have occasion to
ask about the foundation and significance of these figures, whose *deformation*—
for circular orbits in Kepler, for spherical shapes in Maupertuis—numbers no less
among the prototypical deeds of the modern age than the reform of Copernicus,
without standing in anything like as close and consequential a relationship to it as
the infinitization of the universe through Giordano Bruno.

Ever since Plato and Aristotle, circular orbits and spherical forms have epito-
mized the 'cosmicity' of the cosmos, its perfection and rationality. It does not suffice
to refer here to the Pythagorean background of geometric symbolism, as can already be seen by the fact that Aristotle, who otherwise paid short shrift to anything
that smacked of Pythagoreanism, never deviates in this point from the findings of
the "Timaeus." Such consensus is the sure sign of a necessity that reaches far deeper
than the symbolic. From Parmenides and Empedocles on, the spherical form of
Being functions as a metaphor for indivisible unity, for homogeneous inviolabil-
ity and atomicity. In Plato, there is the additional factor that the ideal norm of
the completeness of the demiurgic imitation of the "intelligible organism" (ζῷον
νοητόν) finds expression in the sphere's optimal volume. Nowhere is it stated that
the totality of Ideas takes this form as well; that is a misunderstanding of the relevant passages in the "Timaeus," first put into circulation by Plotinus, which reduces
the metaphorical to the symbolic function.[1] Yet the sphere not only illustrates the
maximum capacity of the work commensurate with the demiurge and his original
model; it represents the identity of *completeness and limitation* as well. Democritus's
attempt to construct a cosmology upon the *straight line* as the most rational geometric element, and accordingly to imagine the original state in atomic trajectories
running parallel through the infinite void, necessarily evoked in Greek minds the
terrifying prospect of the ἄπειρον, the abyss of limitless and formless emptiness in
which Being, presumed to be finite in its formative possibilities, threatened to dis-
sipate and dissolve into nothingness. We can only understand the negativity of the
infinite for the Greeks by recalling that, in their view, the finite reserve of eidetic-
substantial archetypes had exhausted itself in what had already been realized in
this world, so that even a plurality of worlds could do no more than repeat this

---

1. The passages in Plato and Plotinus are juxtaposed in the notes to Mahnke, 229–30; but Mahnke
interprets Plotinus's misunderstanding as surpassing Plato in the direction of the 'infinite sphere' he
makes his theme. In reality, the metaphor thereby loses its expressive content and becomes merely
symbolic.

canon; the infinite was thus equated with the nonexistent, which, as such, could not be mastered by Being. The spherical shape of the Platonic cosmos is a bastion against the threat of the ἄπειρον revived by Democritus. The circular form of the stellar paths is accordingly the form of movement that unites rational evenness and endlessness in time without requiring unlimited space. It is telling that the Platonic endorsement of circular movement first loses its binding force at the very moment when the idea of cosmic infinity also begins, with Nicolaus of Cusa, to appear in a positive light: once the creator and his work prove commensurate with the infinite, the 'exactness' of the geometric figures loses its stabilizing relevance against the nonexistent.

Yet this is not yet to exhaust the metaphorical content of sphere and circle. In the "Timaeus," the cosmos is described as a sphere "spinning uniformly in the same spot and within itself and . . . revolving in a circle" (34A).[2] This stationary spinning of a sphere represents the most perfect union of motion and rest; as such, it stands between the unmoved divine (here, the Ideas) and the inner-cosmic motions, leading all the way down to irregular movements. From Xenophanes on, the divine was seen to combine the attributes of immobility and pure thought. If 'activity without motion' is to be more than a mere play on words, a metaphorical representation must lie behind it, and it would seem that the sphere spinning within itself and the circle returning to itself *imitate* the nature of the divine precisely because they are already implicitly *contained* in the notion of an actively restful, restfully active deity. The circular motion of the stars becomes the sign of their divinity and assumes normative character for human reason, which is invited to contemplate the celestial pageant because it finds the inner lawfulness of truly rational Being paraded there before it:[3] reason must imitate the strictly regular revolutions of the divine in order to give itself this 'form' (47C; 90 CD). Already in Plato, the normative characteristics that were originally entirely inherent in the Ideas thus begin to pass over to the cosmos. The heavenly revolutions are the first innerworldly phenomena to be so affected;[4] their origin in imitation is overlooked in the appeal to imitation that they themselves convey. Here, the metaphysical groundwork is laid for the ethical and aesthetic dignity accorded the 'starry sky' in Stoicism. With this in mind, we can see why Plato, according to a report communicated by Simplicius,[5] could prescribe for astronomy a theoretical 'program' that would keep it occupied for the rest of antiquity (and far beyond, right up to Kepler): namely, that of referring the

---

2. [*Timaeus,* trans. Bury, 63.]

3. See W. Theiler, "Zur Geschichte der teleologischen Naturbetrachtung bis auf Aristoteles" (Diss., Basel, 1924), 73–74. Theiler points out that even in the "Politeia" (436CE), circular movement is not yet invested with any particular distinction, as in *Tim.* 36C sqq.

4. Theiler points to the similarity between the key ideas in the "Republic" 500C (imitation of the ideas) and "Timaeus" 47C (imitation of the celestial revolutions). This displacement in a basic schema presupposes a shift in position. See further *Nom.* 898A, *Epin.* 982B.

5. *Commentarium in Aristotelis De caelo* 498a46–b3. According to Simplicius, Eudoxos of Knidos was the first to have framed his hypotheses according to this principle.

movements of the planets back to pure circular motions. With that, the originally mythic *symbol* has become so fraught with content, so 'meaningful', that it could become a *metaphor* for the immanent homogeneous structure of the divine and the human, the cosmos and reason, theory and ethos.

For Aristotle, the pure circulation of the first celestial sphere was practically the model for eliminating the Platonic χωρισμός,[6] for the possibility of an ideal reality that now formally perpetuates itself throughout *all of nature*. When Aristotle describes the circulation of water, for example,[7] its evaporation in fine weather and its renewed condensation to mist, clouds, and rain in cooler conditions, he sees in the circular journey of the approaching and withdrawing sun not just the efficient cause (κινοῦσα ἀρχή) of this self-contained process, but equally its formal model: "This cycle of changes imitates the sun's annual movement."[8] The Stoics took the final step here by attributing even the inner cohesion and solidity of all physical things to an encompassing circulation of the soul (πνεῦμα) within (*SVF* II 458): the πνεῦμα is the binding force that acts like a chain to preserve the integrity not just of the organism, but of stone and wood as well; starting at the center, it extends from there to the outline of the body, then loops back to its point of origin upon reaching the surface. The structure of the universe and the structure of each individual thing are isomorphous (*SVF* I 497 = II 458). They bear the index of godliness and perfection—truly an optimistic metaphysics! The Stoic centripetal movement discussed in the previous section is cyclical in effect, since each element that arrives at the center is jostled along by all the other elements thronging in the same direction before being pushed back by those same elements toward the circumference. All the same, circular movement is no longer *the* 'natural' movement that it had been for Aristotle, but a product of natural (centripetal) movement and a violent movement that results from it. It is true that, apart from circular movement, Aristotle had recognized the vertical (upward and downward) movements of the elements to their proper places (τόποι οἰκεῖοι) as 'natural' movements; but these can only follow secondarily from violent movements, since in an eternal cosmos each element would long since have arrived at its definitive place were it not subject to continuous and 'violent' dislocation. Such violence, however, can only arise as an accidental side effect from the 'natural' cycles of the spheres. Strictly speaking, then, only circular movement is 'natural', and traces of the effort required to adhere to this consequence are still clearly visible.[9] In the supralunary realm, at any rate, this one

---

6. [In Platonic metaphysics, the *chorismos* is the gap separating the physical realm of the senses from the noetic realm of the intellect.]

7. *Meteorologica* I, 9; 346b16–347a5. On the circle's perfection, see *Metaphysics* V 6; 1016b16–17.

8. γίνεται δὲ κύκλος οὗτος μιμούμενος τὸν τοῦ ἡλίου κύκλον (b 35/6). [Aristotle, *Meteorologica*, trans. H. D. P. Lee (Cambridge, MA: Harvard University Press, 2004), 71; translation modified.]

9. It would only be consequential for Aristotle to have sacrificed the view advanced in his early dialogues on the voluntariness of the planetary motions to his conception of 'natural movement', as W. Jaeger, *Aristoteles,* 154–55, assumes him to have done; however, H. E. Cherniss (in *Aristotle's Criticism of Plato* [Baltimore, 1944], 1: 598) has invalidated the reference to *Eth. Nic.* III 5. See now F. Dirlmeier's

type of movement alone befits the celestial orbs, so that Aristotelian metaphysics, as the most influential factor in the tradition, could provide the Platonic 'program' of astronomy with its most emphatic and effective source of support.

The entire horizon of ancient circle metaphorics is present in the occasionally cryptic allusions made by Plotinus in his tractate "The Heavenly Circuit."[10] The thesis explaining why the sky moves in a circle is a re-Platonized version of Aristotle: "In imitation of the Mind."[11] That this thesis alludes to, and interprets, the conception advanced by Aristotle in the seventh chapter of "Metaphysics" XII can be seen above all in the treatise's closing words. These fully explicate the opening thesis: "The Mind has no such progress in any region; its movement is a stationary act, for it turns upon itself. And that is why the All, circling as it does, is at the same time at rest."[12] In Plato, the demiurge shapes the cosmos in accordance with the requirement of the utmost rationality, and that is why he prescribes circular orbits for the heavenly bodies; in Aristotle, the absolute uniformity of the ultimate circular movement is deduced from an analysis of the concept of time, which requires an eternally homogeneous movement as its substrate, such that the intransient pure actuality of the unmoved mover is the norm grasped by the eros of the first sphere. Plotinus does not simply harmonize the two positions; he goes beyond them both. With an eye to demiurgic mimesis, he interprets the eros of the first sphere as an *imitation* of the highest (Aristotelian) principle, the unmoved mover as pure Mind (νοῦς). But what is the nature of that which circular movement first makes imitable? The Aristotelian prime mover is unmoved under the criterion of *physical* movement, whose final principle it is meant to be; as thought thinking

---

commentary (Berlin, 1956), 329–30. In my opinion, the difference between 'natural' and 'voluntary' motion, whose influence on ancient astronomy is obscured from us only by the authoritativeness of Ptolemy's achievement for the tradition, seems ultimately to go back to the *ambiguity of mechanical and organic metaphorics* in Plato's "Timaeus." The idea of the *motus voluntarius* belongs to an organic background metaphorics and therefore came to the fore in Stoic cosmology, whereas the idea of the *motus naturalis* is axiomatic for an economic mechanics whose rational achievement can only be compared with that of the principle of inertia.

The vitalistic-voluntaristic interpretation of the planetary movements, which admittedly could not be resolved in constructive terms, posed a mortal threat to astronomy as a science, since researchers searching for rules and laws could only adopt an attitude of resignation when faced with 'voluntariness'; Cleomedes and Geminos both took refuge in such formulae of resignation (see K. Reinhardt, *Poseidonios* [Munich, 1921], 202–3, which nonetheless downplays the commonalities in drawing out the differences). To be sure, the Aristotelian doctrine of a unique essence peculiar to the heavens also provided astronomy with just such a formula of transcendence, permitting it to shirk the demand for final exactness, as can still be seen in Ptolemy (*Syntaxis math.* XIII 2). On this point, see also Hans Blumenberg, "Kosmos und System: Aus der Genesis der kopernikanischen Welt," *Studium Generale* X (1957): 75–76.

10. *Enn.* II 2. I draw on the edition of Henry-Schwyzer (I, 158–63). In several passages I have preferred R. Harder's version (vol. I; Hamburg, 1956). Marsilio Ficino's Latin translation is cited from the Didot edition of Creuzer-Moser (Paris, 1855).

11. ὅτι νοῦν μιμεῖται. [Plotinus, *The Enneads,* trans. Stephen MacKenna (London: Faber & Faber, 1980), 88; translation modified.]

12. ὁ δὲ νοῦς οὕτω κινεῖται · ἕστηκε γὰρ καὶ κινεῖται · περὶ αὐτὸν γάρ. οὕτως οὖν καὶ τὸ πᾶν τῷ κύκλῳ κινεῖσθαι ἅμα καὶ ἕστηκεν. [Plotinus, *The Enneads,* trans. MacKenna, 91; translation modified.]

itself, however, as νόησις νοήσεως, it is at the same time pure ἐνέργεια in *theoretical* activity. Circular movement, as an imitation of the νοῦς, refers to a relationship that Mind has to itself: Marsilio Ficino translates περὶ αὐτὸν γάρ ["it turns upon itself"] with *nam reflectitur in se ipsum*. The cosmic soul is incapable of such purely theoretical self-reflection; through imitation, it repeats at its own level: it encompasses the whole to make it a unity, brings it to itself. The difference between the cosmic soul and Mind is thus that the latter tarries within itself, whereas the former brings an other to itself in an all-encompassing circular movement, "a movement towards itself, the movement of self-awareness, of self-intellection, of the living of its life, the movement of its reaching to all things so that nothing shall lie outside of it, nothing anywhere but within its scope."[13] The organic, not the mechanical, is the direct imitation of pure Mind. To be sure, this is only the tendency of the cosmic *soul*; the motions of the heavens, however, are those of the cosmic *body*. Here it is significant that Plotinus departs entirely from Aristotle's 'natural' movement in ascribing a naturally straightforward motion to the body, which the soul endeavors to steer toward the center; the circular motion of the sky thus comes about as a 'mixed' movement from two divergent rectilinear movements. That appears on first glance to anticipate the Newtonian understanding of the genesis of planetary movements, yet it can be sufficiently explained by Plotinus's metaphysical need to interpret the body as heterogeneous to the mind and pitted against it, as its deformation and falsification. By its very nature, bodily movement cannot have the form adequate to the mind; natural phenomena arise from the commingling of metaphysical opposites. The relationship between body and soul in man is already prefigured in the cosmic dimension. That, too, is hinted at in our tractate: in the human body, the soul finds it even more difficult to perform 'its' mimetic circular movement, since drives directed to other ends (πρὸς ἄλλα αἱ ὁρμαί) operate in conjunction with the body's rectilinear form of movement. In his tractate "Nature and Source of Evil" (I 8, 4), Plotinus presents circular movement around the Mind as the primordial state of the cosmic soul, whose 'fall' and overpowering by primal matter is precipitated when the soul turns its gaze from the νοῦς and thereby loses its bearings, as it were, in the course of its mimetic performance; this initial vertical movement of the soul is the abandonment of its original, unsullied condition and must be revoked through a corresponding movement of flight in the inverse direction. Through this dualistic classification of circular and rectilinear figures of movement, geometric metaphorics becomes so wedded to Neoplatonic metaphysics that it henceforth takes up residence in that tradition, as Mahnke has shown.

The origin of this tradition in Plotinus is of specific interest to us here because, in his deduction of the circular movement of the sky from the cosmic soul's imitation

---

13. εἰς αὐτὴν συναισθητικὴ καὶ συννοητικὴ καὶ ζωτικὴ καὶ οὐδαμοῦ ἔξω οὐδ' ἄλλοθι · καὶ τὸ πάντα δεῖν περιλαμβάνειν τοῦ γὰρ ζῴου τὸ κύριον περιληπτικὸν καὶ ποιοῦν ἕν. [Plotinus, *The Enneads,* trans. MacKenna, 88.]

of pure Mind, *the structure of metaphor itself is metaphysically hypostasized*. In its nature, in the 'language' of its being, the soul can neither grasp nor adequately 'replicate' the Mind; its mimesis can hit its target only in missing it, be true only by being different: in structural terms, it already preempts Cusanus's 'learned ignorance' (a fertile source of metaphysical metaphorics). For this is an exact representation of the function of 'absolute metaphor', which springs into a nonconceptualizable, conceptually unfillable gap and lacuna to express itself in its own way. The cosmic soul moves in a circle because it *must* lovingly imitate the Mind yet *cannot* adequately do so; it supplies an 'image' in place of the concept and conceptual understanding; it literally reproduces the Mind, and its reproduction is *at the same time* a metaphor for what it reproduces *and* a metaphor for its failure to reach its goal: "The soul exists in revolution around God to whom it clings in love, holding itself in the utmost of its power near to Him as the Being on which all depends, and since it cannot coincide with God it circles about Him."[14] Circular movement is the most that can be attained by a love that, unrequited and unrequitable, is separated from its object by the hiatus of transcendence (inasmuch as love strives to become one with the beloved), *and* it is simultaneously the metaphor for unrequitability: *because* the soul cannot attain the Mind but equally cannot desist from it, it circles around it and thereby finds—by the gift of grace, one could say in theological amplification— the most precise 'absolute metaphor' in which its mimesis is fulfilled. One cannot talk of 'symbolism' here: the symbol stands in the service of knowledge and must therefore be fixed and static, whereas here we can already detect the highly complex movement that must be represented, indeed 'accomplished', in the geometric expression. Metaphor is capable of movement and can represent movement; there can be no more impressive confirmation of this than Cusanus's self-transcending

---

14. εἰ δὴ ψυχῆς ἐστι, περιθέουσα τὸν θεὸν ἀμφαγαπάζεται καὶ περὶ αὐτὸν ὡς οἷόν τε αὐτὴ ἔχει · ἐξήρτηται γὰρ αὐτοῦ πάντα. ἐπεὶ οὖν οὐκ ἔστι πρὸς αὐτόν, περὶ αὐτόν (II 2, 2). In Ficino's translation: *Quodsi ita est, anima rursus revolvitur circa deum affectatque complecti, et, utcunque potest, circa ipsum sese habet; cuncta enim a deo pendent. Quoniam vero non permanet penes ipsum, saltem se versat circa ipsum* . . . [Because if it is thus, the soul revolves perpetually around God and aspires to His embrace, and, insofar as it is able, holds itself [in a course] around Him; for all things are suspended from God. Although it cannot endure permanently in His charge, at least it can orbit around Him.] Here an ecstatic approximation of the cosmic soul to cosmic reason has obviously been interpolated into the text. In its 'normal state', however, the cosmic soul presupposes circular movement as its minimum (*saltem*) proximity to the Mind, after the effort to go beyond this has proved incapable of 'enduring' (*permanet*). The mimesis of reason's self-sufficiency is downplayed in this reading; circular movement is understood as the 'second best' theoretical comportment after ecstatic union; the soul wants to gaze upon its beloved from all sides. Once circular movement is thus regarded primarily as a theoretical bearing turned toward a single object, the metaphorical aspect disappears; what is described is merely a 'technique' of actualization. With the addition of this nuance, the link to the Aristotelian conception (*Metaph.* XII 7), which was to be interpreted here precisely by being brought into connection with Platonic mimesis, also goes missing. In Aristotle, the sky does not circle *around* pure reason but *beneath* it; this circling is already theory *converted* into practice (in Plotinus's terms, it is 'mimetic action'), whereas Ficino's interpretation suggests that practice should be understood as an activity *subserving* the integration of theory. That does not accord with the tenor of the tractate's concluding thesis on circular movement as the mimesis of pure reason.

'explosive metaphorics', which operates with geometric figures even as it trans-forms them.[15]

The negative theology of both late antiquity and Christianity, where it bore a Neoplatonic stamp, demanded a new language. Naturally, one could always argue that any theology that believes itself unable to predicate anything about God has no need of speech. But an essential difference is drawn here between silence and silenc-*ing*; that is what "learned ignorance" (*docta ignorantia*) intends to signify. Negative theology does not represent a body of knowledge; it is a path, a spiritual exercise, a method for cultivating a stance or attitude. Even where negative theology is not systematically elaborated, as in Augustine, we encounter those characteristic 'meta-phors which baffle intuition'.[16] What we are here calling "explosive metaphorics" achieves something more: it draws intuition into a *process* in which it can keep up at first (for example, by mentally doubling and then continuously redoubling a circle's radius), only to be compelled to give up—and that is understood as meaning to give itself up—at a certain point (for example, by thinking a circle with the greatest possible radius, a radius of infinite magnitude). The aim is to make transcendence something that can be 'experienced' as the limit of theoretical apprehension, and *eo ipso* as a challenge to heterogeneous apprehensive modes. The 'blasting agent'

---

15. Mahnke (219–20) has elaborated the curious plasticity of Plotinus's metaphorics (albeit still under the heading of 'symbolism') with reference to the example of the "mental sphere" (σφαῖρα νοητή), which recurs on several occasions in Plotinus (V 1, 9; VI 5, 4. 10; II 9, 17). Here, the sphere does not function metaphorically as a geometric figure of a certain size and optimal capacity, as it does in Plato's "Timaeus," and more subtly still in Kepler's "Harmony of the World"; rather, it func-tions metaphorically insofar as it is a *concept* at all, and could therefore be replaced by any other con-cept. In terms of its *scope*, the concept 'contains' everything that falls under its definition; in terms of its *content*, it is the immanent constitutive principle that establishes such logical subsumption under the concept (form). This is a wholly Aristotelian conception and, as such, becomes a metaphor for the identity of God's immanence and transcendence: "Just as one can say with equal justice of the 'sphere as such' that its conceptual scope encompasses all particular spheres, great and small, and that its con-ceptual content is contained in the essence of every particular sphere, so one can equally say of God that he is 'all-encompassing' and that he dwells 'in the depths' (VI 8, 18). That is why Plotinus trans-fers the Aristotelian image of the celestial spheres, kept in motion by God from the outermost circle, onto the intellectual cosmos, whose 'first sphere encompasses all others', while at the same time agree-ing with Plato that the soul is 'in the body, the intellect in the soul', and God, as the innermost cen-ter, in all. For even though these expressions may evoke opposing images, conceptually they mean the same thing" (Mahnke, 220). The metaphorical aspect does not lie here in the material, which has been adopted solely as a traditional Platonic topos, but on the formal plane, in the immanent and transcen-dent achievement of the concept as such. Plotinus does not yet know the technique by which meta-phorics can cast aside its material cloak: it consists in exploding what avails itself to the mind's eye by adding the *infinitum* and withdrawing it from apperception. Plotinus wants to achieve the same result through the innocuous *noeton*. What Mahnke fails to notice in his account of the history of the sup-posed symbolism of the 'infinite sphere' is precisely this tendency to 'detonate' the metaphor materi-ally so that it may be formally deployed. P. Henry, in his introduction to the English translation of the "Enneads" by Stephen MacKenna (London, 1956), xlv-xlix, has drawn attention to the metaphorical character of Plotinus's 'symbols'.

16. E. R. Curtius, *Europäische Literatur und lateinisches Mittelalter* (Bern, 1948), 145 [*European Lit-erature and Latin Middle Ages*, 135]: 'the hand of my tongue' (*Conf.* V 1), 'the hand of the heart' (X 12), 'the head of the soul' (X 7). The barrier to comprehension still lies here in the static incompossibility of the perceptualized elements.

in this metaphorics is the concept of infinity, its most enduring model the puta-tively hermetic formula taken from the "Liber XXIV philosophorum": "God is an infinite sphere whose center is everywhere and circumference nowhere."[17] Cu-sanus applied this formula not just to God, but to the totality of the world as well (*Docta ign.* II, 4. 5. 11. 12). Yet in a self-reflective move that already bade farewell to the Middle Ages, he also 'methodically' thought through and justified the use of expressive means of this kind, extracting a 'recipe' from the traditional topos. One chapter of the "Docta ignorantia" bears the title "Mathematics are a very great help in the understanding of different divine truths" (I, 2).[18] Cusanus starts out from the time-honored thesis that "the visible universe is a faithful reflection of the invisible." In his view, however, the created world is no longer primarily the image of its invisible creator; the privileged point of departure is instead the world of *mathematicalia,* engendered by the human mind from its own creative potency. Why this new medium of inauthentic expression? In the first place, the work of man is no less suited to metaphysical metaphorics than the divine work of nature, since man is creative as the 'image and likeness of God'. The advantage of math-ematics is one of 'method': mathematics allows for freely variable manipulation, for experimentation under autonomously selected conditions. 'Experimentation' here means making the radius of a circle infinitely small, for example, in which case the figure shrinks to a point and so surrenders its being, or making it infinitely great, in which case the circumference distends into a straight line, and the figure likewise ceases to be itself. The figure stands between the two infinities schematized in the pseudo-hermetic sentence; transcendence is no longer solely 'up there', and any at-tempt to flee it drives one straight into its arms. At this outer limit, the metaphor, itself a makeshift at the limit of our ability to perceptualize the 'matter itself', must be done away with. Cusanus describes this process in the following terms: ". . . No object that we know or of which we have any idea, can be the Absolute Maximum; and since it is by way of symbols that we intend to conduct our search of it, we must, therefore, look for something more than a simple comparison. In mathemat-ics, in fact, we are always dealing with finite things, for if they were not finite we could form no idea of them at all. If then we want to reach the Absolute Maximum through the finite, we must, in the first place, study finite, mathematical figures as they are, namely a mixture of potency and act; then we must attribute the respective perfections to the corresponding infinite figures, and finally we must, in a much

---

17. *Deus est sphaera infinita, cuius centrum ubique, circumferentia nusquam est.* C. Baeumker, *Das pseudohermetische 'Buch der vierundzwanzig Meister,'* Beiträge z. Gesch. D. Philosophie d. Mittelalters XXV/1–2 (Münster, 1927), 194 ff., prop. 2. Among the lapidary definitions contained in this oft-cited text can be found the following sphere metaphor: *Deus est sphaera, cuius tot sunt circumferentiae, quot sunt puncta.* [God is the sphere that has as many circumferences as points.] Readers interested in the geneal-ogy and reception history of this text should consult Mahnke's monograph.

18. [Nicholas of Cusa, *Of Learned Ignorance,* trans. Germain Heron (London: Routledge & Kegan Paul, 1954), 25.]

more sublime way, attribute the perfections of the infinite figures to the simple Infinite, which cannot possibly be expressed by any figure."[19] Mathematics helps us to grasp the alterity of the divine insofar as the *coincidentia oppositorum* of divine being can be formally reconstructed through the indicated metaphorical method. Our notion of 'absolute metaphor' does not lead to an adequate understanding of what was intended by Cusanus, since from his position, all metaphorical projections are legitimated by a universal structural identity. They thus claim a far deeper legitimacy than we can grant 'absolute metaphor', which appears to spring from a mental *horror vacui,* as it were. Cusanus explicitly restates the metaphysical assumption of the universal homogeneity of Being—an assumption that authenticates metaphor, despite everything, as a means to *knowledge*—at the beginning of the chapters of "Docta ignorantia" that rehearse such examples all the way through to the *coincidentia oppositorum*: "The fundamental reason for the use of symbolism in the study of spiritual things, which in themselves are beyond our reach, has already been given. Though we neither perceive nor understand it, we know for a fact that all things stand in some sort of relation to one another; that, in virtue of this interrelation, all the individuals constitute one universe and that in the one Absolute the multiplicity of beings is unity itself."[20] The metaphysical premise that has the world emerge, as *explicatio,* from the divine unity of the *coincidentia oppositorum* makes 'explosive metaphorics' a legitimate investigation into the inner structure of creation, a descent to the primal ground whence all things have their being.

The twenty-first chapter of book I deals with the "analogy between the infinite circle and unity." The circle is the perfect transposed representation (*figura*) of unity and simplicity. The metaphor marks the coincidence of beginning and end, whose *transsumptio* is given the following striking formulation: "In Him, in fact, the beginning is such that the end and the beginning are one."[21] The coincidence of immanence and transcendence is Cusanus's great theme, and he can demonstrate it on the infinite circle as well: circumference and diameter fall together here, but their unity has absorbed the function of both; as circumference, the infinite circle

---

19. . . . *constat maximum simpliciter nihil horum esse posse, quae per nos sciuntur aut concipiuntur, hinc, cum ipsum symbolice investigare proponimus, simplicem similitudinem transilire necesse est. Nam cum omnia mathematicalia sint finite et aliter etiam imaginari nequeant: si finitis uti pro exemplo voluerimus ad maximum simpliciter ascendendi, primo necesse est figuras mathematicas finitas considerare cum suis passionibus et rationibus, et ipsas rationes correspondenter ad infinitas tales figures transferre, post haec tertio adhuc altius ipsas rationes infinitarum figurarum transsumere ad infinitum simplex absolutissimum etiam ab omni figura. De docta ignorantia* I 12 [Nicholas of Cusa, *Of Learned Ignorance,* trans. Heron, 27]. In this early text, Cusanus is still unclear about his motives for preferring mathematical figures, as we have expounded those motives here; at this point (I, 11), he can only justify this preference for mathematical signs "on account of their indestructible certitude" (*propter ipsorum incorruptibilem certitudinem convenientius uti*).

20. *Hoc autem, quod spiritualia, per se a nobis inattingibilia, symbolice investigentur, radicem habet ex iis . . ., quoniam omnia ad se invicem quadem—nobis tamen occultam et incomprehensibilem – habent proportionem, ut ex omnibus unum exurgat universum et omnia in uno maximo sint ipsum unum* (I, 11). [Nicholas of Cusa, *Of Learned Ignorance,* trans. Heron, 25.]

21. *tantum est in ipso principium, quod et finis est in ipso principium.* [Nicholas of Cusa, *Of Learned Ignorance,* trans. Heron, 182.]

is "infinite in capacity," and "outside all, while all-encompassing"; as diameter, it is "all-penetrating."[22] Metaphor requires each of its elements to be interpreted according to its function; otherwise it lapses into *allegory,* where the wheels on the chariot of some goddess or other can be identified with the four cardinal virtues, and such like. At times, the functional aptness of Cusanus's metaphors can be perceived only with difficulty, or even not at all, as when he purports to make the following inference from the infinite circle: "Because it is the center it is the efficient cause, because it is the diameter it is the formal cause, because it is the circumference it is the final cause. It gives being because it is the center, it governs because it is diameter, it conserves in being because it is the circumference."[23] At the end of this chapter, the circle, which as *sphaera infinita* has become the 'model' of statements about God, is now equally characterized as a key figure of theological thought and procedure: "I would ask you especially to note how all theology is circular and lies within a circle, to such an extent that even the terms of the attributes are truly convertible: infinite justice is infinite truth, and infinite truth is infinite justice, and so it is with all of them . . ."[24] Here it becomes clear that the 'truth' of explosive metaphorics, in keeping with the account we have given of absolute metaphor, is essentially *pragmatic*: it induces an attitude, a stance or behavior that may be classified with broad generality as 'mystical', and in Cusanus's case more specifically as *docta ignorantia,* as that ignorance that 'knows' itself to indicate the surpassing greatness of its indispensable object, thereby distinguishing itself from Scholasticism as a science that falls short of that object. The stance or bearing induced by the metaphor is actualized with each use of the metaphor, whose implication is *docta ignorantia*; this processual circle is reinforced in the peculiarly unprogressive fecundity of Cusan metaphorics, which has no ambition to go 'outside' and 'beyond' itself. Cusanus no longer shares the faith of High Scholasticism in the servile subordination of logic to metaphysics; he snubs logic with a certain apotropaic deviousness, seeing original sin in man's seduction by the idea of knowledge, his will to resemble God *in scientia.* The inner unity and gestalt of a *style of existence* can be grasped here under the dominance of circle metaphorics.[25]

---

22. *capacissimus . . . extra omne omnia ambiens . . . omnia penetrans.* [Nicholas of Cusa, *Of Learned Ignorance,* trans. Heron, 47; translation modified.]

23. *Causa efficiens, quia centrum; formalis, quia diameter; finalis, quia circumferentia. Dans esse, quia centrum; gubernans, quia diameter; conservans, quia circumferentia.* [Nicholas of Cusa, *Of Learned Ignorance,* trans. Heron, 48.]

24. *Hoc tantum notandum esse admoneo, quomodo omnis theologia circularis et in circulo posita existit, adeo etiam quod vocabula attributorum de se invicem verificentur circulariter: ut summa iustitia est summa veritas et summa iustitia et ita de omnibus . . .* [Nicholas of Cusa, *Of Learned Ignorance,* trans. Heron, 48.]

25. The circle metaphor, along with the idea of the *coincidentia oppositorum,* can perhaps be traced to a common historical source as well. Ten years after the "Docta ignorantia," Cusanus published his "Idiota" dialogues (1450), which included the "Experiments with the Scales." It is likely that he had already been reflecting on these mechanical thought experiments for some time; perhaps he had stumbled across the pseudo-Aristotelian "Quaestiones mechanicae" in the process, at the beginning of which the circle is conceived as a coincidence of opposites, a 'wonder' said to be the cause of leverage as well:

Mahnke has shown that Kepler was influenced by the geometric metaphorics of Cusanus and what form this influence took.[26] A massive *metaphorical realism* is generally characteristic of Kepler's cosmological speculations. While this sometimes leads him somnambulistically to new insights, it also prevents him from adequately comprehending the rationalization of anthropocentric teleology ushered in by Copernicus. The heliocentric idea, already abandoned by Giordano Bruno in favor of an acentric universe, is given a far stronger metaphysical accent in Kepler than in Copernicus; and while this prompts him to discover his laws of planetary movement, it also signals what is, in effect, a pre-Copernican dependence on circle-centered (and center-circling) metaphorics. Ample evidence of this is provided in a letter to Wackher from early 1618. Kepler writes his friend in Prague of his progress on the "Harmony of the World," observing that the real effect of the cosmic harmony could only be perceived and experienced as a spectacle upon the sun: "It is therefore to be believed that there are far nobler creatures living on the sun, quasi-divine beings who delight in these phenomena and are stimulated by them in the most natural manner. For we earth-dwellers are circled solely by the moon, it alone is subservient to us . . . But the sun is circled and served, so to speak, by us and the entire choir of planets, who are its family and chattels."[27] Kepler himself senses that there is more than a hint of paganism in such massive metaphorical realism, continuing: "If I were a heathen and had heard nothing of Christian teaching, I would say that there is a place of refuge open to us and all brave Wackher-souls on that most excellent of orbs in the entire universe."[28] This is a thoroughly un-Copernican idea; for the fact that the appearance of the stellar orbits fails to agree with their

---

πάντων δὲ τῶν τοιούτων ἔχει τῆς αἰτίας τὴν ἀρχὴν ὁ κύκλος. καὶ τοῦτο εὐλόγως συμβέβηκεν · ἐκ μὲν γὰρ θαυμασιωτέρου συμβαίνειν τι θαυμαστὸν οὐδὲν ἄτοπον, θαυμασιώτατον δὲ τὸ τἀναντία γίνεσθαι μετ' ἀλλήλων. ὁ δὲ κύκλος συνέστηκεν ἐκ τοιούτων · εὐθὺς γὰρ ἐκ κινουμένου τε γεγένηται καὶ μένοντος, ὧν ἡ φύσις ἐστὶν ὑπεναντία ἀλλήλοις (847b15–21). [The original source of the cause of all these things is the circle. And quite rightly: for it is nothing strange for something amazing to be produced by some other amazing thing, but for opposites to be produced, associated one with the other, is a wonder. Now the circle is made up of opposites. For it came into being from movement and rest, which are opposite in kind.] The problem of leverage—likewise a coincidence of opposites, inasmuch as it allows substantial loads to be lifted with a minimum of effort—is shown to stem from the even more wondrous phenomenon of circular movement, since the latter consists of the *coincidentia oppositorum* of repose (center) and motion (periphery). The effects of mechanical art rest on this supreme, self-contradictory, and therefore counternatural principle, "by which we gain mastery over what tends naturally to overwhelm us" (847a20 f., quoting Antiphon).

26. Mahnke, 129 ff.

27. *daher ist es glaubhaft, daß es auf der Sonne viel edlere Lebewesen gibt, die sich an diesen Erscheinungen ergötzen und in natürlicher Weise von ihnen angeregt werden, Lebewesen, die dem göttlichen Wesen ähnlich sind. Denn uns Erdbewohner umkreist einzig der Mond, er allein ist uns dienstbar . . . Die Sonne aber wird von uns und dem ganzen Chor der Planeten umkreist, indem wir ihr gleichsam dienen, eigentlich ihre Familie und ihren Besitzstand ausmachen. Johannes Kepler in seinen Briefen*, ed. M. Caspar and W. v. Dyck (Munich, 1930), II 99.

28. *Wenn ich ein Heide wäre und von der christlichen Lehre nichts erfahren hätte, so würde ich sagen, auf dieser vortrefflichsten Kugel in der ganzen Welt steht uns und allen Wackher-Seelen eine Zuflucht offen.* [Trans. Carola Baumgardt in *Kepler's Life and Letters* (London: Victor Gollancz, 1952), 131; translation modified.]

essence, that their equal motions appear to us as unequal (*aequales illorum motus apparere nobis inaequales*), is seen by Copernicus to lie only in the inferior and provisional sphere of sensory data, which are rationally traced back to the universe's adequately conceivable 'ground plan'. The anthropological presupposition of a split between the sphere of the senses and reason plays a role here, but astronomy is also tied to the ethical schema of sensuality's subordination to reason.

Kepler's realistic use of circle metaphorics leads him to endow the sun with metaphysical attributes that appear to have been borrowed from the Aristotelian unmoved mover, the theologically fateful confusion of kinetic causality and creation made by High Scholasticism now being eliminated: "As the sun stands amidst the moving stars, *itself stationary and yet the source of motion,* it shows the image of God the Father, the Creator. For that which, in God, is creation is movement in the sun."[29] Kepler imagines the sun's kinetic function in such a way that "the solar body is magnetic all around it and rotates in its place, making the circle of its force move around with it. This force does not attract the planets but causes them to continue moving in their course ... For me, magnetism is a simile, not fully the matter itself."[30] The Aristotelian kinetic theory was structured to allow movement to enter the universe 'from outside'; the regular movement of the first sphere dissipated into other, irregular modi as it trickled down the causal chain, so that, as Theophrastus had already objected, the actuality of pure existence no longer even reached the cosmic center. Kepler breaks with this model, transposing the *causa motrix* [cause of motion] to the middle of the universe as *fons et principium circuli in loco Solis* [the source and principle of circulation in the sun's place], such that motion now radiates centrifugally. This 'naturalization' of planetary motion leads for the first time from a purely phoronomic astronomy, which could provide no explanation for the various mechanical problems posed by the stellar world, to a causal celestial physics. Here, it is quite striking how the shift in viewpoint that was to prove so decisive in driving forward the theoretical process, the attainment of new possibilities and means of rational construction, is initially realized in the medium of metaphorics. The essential precondition for Kepler's laws was not a conceptually adequate grasp of gravitational processes, but the pure representational schema of a radiating sphere of kinetic force constituted from its midpoint, the sphere as projection of the center: "The surface is ... the image of the center, resembling both a brilliant flash from it and a path toward it."[31] Kepler's most astonishing and daring feat, his abandonment of circular form as the constructive principle for the planetary orbits, is likewise

---

29. *Wie nun die Sonne inmitten der Wandelsterne steht, selber ruhend und doch Quelle der Bewegung, zeigt sie das Abbild Gottes des Vaters, des Schöpfers. Denn was bei Gott die Schöpfung ist, das ist bei der Sonne die Bewegung.* Letter to Mästlin, 3 October 1595 (op. cit., I, 19).

30. *der Sonnenkörper rings im Kreise herum magnetisch ist und an seinem Ort rotiert, wobei er den Kreis seiner Kraft mit herumbewegt. Diese Kraft zieht die Planeten nicht an, sondern besorgt ihre Weiterbewegung ... der Magnetismus ist mir ein Gleichnis, nicht vollkommen die Sache selber.* Letter to Mästlin, 3 March 1605 (op. cit., I, 222).

31. *superficies est ... imago centri et quasi fulgor ab eo et via ad id.* Cited in Mahnke, 135. I refer the interested reader to the wealth of material in Mahnke.

embedded in the fundamental metaphorical stratum: his representation of the sun as the source of planetary movements enables him to see the orbital forms as products of a process and no longer as examples of an *eidos:* "You ask me why I teach equations from triangular planes. No doubt you are thinking of my treatment of this matter in the Epitome. Answer: because I have set out to derive my calculations from the theory of natural causes, just as the ancients derived theirs from the hypothesis of perfect circles and the uniform movements arising therefrom. The cause of the real slowing down or speeding up of a planet on its path through the ether, however, is its greater or lesser distance from the sun, the source of motion."[32] Here Kepler already shows a keen awareness of the peculiarity of his method. A planetary orbit is not something that could be constructed eidetically as a total form. It cannot be immanently charted but is 'built up' from elements whose constant is the triangular plane measured out by the sun-planet radius over a given unit of time. The orbital form has become secondary; intransience is to be found not in the orbital form, but in the chronometric proportion between a planet's path and its distance from the sun. This metaphorically 'mediated' detachment from geometric eidetics is what makes Kepler's achievement a truly 'modern' one. In tackling the thorny problem of the orbit of Mars, Kepler proceeds by seeking to accommodate the data observed by Brahe first to the circle, then to the ellipse. When that attempt fails, it occurs to him that the eidetic distinction between the two only isolates polar phases within an ongoing transformational process. The singular case of the circle should not be regarded as an elemental figure, nor the ellipse as a specifically heterogeneous figure; rather, the circle is to be grasped as the limit case reached through a continuous diminution in the ellipse's distance from the focus. Kepler takes from this the methodological insight that the circle-ellipse alternative is insufficient, but that, in principle, an infinite number of ellipses would have to be tested. Moreover, the circle *qua* hypothesis enjoys no methodological advantage over any of the elliptical hypotheses. Overcoming the eidetic disjunction allowed Kepler to arrive at his new insight from the paradigm of the orbit of Mars. It no longer makes sense to cling to the circle, this most improbable of figures, as the figure of 'natural movement'.

Newton referred Kepler's metaphorically inferred and empirically verified laws back to the principles of Galilean mechanics. The planetary orbits result in their homogeneous phenomenality from divergent (namely, centripetal and centrifugal) mechanical factors: this insight, formulated now in purely theoretical, mathematical terms, becomes, in the course of Newton's wide-ranging reception, a background metaphor that 'shines through' in various ways. Hence, it can scarcely be

---

32. *Ihr fragt mich, warum ich die Gleichungen aus den Dreiecksflächen zu berechnen lehre. Ihr denkt ohne Zweifel an meine diesbezügliche Darstellung in der Epitome. Antwort: weil ich mir vorgenommen habe, die Berechnung aus der Theorie der natürlichen Ursachen herzuleiten, gleichwie die Alten sie aus der Hypothese der vollkommenen Kreise und der gleichförmigen Bewegungen auf diesen herleiten. Nun aber ist die Ursache für die wirkliche Verzögerung oder Beschleunigung des Planeten auf seinem Weg durch die ätherische Luft der größere oder kleinere Abstand des Planeten von der Sonne, der Quelle der Bewegung.* Letter to Crüger, 9 September 1624 (op. cit. II, 206).

doubted that the theory of the division of powers in the state developed in Montesquieu's "Esprit des lois" [Spirit of the Laws], for example, is 'read off' the model
of the polygon of forces. Montesquieu showed great enthusiasm in his youth for
reasearch in the natural sciences, and the influence of mechanical conceptions is
evident throughout his magnum opus in the metaphors in which they are deposited.[33] The autonomous factors in the state must always act in accordance with their
own interests, tasks, and motivations while nonetheless ensuring the smooth functioning of the whole; total stillstand would be the ideal, but it is an ideal not permitted by historical life, and so the division of powers must determine a trajectory
in which motion is assimilated to repose (just as, in ancient metaphorics, the circle
was the union of rest and movement): "The form of these three powers should be
rest or inaction. But as they are constrained to move by the necessary motion of
things, they will be forced to move in concert."[34] Mandeville's "Fable of the Bees or
Private Vices, Publick Benefits" (1714), its zoological trappings notwithstanding,
was already dominated by the Newtonian structural model, which Montesquieu
elsewhere formulates in the following terms: "Each person works for the common
good, believing he works for his individual interests."[35] In Kant, too, who made the
most comprehensive attempt to 'translate' the immanent structure of the Newtonian physical universe into the moral realm, the metaphorical background of the
polygon of forces is palpable when he writes in the fourth thesis of his "Idee zu
einer allgemeinen Geschichte in weltbürgerlicher Absicht" [Idea for a Universal
History from a Cosmopolitan Point of View]: "The means employed by Nature
to bring about the development of all the capacities of men is their antagonism in
society, so far as this is, in the end, the cause of a lawful order among men."[36]

Those who are partial to lapidary statements (which, admittedly, this study had
resolved to avoid) might venture to say that the essential processes in the intellectual
history of the modern age can be understood in their structural homogeneity as des-
titutions of circle metaphorics. This is confirmed by the fact that those who oppose
the spirit of the modern age typically resort to circle metaphors and set out to renew
their validity—a tendency that is especially pronounced, of course, in Nietzsche.
Before coming to him, we will cite two further examples. The adaptation of theological speculation to the new state of affairs is very nicely illustrated in Friedrich

---

33. See Maria Ruchti, "Raum und Bewegung im *Esprit des Lois:* Versuch einer Deutung des Stils
von Montesquieu" (Diss., Zurich, 1945) (valuable from the viewpoint of the material but unhelpful as
an interpretation).

34. *Ces trois puissances devroient former un repos ou une inaction. Mais comme, par le mouvement nécessaire des choses, elles sont contraintes d'aller, elles seront forcées d'aller de concert* (XI 6). [Montesquieu, *The
Spirit of the Laws,* trans. Anne M. Cohler et al. (Cambridge: Cambridge University Press, 1989), 164.]

35. *il se trouve que chacun va au bien commun, croyant aller à ses intérêts particuliers* (III 7). [Montes-
quieu, *Spirit of the Laws,* trans. Cohler et al., 27.]

36. *Das Mittel, dessen sich die Natur bedient, die Entwickelung aller ihrer Anlagen zustande zu bringen,
ist der Antagonism derselben in der Gesellschaft, sofern dieser doch am Ende die Ursache einer gesetzmäßi-
gen Ordnung derselben wird.* [Trans. Lewis Beck White in Kant, *Philosophical Writings,* ed. Ernst Behler
(New York: Continuum, 1986), 252.]

Christoph Oetinger, who, reversing the roles traditionally ascribed to nature and God, now deduces an intervention of the divine will, in the form of the "supramechanical power of gravity" (*potentia supramechanica gravitatis*), from the fact that the heavenly bodies move in near circles when they ought 'really' to move in a straight line.[37] The "rotation of life" (*vitae rotatio*) is also present in Oetinger as an existential model,[38] and with an obvious barb against philosophical rationality at that: "De nimia philosophorum continua abstractione cyclum vitae turbante et ab eodem turbata" [On the Excessive and Persistent Withdrawal of Philosophers, Disturbing the Cycle of Life and Disturbed by It] (§15) is the title of a chapter in which the *ratio,* as "often without god" (*saepe sine deo*), is confronted with the "awareness of god" (*sensus cum deo*), and this antithesis is inscribed into the cyclical model of existence as follows (§19): "True cognition, therefore, does not proceed at a tangent to the cycle of life, but straight from the center, whence the sense of the soul, which has its center in the heart, is perceived to be the light of God . . ."[39] From there, Oetinger veers on to the no less well-trodden path of illumination metaphorics.

Reprising the Stoic metaphor of the wise man as a sphere, Horace (*Sat.* II, 7) had described the sage as perfect in himself, polished and round, so that nothing coming from outside can make him lose his balance. Nicolas Chamfort draws on the metaphor in the following reflection: "The man of the world, the friend of fortune, and even the lover of glory, draws a straight line before him which leads to an unknown end. But the man who is his own companion, the wise man, describes a circle which ends with himself. He is the *totus teres atque rotundus* of Horace."[40] That seems to have been inspired by the ancient model, evoking a mood of humanistic serenity amid the tumult of the great revolution. But the Stoic metaphor of the sphere for the wise man's unblemished soul is static: round, smooth, and self-contained, it repels everything that bombards it from outside, offering no point of entry or attack. The metaphor is dynamized here under duress, confronted with

---

37. *Inquisitio in sensum communem et rationem* (Tübingen, 1753), 147. §88. *Quaestiones de liberrimis Dei operationibus in universo* [Questions on the Entirely Free Actions of God in the Universe]. There the argument is put forward under point 2: *quum corpora coelestia in orbitis circulariter moveantur, quis nisi Deus motum naturalem rectilineum in curvam urget? . . . annon potius liberrima Dei actio est effectrix huius motus ex oppositis directionibus constantis?* [If the celestial bodies move in circles, who, if not God, bends their naturally straight course into a curve? . . . Is it not the entirely free action of God that produces such a movement, which remains constant despite coming from opposite directions?] The supramechanical, voluntaristic intervention of gravitation (p. 148) is immediately blunted by the characterization of this power (*potentia*) as *constanter in mundo adhibita* [applied constantly in the world]. Whence, in the parameters of a voluntaristic theology, does this claim of constancy have its sufficient *reason*? It is easier to say whence, in the eighteenth century, it has its *motivation*.

38. *Brevissima Theoriae Musicae Analysis* (an appendix to the "Inquisitio" mentioned in the previous note) II 2, 50: *animae simplicitas . . . centrum illud leniter videatur moveri in generali totius vitae rotatione* [the simplicity of the soul . . . this center appears in general to want to be gently moved by the rotation of all life].

39. *vera igitur cognitio non in linea cycli vitae tangentiali abstractiva sed in directa ex centro progreditur, unde intelligitur sensum animi, qui centrum habet in corde, esse lucernam dei . . .*

40. Cited in Schalk, *Die französischen Moralisten,* I, 262. [Nicolas Chamfort, *Maxims and Considerations,* trans. E. Powys Mathers (London: The Cockerel Press, 1926), I 79; translation modified.]

the infinite straightness of a 'lifeline' that can never be 'rounded out' into complete self-assurance. The sphere is thus flattened into a circular trajectory: what matters most is not that substantial plentitude be maintained but that the figure be held. The wise man preserves what was lost through infinite space and the principle of inertia; he is pre-Copernican and pre-Newtonian insofar as he plots his existence as a circle, without confirmation and consolidation from the great cosmic prospect that had supported the Stoic idea of wisdom.

Nietzsche numbered the aforementioned Chamfort among the half dozen authors in whom "the spirit of the last centuries of the old era has arisen anew," and whose works, "written in Greek, would have been understood by Greeks."[41] With perceptive consequentiality, Nietzsche opposed the circle metaphor not only to the modern scientific view of nature, but also to the voluntaristic notion of God that underpinned it: "Whoever does not believe in the cyclical process of the universe must believe in an arbitrary God—that is my view of things, in contrast to all previous theistic viewpoints!"[42] Under the title "The Developed Circle," he polemicizes against the Newtonian mechanics of stellar circles as the ideal of the natural-scientific understanding of the universe: "Let us beware of thinking of the law of this circle as something that has developed, in false analogy to circular movements within the ring ... The cycle is not something that has developed, it is the primal law ... thus we should not by false analogy use rising and falling cycles, for example the wheeling of the stars, the ebb and flow of the tides, the alternation of day and night, or the regular succession of the seasons, when characterizing the eternal cycle."[43] In Aristotle, the contention that circular movement was the 'natural' movement could still draw on a whole background of metaphorical and rational support;[44] for Nietzsche, it signifies an ultimate, no longer justifiable principle: "... Rationality and irrationality are not predicates of the universe, the circle is a nonrational necessity, free of all formal, ethical, or aesthetic considerations."[45] As we have seen, absolute metaphor leaps into a void, inscribing itself on the *tabula rasa* of theoretical unsatisfiability; here it has occupied the position of the defunct absolute will. Metaphysics has often revealed itself to us to be metaphorics taken at its word; the demise of metaphysics calls metaphorics back to its place.

---

41. *der Geist der letzten Jahrhunderte der alten Zeitrechnung wieder erstanden sei ... wären, griechisch geschrieben, auch von Griechen verstanden worden. Menschliches, Allzumenschliches* II, 2 (Musarion ed., IX, 295). The sequence, ending with Chamfort, reads: Montaigne, La Rochefoucauld, Labruyère, Fontenelle, Vauvenargues.

42. *Wer nicht an einen Kreisprocess des Alls glaubt, muß an den willkürlichen Gott glauben – so bedingt sich meine Betrachtung im Gegensatz zu allen bisherigen theistischen!* From the period of the "Gay Science," 1881/2 (Musarion ed., XI, 178).

43. *Hüten wir uns, das Gesetz dieses Kreises als geworden zu denken, nach der falschen Analogie der Kreisbewegungen innerhalb des Ringes ... Der Kreislauf ist nichts Gewordenes, er ist das Urgesetz ... also nicht durch falsche Analogie die werdenden und vergehenden Kreisläufe, zum Beispiel die Gestirne oder Ebbe und Fluth, Tag und Nacht, Jahreszeiten, zur Charakteristik des ewigen Kreislaufs verwenden.* (XI 181)

44. *Metaphysics* V 6; 1016b 16f.

45. *... Vernünftigkeit oder Unvernünftigkeit sind keine Prädicate für das All ... eine unvernünftige Notwendigkeit, ohne irgendeine formale, ethische, ästhetische Rücksicht.*

TRANSLATOR'S AFTERWORD

Metaphorology: A Beginner's Guide

Paradigms for a Metaphorology was first published in 1960 in the *Archive for the History of Concepts* (*Archiv für Begriffsgeschichte*), simultaneously appearing in book form with the Bouvier Verlag in Bonn.[1] At the time, Hans Blumenberg (1920–1996) was known to the philosophically interested public only as the author of a half dozen or so articles scattered in various journals and reference works, one of which—"Light as a Metaphor of Truth" (1957)[2]—deserves to be mentioned as a preliminary study, or "proto-paradigm,"[3] for *Paradigms*. His biography to that point may be sketched in a few strokes. Persecuted by the Nazis as a "half Jew," prevented from enrolling at a state university, and interned in a labor camp during the war, Blumenberg escaped to his hometown of Lübeck, where he found refuge with the family of his future wife. Upon resuming his studies at war's end, he

1. Hans Blumenberg, "Paradigmen zu einer Metaphorologie," *Archiv für Begriffsgeschichte* 6 (1960): 7–142; Blumenberg, *Paradigmen zu einer Metaphorologie* (Bonn: Bouvier Verlag, 1960).

2. Hans Blumenberg, "Light as a Metaphor of Truth," trans. Joel Anderson, in *Modernity and the Hegemony of Vision,* ed. David Levin (Berkeley: University of California Press, 1993), 30–62.

3. Anselm Haverkamp, "Die Technik der Rhetorik: Blumenbergs Projekt," in Hans Blumenberg, *Ästhetische und Metaphorologische Schriften,* ed. A. Haverkamp (Frankfurt am Main: Suhrkamp, 2001), 446.

seemed determined to make up for lost time, writing his doctoral and postdoctoral dissertations at great speed. By 1950, he had satisfied all the formal requirements for embarking on an academic career. In retrospect, the relatively quiet decade that ensued can be seen as a period of gestation that issued not just in *Paradigms,* but equally in the hefty tomes that appeared in steady succession from the mid-1960s on, occasionally supplemented by slimmer volumes. Three of those books, in particular—*The Legitimacy of the Modern Age* (1966), *The Genesis of the Copernican World* (1975), and *Work on Myth* (1979)—established Blumenberg's reputation as one of Germany's most erudite and original thinkers, and they remain, alongside *Shipwreck with Spectator,* his only titles to have previously appeared in English translation.[4]

Paradigms, then, was merely the "first vintage" (to borrow a Baconian metaphor cited in that work) in a series that seemed to grow more full-bodied and sophisticated with each new release. Like most first vintages, it is robust, crisp to the point of acerbity, and ought not to be consumed too quickly if one wants to avoid coming away from it with a buzzing head. In contrast to the expansive style of argumentation and lofty architecture characteristic of the works that were to come, its diction seems checked, almost constrained, as if Blumenberg had tried to cram into its pages everything he would later elaborate at leisure and at far greater length; thus, excurses on the book of nature, on the parable of the cave, and on the metaphor of the ship at high seas would each mature into a monograph in its own right.[5] *Paradigms* may accordingly be read as a kind of beginner's guide to Blumenberg, a programmatic introduction to his vast and multifaceted oeuvre, and it is primarily for this reason that I have chosen to make it available to an anglophone audience. Its very brevity—not a virtue usually associated with this author—makes it an ideal point of entry for readers daunted by the sheer bulk of Blumenberg's later writings, or distracted by their profusion of historical detail. In keeping with the generic requirements of a beginner's guide, *Paradigms* expresses many of Blumenberg's key ideas with a directness, concision, and clarity he would rarely match elsewhere. What is more, because it served as a beginner's guide for its author as well, allowing him to undertake an initial survey of problems that, under the general heading of "nonconceptuality" (*Unbegrifflichkeit*), would preoccupy him for the remainder of his life, it has the additional advantage that it can offer us a glimpse into what might be called the "genesis of the Blumenbergian world." This, too, justifies its translation into English.

---

4. All three works were translated in the 1980s by the admirable Robert M. Wallace: *The Legitimacy of the Modern Age* (Cambridge, MA: MIT Press, 1983); *The Genesis of the Copernican World* (Cambridge, MA: MIT Press, 1987); *Work on Myth* (Cambridge, MA: MIT Press, 1985). Paul Fleming's translation of *Care Crosses the River* is forthcoming from Stanford University Press.

5. See Hans Blumenberg, *Die Lesbarkeit der Welt* (Frankfurt am Main: Suhrkamp, 1981); Blumenberg, *Höhlenausgänge* (Frankfurt am Main: Suhrkamp, 1989); Blumenberg, *Shipwreck with Spectator: Paradigm of a Metaphor for Existence,* trans. Steven Rendall (Cambridge, MA: MIT Press, 1997).

There is a third, still more pertinent sense in which *Paradigms* can be understood as a beginner's guide that I would like to explore here. Composed of ten interlinked case studies dealing with the relationship between conceptual thought and metaphorics, their functional limitations and pragmatic implications, their areas of convergence, divergence, and interference, *Paradigms* is a beginner's guide to metaphorology rather than a systematic exposition of the "new science"—if it is one—that goes under that name. Through its title alone, it raises a claim to systematicity, to a *logos* of metaphor, that it simultaneously disavows on two levels: on the level of form, by presenting its findings in a fragmentary, inconclusive fashion, and on the level of content, by showing how metaphor eludes the logocentric schema that the philosophical tradition had tried to impose upon it ever since Plato.[6] From Blumenberg's explicit refusal to speculate on whether such a systematics would be possible,[7] it seems but a short step to Derrida's verdict, made a decade after the publication of Blumenberg's text and presumably in ignorance of it, on the impossibility of any metaphorology: "I am trying to speak *about* metaphor, to say something proper or literal on this subject, to *treat* it as my subject, but I am obliged, by metaphor (if one can say that) to speak of it *more metaphorico,* in its own manner."[8] Can metaphorology, then, be anything other than a beginner's guide, an enterprise as provisional and premature as the status traditionally ascribed by philosophy to metaphor itself—and this because, as Derrida suggests, it is inextricably enmeshed in the object it purports to analyze?

One way of approaching the question is to pay close attention to the metaphors used by Blumenberg to characterize his project, an approach sanctioned by his own insight into the symptomatic value of metaphor for patterns of thinking and feeling that ordinarily withdraw from conceptual formulation without thereby sinking into chthonic irretrievability. Perhaps the most prominent such metaphor in the present work is to be found just after he has regretfully closed down a line of inquiry he cannot pursue any further: "What I am submitting here is only semifinished product [*Halbzeug*]."[9] Anselm Haverkamp has noted that *Halbzeug,* a term used in industrial manufacture to designate material that is midway between a raw and a finished state, very precisely captures the "half-conceptual" status that Blumenberg ascribes to metaphor, which still reveals traces of a human lifeworld—the inexhaustible primary resource, as it were, from which all significations arise—that

---

6. See David Adams, "Metaphors for Mankind: The Development of Hans Blumenberg's Anthropological Metaphorology," *Journal of the History of Ideas* 52 (1991): 152–66. Blumenberg ignores the twentieth-century tradition that, from I. A. Richards to Max Black, had investigated the ways in which metaphor operates at the level of the utterance.

7. See above, p. 63.

8. Jacques Derrida, "The *Retrait* of Metaphor," trans. Peggy Kamuf, in *Psyche: Inventions of the Other* (Stanford: Stanford University Press, 2007), 49; Derrida, "White Mythology: Metaphor in the Text of Philosophy," in *Margins of Philosophy,* trans. Alan Bass (Chicago: University of Chicago Press, 1982), 219.

9. See above, p. 17.

can no longer be discerned in the end state of conceptual refinement.[10] "Semifinished product" thus refers as much to the material of metaphorology as it does to the paradigms *toward* a metaphorology (as the book's title could also be rendered) in which that material is incompletely processed. Both are "worked on" and "worked up" rather than "worked out"; and while this means that they lack the functional specificity proper to concepts (and to investigations into concepts), they are for that reason more flexible and versatile in the uses to which they can be put.

Fittingly, however, the meaning of *Halbzeug* cannot be translated without remainder into the terms of the theory that, in operating upon it, first makes it fully operational. What interests me here is the discrepancy between this metaphor for the intermediacy of metaphor and the "background metaphorics" of the journal in which it appeared, a discrepancy that reflects a broader tension, otherwise smoothed over in *Paradigms,* between the discipline of conceptual history and the subsidiary enterprise pioneered in the pages of its official organ. The *Archive for the History of Concepts* was founded by Erich Rothacker in 1955 with the aim of supplying what the journal's subtitle, employing a metaphor that tapped straight into the zeitgeist of 1950s Germany, called "Building Blocks [*Bausteine*] for a Historical Dictionary of Philosophy." Since construction of the dictionary in question would not get underway for several years—indeed, the multivolume work has only recently reached completion—the journal was to function both as a storehouse for materials awaiting deployment and as a showcase for what research into the history of concepts could achieve. The sequence and division of labor were clear: first Rothacker's team of stonecutters would work directly at the quarry, so to speak, preparing treatises on the history of individual concepts without regard for their eventual alphabetic and redactional arrangement; then a team of master builders would fit the stones one by one into the edifice of the dictionary under the watchful eye of its architect, Joachim Ritter. This procedure seemed especially advisable given that the discipline of conceptual history was still in its infancy, as Ritter remarked in his foreword to the first volume, meaning that the dictionary was unable to draw on a well-established research tradition. For the same reason, the editorial board resolved, albeit "with a heavy heart," not to include entries on philosophical metaphors; given the state of the field, any attempt to do them justice could only result in "inadequate improvisations."[11]

---

10. Anselm Haverkamp, "Editorisches Nachwort," in Hans Blumenberg, *Theorie der Unbegrifflichkeit* (Frankfurt am Main: Suhrkamp, 2007), 115.

11. Joachim Ritter, "Vorwort," in *Historisches Wörterbuch der Philosophie,* ed. Joachim Ritter (Darmstadt: WBG, 1971), vii, viii-ix. It is an indication of the steadily growing influence of the metaphorological model that Ritter's omission has since been made good; see Ralf Konersmann, ed., *Wörterbuch der philosophischen Metaphern* (Darmstadt: WBG, 2007). As the editor remarks in his foreword, this work unintentionally evolved into a "homage to Hans Blumenberg." Konersmann, "Vorwort: Figuratives Wissen," in *Wörterbuch der philosophischen Metaphern,* 12–13.

Rothacker, an influential figure at the time known above all for his work in the philosophy of culture, was on friendly terms with Blumenberg and had invited him to contribute to the journal at an early stage.[12] In a letter from February 1958 in which he sketched the project that was to become *Paradigms,* Blumenberg responded positively to the offer, although an undertone of skepticism was not to be overheard:

> Your . . . invitation to collaborate on the *Archive for the History of Concepts* is important to me because my own way of working has made me interested in this enterprise from the beginning. I must confess that the first publications rather deterred me from applying to contribute something myself; so self-contained and apparently definitive a work as the cosmos issue, while it has my admiration, does not exactly make one keen to plug holes here and there with one's own material, to fill in gaps, to deliver "building blocks." Without wanting to criticize, I find it characteristic of our situation that an undertaking so clearly reliant on summative and integrative work will, in the end, only consist of erratic individual achievements.
>
> Nonetheless, you have given me a new impulse, and I will act on it. With your permission, however, I will work in a more fragmentary fashion—and leaving the gaps showing—than has previously been the case in the *Archive.*[13]

Between the lines, Blumenberg was here already stating his intention to provide Rothacker with "semifinished product" rather than the expected masonry—not because he thought himself ill-qualified to deliver the goods, but from a sure awareness that the pretension to solidity and permanence conveyed by previous contributions to the journal would be out of keeping with his approach. Blumenberg indicates why this is the case in his only subsequent contribution to the *Archive,* an even more sporadic collection of "Observations on Metaphors" that appeared in 1971, occasioned by the long-awaited publication of the first volume of the *Historical Dictionary.* Blumenberg commends Ritter for trying to strike a balance between "the Cartesian ideal of unambiguous terminology" to which the predecessor to his dictionary, Rudolf Eisler's *Dictionary of Philosophical Concepts* (4th ed., 1927–30), had still adhered, and an essentially historical self-understanding of philosophy that has abandoned the goal of absolute terminological precision, seeking instead to clarify and interrogate the present usage of concepts by confronting them with their past meanings. Blumenberg's criticism is that the precarious balancing act between positivism and hermeneutics sketched in Ritter's foreword was not sustained and could not be sustained in the entries that followed, and this by virtue of an "unavowed bias toward the Cartesian ideal and its successors" built into the

---

12. Erich Rothacker to Hans Blumenberg, 31 January 1958, Hans Blumenberg Nachlaß, Deutsches Literaturarchiv.

13. Hans Blumenberg to Erich Rothacker, 7 February 1958, Hans Blumenberg Nachlaß, Deutsches Literaturarchiv.

methodology of conceptual history itself.[14] The impurity and equivocity of the sources with which the discipline operates, their unfitness for formalization, stand in the way of its efforts to reduce them to the lowest common denominator of a definable meaning; its innate teleological (or logotelic) drive blinds it to the historical depth dimension from which the concepts it selects, orders, and exhibits first emerge.[15] Conceptual history is constitutively incapable of conceptualizing nonconceptuality and therefore feels justified in ignoring it. If figurative language appears at all on its horizon, then it is only as an irritant to be put behind it as quickly as possible. This is where metaphorology can lend a helping hand. Far from playing the role of a junior partner whose services conceptual history can afford to decline, as Ritter assumed, metaphorology enters the scene as a necessary complement and corrective to conceptual history's striving for ultimate definitional clarity: "Metaphorology performs conceptual history the auxiliary service [*Hilfsdienst*] of guiding it to a genetic structure of concept formation that, while it may not meet the requirement of univocity, nonetheless permits the univocity of the end result to be recognized as an impoverishment of the imaginative background and the threads leading back to the lifeworld."[16]

We can see how this position is already indicated and discreetly defended in the countermetaphor of "semifinished product," which plays a transitional phase in the production process off against its fully reified and instrumentalized consummation. At the same time, we should be wary of concluding, even from Blumenberg's later statements on the matter, that "a history of concepts must make way for a history of metaphors,"[17] or that metaphorology "would not only have 'burst the bounds'" of the historical dictionary, it would have "liquidated it altogether."[18] Such claims overcompensate for Blumenberg's willingness to make strategic accommodations by transforming *Paradigms* into a coded manifesto against conceptual history, a tract so subversive that it could be mistaken by its target for a contribution to its cause; a "stereoscopic" reading that keeps both aspects in view would be closer to

14. Hans Blumenberg, "Beobachtungen an Metaphern," *Archiv für Begriffsgeschichte* 15 (1971): 163.

15. Corroborating evidence can be found in the entry on "conceptual history" in the volume to which Blumenberg was responding: concepts, one reads there, are to be made "systematizable" in their "unambiguously clarified semantic context." H. G. Meier, "Begriffsgeschichte," in *Historisches Wörterbuch der Philosophie* (Darmstadt: WBG, 1971), 1: 789.

16. Blumenberg, "Beobachtungen an Metaphern," 163.

17. Jean-Claude Monot, "Postface: La patience de l'image," in Hans Blumenberg, *Paradigmes pour une métaphorologie,* trans. Didier Gammelin (Paris: Vrin, 2006), 178.

18. Anselm Haverkamp, "Metaphorologie zweiten Grades: Geld oder Leben," *www.kuwi.euv-frankfurt-o.de/de/lehrstuhl/lw/westeuropa/Lehrstuhlinhaber/publikationen/Neues/Metaphorologie_zweiten_Grades_2005.pdf,* 3 (accessed 22 July 2009). See also the instructive debate in the *Zeitschrift für Ideengeschichte* between the "left-Blumenbergian" Hans Ulrich Gumbrecht, who defends Haverkamp's claim, and the "right-Blumenbergian" Carsten Dutt, who contests it. Dutt, "Postmoderne Zukunftsmüdigkeit: Hans Ulrich Gumbrecht verabschiedet die Begriffsgeschichte," *Zeitschrift für Ideengeschichte* I/1 (2007): 118–22; Gumbrecht, "(Un)dankbare Generationen: Eine Replik auf Carsten Dutt," *Zeitschrift für Ideengeschichte* I/3 (2007): 122–24; Dutt, "Keine Frage des Alters: Eine Duplik," *Zeitschrift für Ideengeschichte* I/3 (2007): 125–27.

its intentions.[19] Metaphorology radicalizes conceptual history, in the literal sense that it directs its attention to the roots of concept formation, yet the two approaches are compatible in their common endeavor to "return to the concrete analysis of the genesis of historical formations," as Blumenberg assured Ritter when sending him a copy of the book.[20] Otherwise he would hardly have thought it worthwhile to enter into a tactical alliance with Rothacker, whose own understanding of conceptual history—as a means for disclosing the history of "problems" lying beneath a "terminological stratum"[21]—displays clear parallels with Blumenberg's philosophically more ambitious attempt to identify metaphor as the point in discourse where it "reaches down into the unknown" (to cite a famous Freudian formulation),[22] into "the substructure of thought."[23]

Blumenberg's contention that metaphors are historical "in a more radical sense" than concepts, that they point the way to an occluded, subterranean realm where the basic questions posed in the "ground of our existence" (*Daseinsgrund*) have already been decided, resonates unmistakably with another contemporary type of theory design: the late philosophy of Martin Heidegger, whose influence on West German philosophy in the 1950s it would be difficult to overestimate.[24] That Blumenberg grasped metaphorology as a rival conception to fundamental ontology, rather than as a rhetorically subdued, philologically disciplined retelling of Heidegger's grand narrative of the withdrawal and self-concealment of Being, can again be illustrated with reference to his leading metaphor. The sentence in which it stands reads in full: "What I am presenting here is only semifinished product, and the perfection and comprehensiveness with which one can deal [*handeln*] with 'Being' is quite unattainable in this field." It does not take much ingenuity to conclude from this backhanded compliment that, for Blumenberg, the price paid by fundamental ontology for its "perfection" and "comprehensiveness" is vacuousness and vapidity; the metaphor all but identifies the "jargon of authenticity" cultivated by Heidegger and his followers with *Zeug*, the term introduced in *Being and Time* to designate the equipment whose "ready-to-handedness" we accept without a second thought

---

19. I refer to Albrecht Wellmer's justly influential "stereoscopic" reading of Adorno's *Aesthetic Theory*. See Wellmer, "Adorno, Modernity, and the Sublime," in *Endgames: The Irreconcilable Nature of Modernity,* trans. David Midgley (Cambridge, MA: MIT Press, 1998), 155–82.

20. Hans Blumenberg to Joachim Ritter, 6 December 1960. See also Ritter to Blumenberg, 1 September 1960: "The fateful separation of systematic philosophy and history of philosophy is itself at long last becoming history. You have significantly contributed to this." Hans Blumenberg Nachlaß, Deutsches Literaturarchiv.

21. Erich Rothacker, "Geleitwort," *Archiv für Begriffsgeschichte* 1 (1955): 5.

22. Sigmund Freud, *The Interpretation of Dreams,* trans. James Strachey (Harmondsworth: Penguin, 1991), 671. Blumenberg makes the analogy with psychoanalysis explicit in his postdoctoral dissertation; see Blumenberg, "Die ontologische Distanz: Eine Untersuchung über die Krisis der philosophischen Grundlagen der Neuzeit" (Postdoc. diss., Christian-Albrechts-Universität, 1950), 104–5, Hans Blumenberg Nachlaß, Deutsches Literaturarchiv.

23. See above, p. 5.

24. See above, p. 14. On the relationship between metaphorology and fundamental ontology, see also Jean-Claude Monod, *Hans Blumenberg* (Paris: Belin, 2007), 53–57.

so long as it continues to function smoothly and purposefully in our practical deal-ings with our surroundings (*das Handeln*).[25] Blumenberg thus ironically associates fundamental ontology with the very sphere of "inauthenticity" against which it had originally defined itself. The Heideggerian *Zeug* will never break down, he implies, because it can never meet with any resistance from the "everyday" world of beings. As he wrote to Rothacker in the same year, this time expressing himself with all desirable candor, "Expositions in the history of concepts quite simply de-mand the spreading out of 'material', otherwise everything becomes as unreal as if one were talking about Being."[26]

Heidegger's name appears only twice in *Paradigms,* each time in exemplifica-tion of a particular metaphorical model, so we are forced to look elsewhere if we want to gain an understanding of what is at stake in the confrontation—hinted at rather than staged in that work—between metaphorology and ontology, *Halb-zeug* and *Zeug.* The first of these references occurs in a quotation from a book by Walter Bröcker. The constellation is hardly fortuitous: Bröcker, a former student and assistant of Heidegger's, had supervised Blumenberg's (still unpublished) post-doctoral dissertation at the University of Kiel, and it is here that Blumenberg's most sustained engagement with Heidegger's philosophy can be found. The en-gagement assumes the double form of appropriation and critique, as the title of the dissertation, "The Ontological Distance," already suggests. Blumenberg follows Heidegger in arguing that the crisis of traditional ontology, driven to its ultimate consequence and turning point in Husserl's attempt to ground phenomenology in transcendental subjectivity, opens the way for an understanding of the essential historicity of Being. The task he sets himself is accordingly to develop an ontologi-cal model of history that will enable him "more thoroughly to articulate the crisis of the modern age using the paradigm of Husserl's phenomenology," in other words, to illuminate the conditions under which Heidegger's break with phenomenology, and his subsequent destruction of the metaphysical tradition, became both possible and necessary.[27]

For the early Blumenberg, history unfolds in the interspace between the two limit terms or poles of the "ontological distance," which he labels "oppositionality" (*Gegenständigkeit*) and "extrapositionality" (*Inständigkeit*). The former, methodi-cally secured by Descartes and reinforced at an even more fundamental level by Husserl, situates human existence over against a world of objects upon which it can impose itself in willful activity or from which it can retreat into an attitude of theoretical repose. Oppositionality can first be recognized and determined as a manifestation of the ontological distance from the counterpole of extrapositionality,

25. Martin Heidegger, *Sein und Zeit* (Frankfurt am Main: Klostermann, 1977), 90–97, esp. 93.

26. Blumenberg to Rothacker, 13 August 1960, Hans Blumenberg Nachlaß, Deutsches Literaturarchiv.

27. Blumenberg, "Die ontologische Distanz," 8.

in which human existence spurns the assurances offered it by reason, religion, and tradition to face up to its own contingency; here the resolute acceptance of finitude elaborated in Heidegger's analysis of *Dasein* stands as model. The concept of "ontological distance" is meant to cover both poles as well as the "dimension of historical metakinetics"[28] that stretches between them: "In a narrower sense, 'distance' is the antonym of proximity, immediacy, urgency, ineluctability; it is what we will convey in the name 'oppositionality'. In a more comprehensive sense, however . . ., the concept of 'distance' includes both 'oppositionality' and 'extrapositionality' as possibilities of distance as such, as distantiation and de-distantiation."[29] Shifts within the space spanned by these two poles define the options available to thought within a given epoch, what *Paradigms* will call "the fundamental certainties, conjectures, and judgments in relation to which the attitudes and expectations, actions and inactions, longings and disappointments, interests and indifferences, of an epoch are regulated";[30] and it is the task of a "morphology of the ontological distance," given a trial run in the dissertation before being unveiled to the public in *The Legitimacy of the Modern Age,* to trace these shifts from one epoch to the next.

Blumenberg's criticism of Heidegger flows from his insight that neither limit position can be maintained in the rigor and finality it claims for itself. Just as the oppositional extremism of Husserl, in trying to shut out the dimension of history from its act of self-foundation, causes the repressed to return with the full weight of its facticity, so too the extrapositional extremism of Heidegger, in seeking to tarry in the sublime isolation of "poetic thinking," turns its back on the historical world from which alone human existence draws its meaning. Blumenberg marks his own position by vindicating the "fallen" or "inessential" realm of history against those who would transcend it in either direction, whether by barricading the subject within a stronghold of its own making or by sacrificing the subject at the altar of Being. Here, for the first time, we encounter that "philosophical antiabsolutism" that Odo Marquard identifies as the vital element of Blumenberg's thought,[31] still struggling to liberate itself from a ponderous Heideggerian idiom that now resiles from the humanly intolerable demands made by Heidegger himself. In Husserl, Blumenberg notes,

> the absolute extreme of the oppositional terminus of the ontological distance showed itself to be the *self-cancellation* of this self in its possibility. Anxiety, too, must be characterized in its "pure" phenomenality as an "absolute" extreme of the ontological

---

28. Blumenberg, "Die ontologische Distanz," 10d.

29. Blumenberg, "Die ontologische Distanz," 219n.

30. See above, p. 14.

31. Odo Marquard, "Laudatio auf Hans Blumenberg," in *Deutsche Akademie für Sprache und Dichtung, Jahrbuch 1980* (Heidelberg: Verlag Lambert Schneider, 1981), 54. See also Marquard, "Entlastung vom Absoluten," in *Die Kunst des Überlebens: Nachdenken über Hans Blumenberg,* ed. Franz Josef Wetz and Hermann Timm (Frankfurt am Main: Suhrkamp, 1999), 17–27.

distance, this time from its *extrapositional* terminus; and here, too, the "absoluteness" of this extrapositionality signifies the self-cancellation of the ontological distance in its possibility as such. . . . The fact that the "space" of existential motility, and hence of ontological understanding, cancels itself out at its oppositional and extrapositional termini, insofar as these are claimed or endured "absolutely," means nothing less than that this movement space [*Bewegungsraum*] of ontological understanding is the inter-space [*Spielraum*] of *history* itself, whose essence is defined purely negatively as opposition to the "absolute."[32]

The criticism is made even more explicit in a draft version of the chapter from which the previous quotation is taken. "It can scarcely be doubted that the reality of human language is nowhere the reality of such [authentic or poetic] saying," Blumenberg remarks there. "If that is a fact of ontological forgetfulness, then one would have to say that man can only *live* in such forgetfulness."[33] In abandoning the "movement space of history" for the waiting room of *posthistoire,* Heidegger abolishes the breathing space that is indispensable for human self-affirmation.

The notion that human existence must assert itself against the absolute recurs in many different guises in Blumenberg. It can be found in the "absolute father" of his 1952 essay on Kafka, the placeholder for transcendence in a godless world;[34] in the theological absolutism he ascribes to the late Middle Ages, to which the modern age opposed the pathos of its will to attain mastery over a limited but inalienable field of action;[35] in the "absolutism of reality" evoked in the opening pages of *Work on Myth,* progressively (though never completely) depotentiated through the conversion of anxiety into fear, fear into ritual, ritual into myth, myth into mythology, mythology into fiction;[36] in the "absolutism of wishes and images" that originally prevailed inside the cave, the imagined birthplace of human culture, no less than in the "absolutism of institutions" preached by those of its latter-day self-appointed guardians who think its dwellers in need of tighter discipline;[37] and—last in order of publication but first in order of priority—in the absolute danger of annihilation to which our apelike ancestors found themselves exposed upon emerging from the tertiary rainforest onto the open steppe, and from which they could save themselves, defying all the odds of evolution, only by taking the emergency exit of hominization.[38] In *Paradigms,* the place of the absolute is occupied by "absolute metaphor," and this in a twofold sense: the absolute is *metaphorized,* "translated" into significations that

32. Blumenberg, "Die ontologische Distanz," 198.

33. Hans Blumenberg, "Die ontologische Distanz: Eine Untersuchung über die Strenge der Philosophie; Erste Fassung" (1949), 206–7, Hans Blumenberg Nachlaß, Deutsches Literaturarchiv.

34. Hans Blumenberg, "Der absolute Vater," *Hochland* 45 (1952–53): 284.

35. Blumenberg, *The Legitimacy of the Modern Age,* 75–200.

36. Blumenberg, *Work on Myth,* 9–14.

37. Blumenberg, *Work on Myth,* 14; Blumenberg, *Höhlenausgänge,* 29–38; Blumenberg, "Anthropologische Annäherung an die Rhetorik," in *Ästhetische und metaphorologische Schriften,* 415.

38. Hans Blumenberg, *Beschreibung des Menschen* (Frankfurt am Main: Suhrkamp, 2006), 550–88.

address certain vast, theoretically unanswerable, yet pragmatically uncircumvent-able questions about our place in the universe; and it is *metaphorized absolutely,* made "untranslatable" through its function of opening up a horizon within which translations between figurative and nonfigurative speech (in the conventional sense) could first take place. To be sure, Blumenberg concedes a limited validity to the substitution theory of metaphor hallowed by tradition, according to which, in the words of Paul Ricoeur, the metaphorical term "carries no new information, since the absent term (if one exists) can be brought back in," and hence "has only an ornamental, decorative value."[39] Some metaphors may well be "leftover elements" that ought to be purged from philosophical language as so many obstacles to clear expression. Yet absolute metaphors say more than this, and they say it differently; they are "foundational elements," incommensurate with the order of discourse in which metaphor appears as a local *dis*order to be tolerated, at best, for its poetic ef-fect, if not eliminated altogether in the interest of terminological exactness.

While crediting Kant with the inspiration for the idea of absolute metaphor, Blumenberg probably picked up the term from the literary critic Hugo Friedrich, who introduced it in his book *The Structure of the Modern Lyric* (1956) to denote a metaphor that establishes an autonomous identity rather than serving as a figure of comparison. Friedrich's prime example is Rimbaud's drunken boat, which has unmoored itself from the "I" it supposedly symbolizes and now careers through an imaginary space that no longer has anything to do with "reality of any kind," leav-ing readers without a compass from which to take their bearings.[40] Blumenberg's absolute metaphor has the opposite effect: it owes its "success" precisely to the fact that it does not permit the question of its relationship to reality to arise in the first place, since it serves to indicate a basic attitude that first gives what we call "reality" its characteristic gestalt, its friendly or forbidding aspect, its homely or hostile phys-iognomy. Indeed, it can be recognized as such only once it has forfeited its binding force, prompting us to ask whether a metaphorologically enlightened philosophy could do without the guidance of absolute metaphors or whether, as seems more likely given their orienting function for intentionality, they would persist with a di-minished truth claim once metaphysics has been unmasked as "metaphorics taken at its word."[41] From this point of view, the feeling of disorientation brought on by Rimbaud's poem can be endured, even "aesthetically" enjoyed, on the condition that the drunken boat sails against the horizon of a world that has long since been rendered navigable.

---

39. Paul Ricoeur, *The Rule of Metaphor,* trans. Robert Czerny (London: Routledge, 2003), 21.

40. Hugo Friedrich, *Die Struktur der modernen Lyrik* (Reinbek: Rowohlt Taschenbuch Verlag, 1985), 73–74.

41. See Barbara Merker, "Bedürfnis nach Bedeutsamkeit: Zwischen Lebenswelt und Absolutismus der Wirklichkeit," in *Die Kunst des Überlebens,* ed. Wetz and Timm, 96–97.

Absolute metaphors compensate human beings for their lack of fit with a world in which they must act in order to stay alive, but in which they can only act at all purposefully if their actions are informed by a foreknowledge of what that world is and how they stand in relation to it.[42] Such foreknowledge, which tends to be prescient rather than prescientific in nature, is acquired by projecting conjectures about the totality of the real onto the blank screen of the absolute, which henceforth (but there is nothing anthropologically "prior" to this "henceforth") projects back an image that helps us to find our way in the world: that of a divinely ordained cosmos, for instance, or a prison cell for the soul or a clockwork universe. These metaphysical conjectures are at once unfounded, since they cannot be verified or falsified, and founding, since they disclose possibilities for making sense of what would otherwise have been senseless. In some cases, notably in Galileo and Kepler, absolute metaphors set the parameters within which the incremental progress of "normal science" can take place; in others, existing scientific achievements are pressed into the service of human self-understanding through their metaphorization, as the history of the Copernican reform demonstrates. The vicissitudes of metaphor—the replacement of one metaphor by another, or the accretions in meaning undergone by a single metaphor—are the subject of a new form of historiography that probes texts for evidence of the conceptually irrecoverable presuppositions on which they operate, the "cultural subconscious" to which they give involuntary expression.[43] The ontological history charted in the postdoctoral dissertation makes way for the conjectural history evoked in the closing sentence of the foreword to *Paradigms,* prompting us to subsume the limit positions of oppositionality and extrapositionality under the broader category of *suppositionalities:* "Metaphorology seeks to burrow down to the substructure of thought, the underground, the nutrient solution of systematic crystallizations; but it also aims to show with what 'courage' the mind preempts itself in its images, and how its history is projected in the courage of its conjectures [*wie sich im Mut zur Vermutung seine Geschichte entwirft*]."[44]

The immediate source for the "conjectural turn" announced in this passage is the negative theology of Nicolaus of Cusa, which Blumenberg had studied intensively in the 1950s and to which he would devote a lengthy chapter in *The Legitimacy of the Modern Age.* Cusanus argues in his treatise *On Surmises (De coniecturis)* that "every human affirmation about what is true is a surmise," since pure truth is reserved for God alone. That is not to say that our striving for knowledge is sinful, the reproach leveled against curiosity by Augustine, nor that it is idle speculation, for we can still be guided toward relative knowledge by what Cusanus calls "the

42. See Vida Pavesich, "Hans Blumenberg's Philosophical Anthropology: After Heidegger and Cassirer," *Journal of the History of Philosophy* 46.3 (2008): 421–48.

43. I borrow the term "cultural subconscious" from Rüdiger Zill, who describes metaphorology as "the cultural-historical pendant to the psychoanalysis of the individual." Zill, "Der Fallensteller: Hans Blumenberg als Historiograph der Wahrheit," *Zeitschrift für Ideengeschichte* I/3 (2007): 31.

44. See above, p. 5.

art of conjecture," the title given by Blumenberg to an anthology of his writings brought out three years before *Paradigms*.[45] Cusanus anchors the prerogative of the human mind to make surmises about what it nonetheless knows to lie beyond its ken in the doctrine of divine likeness, now understood in creative rather than static terms, concluding: "Therefore, just as that Absolute Divine Being is all that which there is [essentially] in each existing thing, so too the oneness of the human mind is the being of its own surmises."[46] Blumenberg adopts the second half of the sentence while rejecting the premise of a universal structural homogeneity that underpins it. Metaphorical projections are backed up by no such transcendental guarantees. They leap into a void, provoked by questions we cannot afford to put off until such time as we may be in a position to answer them with conceptual means. That is why "courage [*Mut*] and conjecture [*Vermutung*] have more than their external homophony in common," as Blumenberg notes in his introduction to the Cusanus volume.[47]

The courage to conjecture could serve as a general formula, not just for the "preemptive" achievement of metaphor, but equally for technique as such, understood as the capacity to come up with practical solutions to problems that cannot, or cannot yet, be made to yield to rational insight. While this theory would not be fully developed until the 1963 essay "Lifeworld and Technicization under Aspects of Phenomenology,"[48] it is already implicit in the rehabilitation of rhetoric against its Platonist detractors carried out in *Paradigms*. And it is foreshadowed, once again, in the metaphor of "semifinished product," which, in assigning metaphorology to the pictorial field of technicization, neatly anticipates and justifies its failure ever to advance beyond the status of a work in progress to its hypothetical final destination, the point at which metaphor would have been dealt with once and for all. Blumenberg's *Halbzeug*, truer to its own theory than he may have realized at the time, springs into a gap that metaphorology, as the science of metaphor, cannot fill; Blumenberg was to draw the consequence from the mid-1970s onward, dropping the old program title and supplanting it with a "theory of nonconceptuality" that, for its part, was destined to remain a "prospect" for such a theory.[49]

---

45. See the article on "Vermutung" in the *Historisches Wörterbuch für Philosophie* (Darmstadt: WBG, 2001), 11: 736.

46. Nicolaus Cusanus, "On Surmises," in *Metaphysical Speculations*, trans. Jasper Hopkins (Minneapolis: Arthur J. Banning Press, 2000), 2: 150–51.

47. Hans Blumenberg, "Einleitung," in Nikolaus von Cues, *Die Kunst der Vermutung: Auswahl aus den Schriften*, ed. Hans Blumenberg (Bremen: Carl Schünemann Verlag, 1957), 22.

48. Hans Blumenberg, "Lebenswelt und Technisierung unter Aspekten der Phänomenologie," in *Wirklichkeiten in denen wir leben* (Stuttgart: Reclam, 1981), 7–54. The essay can be read as a masterly riposte to Heidegger's "On the Question of Technology," although characteristically it never deigns to mention Heidegger by name.

49. See Blumenberg, "Prospect for a Theory of Nonconceptuality," in *Shipwreck with Spectator*, 81–102. The lecture transcripts recently published under the title "Theory of Nonconceptuality" broaden the prospect without going beyond it. Hans Blumenberg, *Theorie der Unbegrifflichkeit*, ed.

Are we to conclude, then, that metaphorology was nothing more than a false start, dogged from the outset by the same "unavowed bias toward the Cartesian ideal" that Blumenberg diagnosed in the project of a history of concepts, and that the identification of absolute metaphors was supposed to rectify? Here it may be useful to recall the double role played by the "example" or "paradigm" (*paradeigma*) in Aristotelian rhetoric. Aristotle stipulates that if enthymemes can be produced in a judicial or deliberative address, if, that is, a deductive proof can be presented, then paradigms should appear after the proof "as a kind of epilogue." If no enthymemes are available, however, paradigms must be employed for purposes of demonstration at the beginning of the argument. "For if they stand first," Aristotle explains, "they resemble induction, and induction is not suitable to rhetorical speeches except in a few cases; if they stand last they resemble evidence, and a witness is in every case likely to induce belief."[50] Depending on where they are placed, paradigms thus either serve to clinch an argument that has already been prosecuted by means of the logically compelling, syllogistic type of reasoning condensed in the enthymeme, in which case only one paradigm is required, or they represent a stopgap measure calculated to generate plausibility in the absence of deductive proof, in which case several will need to be cited if the speaker is to convey conviction. Blumenberg's paradigms clearly fall into the latter category, inasmuch as they seek to persuade the reader of the universal import adduced for absolute metaphor from the individual examples presented in the course of the work. But their plurality and position of priority only highlight the lack of a "more cogent and more efficacious" technique of argumentation, corresponding to Aristotle's enthymemes, for which they could furnish corroborating evidence.[51] Metaphorology, we may infer, cannot exist other than in paradigmatic form: as a beginner's guide rather than as an authoritative compendium; as the bricolage of a skilled amateur rather than as a well-oiled machine subject to expert control; as a *métaphorologie provisoire* that knows of its own reliance on metaphor rather than as a *métaphorologie définitive* that purports to have superseded it. The theoretical project launched in *Paradigms for a Metaphorology,* herein akin to metaphor itself, owes whatever insights it can communicate to us about the strategies by which we cope with an otherwise alien and overpowering reality to the courage of its conjectures.

Anselm Haverkamp (Frankfurt am Main: Suhrkamp, 2007). See also Robert Savage, "Laughter from the Lifeworld: Hans Blumenberg's Theory of Nonconceptuality," *Thesis Eleven* 94 (2008): 119–31.

50. Aristotle, *The Art of Rhetoric,* trans. John Henry Freese (Cambridge, MA: Harvard University Press, 2006), 279 (1394a). See also the entry "Exemplum" in the *Historisches Wörterbuch der Rhetorik* (Tübingen: Max Niemeyer, 1996), 3: 60–70.

51. Aristotle, *Topica,* trans. E. S. Forster (Cambridge, MA: Harvard University Press, 2004), 303 (105a).

Index of Names

Subject Index

CPSIA information can be obtained at www.ICGtesting.com
Printed in the USA
BVOW07*1347090215

386458BV00002B/4/P